The Project Risk Maturity Model

The Project Risk Maturity Model

Measuring and Improving Risk Management Capability

MARTIN HOPKINSON
QinetiQ, UK

Routledge
Taylor & Francis Group

LONDON AND NEW YORK

First published 2011 by Gower Publishing

2 Park Square, Milton Park, Abingdon, Oxon OX14 4RN
52 Vanderbilt Avenue, New York, NY 10017

Routledge is an imprint of the Taylor & Francis Group, an informa business

First issued in hardback 2019

British Library Cataloguing in Publication Data
Hopkinson, Martin.
The project risk maturity model : measuring and improving risk management capability.
    1. Risk management – Mathematical models. 2. Operational risk – Mathematical models.
    3. Project management – Mathematical models.
    I. Title
    658.1'55'015118–dc22

Library of Congress Cataloging-in-Publication Data
Hopkinson, Martin.
    The project risk maturity model : measuring and improving risk management capability / by Martin Hopkinson.
        p. cm.
    Includes bibliographical references and index.
    ISBN 978-0-566-08879-7 (hbk. : alk. paper)
  1. Risk management. 2. Project management. I. Title.

    HD61.H568 2010
    658.15'5–dc22

                                      2010021053

ISBN 978-0-566-08879-7 (hbk)

Contents

Supplementary Resources Disclaimer

Additional resources were previously made available for this title on CD. However, as CD has become a less accessible format, all resources have been moved to a more convenient online download option.

You can find these resources available here: www.routledge.com/9780566088797

Please note: Where this title mentions the associated disc, please use the downloadable resources instead.

List of Figures

List of Tables

Foreword

As I write this Foreword I've just celebrated another birthday. Among the cards are an increasing number that mention memory loss, hair loss, or the fire hazard caused by the large number of candles on my cake. This is confusing. Long-time acquaintances have started referring to me as an 'old friend' and younger relatives appear to think I'm already past it. But a good friend in his late seventies sent a card describing me as 'the Birthday Boy'. And my self-perception is of someone in his prime, finally getting to an age where life is beginning to make some sense. Older? Definitely. Wiser? Maybe.

Apparently I'm not as young as I was. Perhaps I am maturing.

But what is maturity? The word is used in at least two ways. One meaning is to be fully developed, ripe, at the peak of perfection, having reached the maximum level of development. A fully mature cheese or wine is a delight. But the word is also used to mean no longer young, with implications of being old and of no further use. When an investment matures it reaches the end of its life, and some think that the same applies to older people. One-time sex kitten Brigitte Bardot recognised this dual meaning when she was interviewed at the age of 73. Asked how she felt about being old, she defiantly replied 'I have not grown old, I have ripened.'

The Irish poet John Finlay defined maturity as 'the capacity to endure uncertainty', and as we face increasing uncertainty all around us, more and more organisations aspire to maturity in a range of areas of competence. There has been a rapid growth in so-called 'maturity models' which claim to measure degrees of capability in various disciplines, aiming to help organisations become 'more mature'. In 2007 the UK Association for Project Management (APM) surveyed maturity models in the project management space, and found many competing offerings. For example the Project Management Institute (PMI®) offers its Organisational Project Management Maturity Model (OPM3®), the UK Office for Government Commerce has both the Portfolio, Programme and Project Management Maturity Model (P3M3©) and the PRINCE2 Maturity Model (P2MM©), and the International Project Management Association has developed their Project Excellence Model.

Even in the relatively specialised area of risk management, several specific maturity models exist, some of which have a considerable track record of use in different industries and organisations across the world. I have a long-standing interest in the subject dating from the mid-1990s, and in 1997 I published the first framework for assessing the maturity of risk management capability within an organisation. It has always seemed important to me not just to do something and to be seen to be doing it, but to do it well. But how would you know whether your management of risk is good, bad or indifferent? There are many factors that contribute to competence in managing risk, for example, the risk culture of an organisation, as well as its risk processes, its risk infrastructure, and the risk knowledge and skills of its people. The better risk management maturity models incorporate all these areas, and the organisations with more mature approaches to managing risk are competent in each aspect.

So what is 'risk management maturity'? Does it mean that the approach to risk management in a particular organisation is fully ripened, has developed as far as it can, no further improvement is possible, and everything is as good as it's going to get? Or does it imply being past it, with a degree of inflexibility, being set in one's ways, in a rut, and doing things because 'we've always done it that way'? Neither of these seems to be attractive options or worthwhile goals.

The clue is in the full name of the original maturity model first produced by the Software Engineering Institute of Carnegie Mellon University (SEI), which was responsible for triggering my interest in the topic of maturity. Targeting software development organisations, the SEI Capability Maturity Model (CMM) framework was first outlined in 1989 and fully published in 1993, and the key word in its name is 'capability'. The aim is not merely to 'be mature' but to have a 'mature capability'.

Having a mature risk management capability appears to be a desirable goal to which every organisation should aspire. This requires an approach to risk management which is constantly refreshed and renewed, adopting new techniques as appropriate, keeping up to date with the latest thinking and developments, learning from leading practitioners in our own and other industries, offering refresher skills training to our staff and so on.

But something is required to enable us to become and remain mature in the way we manage risk. We need an accepted framework to assess our risk management maturity, allowing us to benchmark ourselves against a recognised standard. We also need a structured pathway for improvement, not just telling us where we are now, but describing the steps required for us to reach the next level. The *Project Risk Maturity Model* detailed in this book provides such an assessment framework and development pathway for risk management capability in projects. It can be used by organisations to benchmark their project risk processes, and it can support introduction of effective in-house project risk management. Using this model, implementation and improvement of project risk management can be managed effectively to ensure that the expected benefits are achieved in a way that is appropriate to the needs of each particular organisation.

We all need to beware of complacency, especially in risk management. In our ever-changing world, what worked yesterday may not be good enough for today or tomorrow. Just because we've been doing something for a long time doesn't mean we're doing it well. Risk management is too important for us to allow it to fade away or become ineffective. We need to assess and monitor our risk management capability, compare ourselves with best practice, identify areas of shortcoming that require improvement, and keep developing. The *Project Risk Maturity Model* provides an answer for those who know that they haven't yet peaked in project risk management capability, or who want to maintain or improve their ability to manage project risk. Martin Hopkinson has done a great job over the past ten years in developing the *Project Risk Maturity Model* into a robust framework, and this book allows others to access and apply his insights and experience. I'm pleased to recommend it.

Dr David Hillson, The Risk Doctor
Petersfield, Hampshire, UK
March 2010

Preface

I joined HVR Consulting Services in 1999, impressed by both its customer reputation and the range of risk management and cost forecasting tools it had developed. Given that it was a company of 60 employees focusing on consultancy rather than tool development, it was clear that its people had been encouraged to engage in development activities as well as fee earning work. I would have a similar opportunity. The most interesting opportunity for development struck me as being the Risk Maturity Model (RMM).

The Risk Maturity Model had originally been conceived by David Hillson during his time leading risk management at HVR. His paper 'Towards a Risk Maturity Model' had been published in the *International Journal of Project and Business Risk Management* in 1997. This paper described four levels of risk management capability that could be found in projects and businesses. It also included a matrix (reproduced in Appendix A) to help organisations measure the maturity of their risk management process by assessing their capability level. The ideas behind this seemed both sound and useful. Given my 14 years' experience of projects, I was interested in building upon these ideas to produce a model specific to project risk management.

On this basis, I compiled and refined a collection of questions to include in the Project RMM. To help in this task, I drew not only on my own experience but also that of other members of the HVR risk management team. This team had established a good reputation amongst its clients over a period of many years. It had a particularly good record for producing realistic risk-based project forecasts; project outcomes tended to fall within the range of forecast possibilities to a much greater extent than I had seen in other organisations. Indeed, where relationships with clients had been difficult, this was usually the consequence of HVR's forecasts being more realistic than the client liked to admit! Lessons learned from HVR's risk management experience could therefore be incorporated into the RMM. Later, as the model was being calibrated, there was also a wide range of projects that could be used for this purpose.

As the model was being developed, I also drew upon other sources. First, with fortunate timing, the Turnbull Guidance[1] was published in October 1999. The Turnbull Guidance recommends the use of a risk-based system for a company's system of internal control. In 1999, it was issued as guidance for companies listed on the London Stock Exchange in order to clarify requirements of the Combined Code and into which it has since been fully incorporated. In effect the Turnbull guidance is a high level guide to corporate risk management. As such it provides context for the project risk management process. Its content is an important source for the RMM stakeholders and risk management culture questions.

In parallel with the Project RMM, I also developed a Business Risk Maturity Model, drawing again from the Turnbull Guidance, together with other relevant standards and sources. The Business RMM can be used to assess the capability of a corporate risk

---

1   N. Turnbull et al. 1999. *Internal Control: Guidance for Directors on the Combined Code*, hereafter referred to as the Turnbull Guidance or the Turnbull Report.

management process used by a company or any other form of organisation. Whilst it shares a lot of common ground with the Project RMM, there are also a number of significant differences. It was useful to understand how, where and why this differentiation was important.

The other external sources for the Project RMM were provided by the project and risk management literature. Of the many books and papers used, two deserve particular mention. First, *Project Risk Management: Processes, Techniques and Insights* by Chris Chapman and Stephen Ward (1st edition 1997, 2nd edition 2003) is widely recognised as being a first-class academic text on the subject. It is also an antidote to approaches that treat risk management as being a procedure that is identical on every project. In practice, following a single recipe is all too common. In contrast, best practice requires the intelligent application of principles and the selection of techniques appropriate to the project in question. The second particularly influential book was the Association for Project Management's guide to *Project Risk Analysis and Management (PRAM) Guide*. The first edition of this guide was also issued in 1997. A key feature of the *PRAM Guide* process is the use of a top-down iterative approach. The importance of this is explained in more detail in several chapters of this book, most notably, Chapter 3.

When finally assembled, the prototype Project RMM was based on 39 questions. It was then calibrated using projects that HVR's risk management team members had been involved with. The key questions addressed by the calibration process were: 1) did the model produce a valid overall result and 2) did it identify the key weaknesses of the project risk management process in each case? Although the prototype frequently passed these tests, a number of adjustments had to be made to the wording of questions and the weightings assigned to them to increase its accuracy. Additional questions were also identified and incorporated into the model.

Amongst the projects used for calibration purposes was one that I had been involved with during the time with my previous company. My opinion was that the risk management process had been ineffective. Not only did the RMM confirm this, but it also now gave me new insight into why this had been so. Previously, my view had been that the team had failed to translate planned risk response into implemented action. Whilst the RMM confirmed that this had indeed been a problem, it suggested that risk identification and risk management culture had been the areas of greater weakness. On reflection, this was correct. In the environment of a project in difficulty, management politics had created barriers to the identification of significant and emerging risks. Actions to improve the risk management process would have had to address these barriers as a priority.

The fact that the Project RMM helped me to identify insights into my own previous project experience was encouraging. The model is not intended to be just a measuring tool. Identifying priorities for process improvement is a fundamental part of its purpose. As clients started to ask for the model to be used to assess their projects, it was encouraging to see that they were similarly pleased with the recommendations for process improvement that were identified. HVR staff also started to use the model for process self-assessment purposes when working on clients' projects.

Since 1999, the model has been continuously updated and improved. The main sources of information used to do this have been experience from the application of the model and advances in the project risk management literature. The current model is based on 50 questions. In the early days, the number of questions increased quite quickly as practice showed that increased differentiation was needed to cover certain issues.

However the number of questions has stabilised, with an increase of only one in the last five years.

The words used in the model have also evolved. Words are used to identify the scope of each question and to describe criteria to be met for alternative answers. This part of the model's content has to be written concisely, yet cover all reasonable possibilities. It also has to avoid being inappropriately prescriptive whilst, nevertheless, setting unambiguous criteria. Over the years, a number of people have been adept at identifying gaps or ambiguities that they can exploit to obtain higher scores. Closure of these loopholes is one of the key reasons for keeping the model's content under continuous review. However, since it has been now used for approximately 250 assessments, the model should have become reasonably robust.

Changes to the model have made high scores slightly more difficult to achieve. Despite having been questioned by some users for 'moving the goalposts', this is something for which I do not apologise. If the art of project risk management is progressing, then so should the Project RMM. Besides, continuous improvement is described as being part of achieving the highest capability levels in similar maturity models. Projects and organisations that stand still over a long period of time should thus not expect to retain the highest level of assessment. With each change, the model is recalibrated against previous project assessments to ensure that it has not become unfair.

Gradual evolution of the Project RMM can be expected to continue. Despite all the work to develop the model to date, it is, inevitably, imperfect. As with any interesting non-trivial subject, project risk management engenders passionate debate amongst the leading academics and practitioners. Disagreements between leaders in the field exist and provide important fuel for improvement. I have been in the fortunate position of being part of this process myself. However, as a result, I am also aware that concepts of what constitutes best practice continue to be contested and to evolve. With regards to the current version of the Project RMM, I have spent ten years updating the model on the basis of both practical experience with assessments and a close involvement in the development of professional standards.

In 2004, HVR was bought by QinetiQ, a leading UK-listed engineering technology and services company. QinetiQ and HVR have reputations for being at the cutting edge of development in their fields, and the ongoing development of the Project RMM has continued to be supported. The model has recently been incorporated into the AWARD toolset owned by QinetiQ and used for the purposes of tender assessment and project approval. It is also, of course, QinetiQ's support and commitment to continuous development that has made it possible to publish this book and its accompanying disc.

The primary purpose of this book is to explain to readers how the Risk Maturity Model should be used. Whilst anyone would be able to take out the disc and skip to 'Software User Instructions' (see pp. 235–41), readers are strongly advised to read other sections of the book before putting it to use! The parts of the book most directly relevant to its purpose are Chapters 1 'Project Risk Maturity Model', 5 'Risk Maturity Model Data Collection', and 6 'Stakeholders'. Chapter 6 and the following five chapters are designed to provide readers with insight into the purpose of each RMM Question and the reasons for its wording. The wording of each question is important, since it defines the criteria to be used for assessments. Thus, Chapters 6 to 11 are the ones to which anyone involved with RMM assessments is likely to refer most frequently.

Chapters 2 and 3 have been designed to provide useful background material for readers. Part of their purpose is to address a problem faced by all risk management practitioners: the lack of agreement on what constitutes best practice. Chapter 2 clarifies the position taken on a number of related issues by defining the model's scope and boundaries. It also identifies features of a risk management process that are important to what the model implicitly treats as being best practice, that is, a Level 4 risk management capability. For example, the chapter differentiates between the concept of overall project risk and the idea of managing risks on a risk-by-risk basis. Managing overall project risk (and its link with quantitative analysis) is a key concept for what is required to achieve RMM Level 4.

Two other major points identified by Chapter 2 are that a mature project risk management process requires risks to be understood broadly as being attributable to conditions of uncertainty (that is, lack of certainty) and that it should be based on a top-down iterative process in its early stages. These are important points that differentiate the model's concept of what is usually required for Level 4 capability from some forms of common practice.

In practice the idea of use of a top-down iterative approach to risk management process is often not well understood. Chapter 3 therefore provides a worked example to illustrate what this can involve. Since a number of the RMM questions refer to the principle of using a top-down process, readers who are less familiar with this should find that Chapter 3 provides useful context.

Chapter 4 is a case study which shows how the RMM has been systematically used for project assessments by a major organisation. This chapter provides evidence that the model works in practice and that its use is likely to improve the performance of projects. It also includes discussion of issues that should be addressed by anyone who is responsible for rolling out an assessment programme of this nature.

Where appropriate, examples have been used to illustrate the points made by the book. There are approximately 45 examples, each describing the circumstances of a different project organisation. Most are derived from real life. However, for reasons that include ease of explanation and the protection of confidentiality, some examples are fictional. Whilst they are fictional, they are nevertheless based on lessons learned from real life. For clarity, fictional examples are described by this book in the present tense, whereas examples derived more directly from real life are described in the past tense.

Inevitably with a work of this nature, there are many people who I would like to thank. The first person on my list has to be David Hillson, both for writing the foreword for this book and for originating the Risk Maturity Model principles. He has also been responsible for a number of other ideas that have influenced this book including his work on opportunity management and risk descriptions.

The most prominent academic sources of inspiration for this book are Chris Chapman and Stephen Ward. You will find their ideas referenced in various places. I have been fortunate enough to have worked with both of them on risk management guides published by the Association for Project Management (APM). In addition, Chris Chapman kindly reviewed Chapter 3, which has a similar narrative structure to the ten tales in the second of his books co-authored with Stephen Ward.

Working on APM risk management guides has given me invaluable contacts with a range of other project risk management professionals including practitioners, consultants, risk tool developers and academics. In particular, I had the pleasure of leading the group that developed the APM guide *Prioritising Project Risks* (Hopkinson et al. 2008). The membership of this group was as strong and constructive as one could hope for, and I thank everyone who is listed in the guide.

Another APM group has also provided me with invaluable ideas and contacts on an aspect of project management which should be closely associated with risk management. This is the Governance of Project Management Specific Interest Group (SIG). Its guidance documents have influenced the Project RMM, particularly from its stakeholders' perspective and I thank all the SIG members who made significant contributions.

As described in the case study in Chapter 4 (see pp. 65–85), the most comprehensive application of the Project RMM across an organisation has been its use by the UK Ministry of Defence (MoD). Three MoD people to whom particular thanks are due are Russell Brown, Graham Lovelock and Greg Truelove. All three have provided constructive ideas and support that have contributed to the model. Russell Brown led the team that managed the RMM programme in its initial stages. Graham Lovelock took over the team leadership and co-authored a paper with me that was presented to the PMI Europe Congress in 2004. Greg Truelove, who remains in the team, and who has probably been involved in more formal RMM assessments than anyone, very kindly reviewed Chapter 4.

Within QinetiQ, I am grateful for the management team's continuous support for investment in the Risk Maturity Model. I am also grateful for the input of all of my consultancy colleagues in HVR and QinetiQ. Over the years, the strength and depth of this resource has provided me with an invaluable source of feedback and suggestions.

Most of all, I need to thank my wife Jane, both for her tolerance of difficulties caused by your spouse writing a book and also for providing such detailed comments on the first draft. As an academic, she was quick to identify loose writing or poorly explained ideas.

Last (and perhaps least!), I thank Jamie Kelly, a colleague on a railways infrastructure project, for his advice: 'Make sure the first line is real humdinger.' I'm sorry Jamie, but looking at it now, I suspect that first line just doesn't cut the mustard.

Introduction to the Project Risk Maturity Model

1 *The Project Risk Maturity Model*

A Risk Maturity Model (RMM) is a tool designed to assess risk management capability. The Project RMM software provided with this book will allow its user to assess the capability of the risk management process being applied on any project. It will also allow capability improvements to be assessed and for the capabilities of different projects to be compared. However, assessing risk management capability is not a simple task. Obtaining reliable results requires an assessor (or auditor) who has insight into the subtleties of project risk management; what is best practice for one project might be inappropriate to another.

This book has been written to describe the issues facing anyone tasked with assessing project risk management capability. Whilst it is possible for any owner of the Project RMM software to load it onto their computer and start their assessment process forthwith, following the guidance in this book should provide them and their organisation with a sounder basis for believing the results.

By way of introduction, the rest of this chapter describes how the Project RMM has been constructed and how its results should be interpreted. Subsequent chapters then describe the issues that assessors should understand before putting the RMM into action or making recommendations for process improvement. The section 'Software User Instructions' at the end of the book (pp. 235–42), provides user instructions for how the Project RMM software should be installed and used.

The Project Risk Maturity Model (RMM)

The Project RMM was first developed by HVR Consulting Services in 1999. Its four-level capability structure, illustrated in Figure 1.1 is derived directly from the structure developed by David Hillson (1997) who used it to establish a generic Risk Maturity Model framework. The matrix for assessments identified by Hillson's paper published in the *International Journal of Project and Business Risk Management* has been reproduced in Appendix A.

In order to adapt the Hillson Risk Maturity Model for project-specific purposes, the following additional sources were used:

- Standard risk management guides, most notably the *Project Risk Analysis and Management (PRAM) Guide* (1997) published by the Association for Project Management (APM).
- The project risk management literature published in academic journals and books.

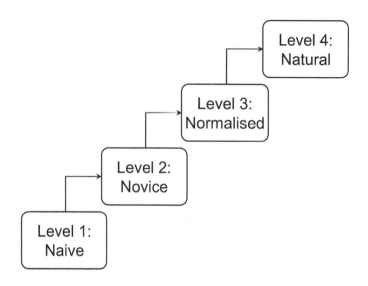

Figure 1.1   Risk maturity model levels

- The Turnbull Guidance[1] (1999) – *Internal Control: Guidance for Directors on the Combined Code.*
- The experience, dating back to 1987, of risk management consultants working for HVR Consultancy Services.

Since its creation the Project RMM has continued to evolve in response to lessons learned from its application. To date, it has been used for approximately 250 assessments on projects with an estimated combined value in excess of £60 Billion. Changes have also been made in response to new literature on the subject. Later chapters in this book identify the sources that have been the most influential. The software on the CD ROM included with this book is the latest version (version no. 6.0.0) of the model, updated in 2010.

The definitions of each level of project risk management capability are:

LEVEL 1 – NAÏVE

Although a project risk management process may have been initiated, its design or application is fundamentally flawed. At this level, it is likely that the process does not add value.

LEVEL 2 – NOVICE

The project risk management process influences decisions taken by the project team in a way that is likely to lead to improvements in project performance as measured against

---

1   N. Turnbull et al., *Internal Control: Guidance for Directors on the Combined Code,* hereafter referred to as the Turnbull Guidance or the Turnbull Report.

its objectives. However, although the process may add value, weaknesses with either the process design or its implementation result in significant benefits being unrealised.

LEVEL 3 – NORMALISED

The project risk management process is formalised and implemented systematically. Value is added by implementing effective management responses to significant sources of uncertainty that could affect the achievement of project objectives.

LEVEL 4 – NATURAL

The risk management process leads to the selection of risk-efficient strategic choices when setting project objectives and choosing between options for project solutions or delivery. Sources of uncertainty that could affect the achievement of project objectives are managed systematically within the context of a team culture conducive to optimising project outcomes.

Advancing through Project RMM Maturity Levels

RMM Level 1 could describe a project that is not implementing any process for managing risk. This would include projects that claim to be implicitly managing risk by virtue of the effectiveness of other project management processes such as planning (thus ignoring the fact that deterministic project management processes such as planning are not designed to manage the implications of uncertainty). However, since it would be unusual for projects to undergo RMM assessments when they have no formal risk management process, the more common cause of RMM Level 1 assessment results is a fundamental flaw with the design or application of the process. In practice, most problems at this level amount to failures of application. Whilst a risk management process might have been initiated, allowing any of its critical components to lapse into disuse will result in the overall process adding no value, hence producing a Level 1 assessment.

Once a project has taken professional advice or followed standard guidance to initiate its process, moving to a Level 2 RMM capability should be a relatively easy target to achieve. Level 2 does not set a particularly demanding standard. In effect, it requires that the value added by applying the risk management process should be greater than the cost and other resource implications of its application. Thus, even a relatively light application of the process can be sufficient to achieve this level.

The step-change difference between Level 2 and Level 3 RMM capability is mainly attributable to two factors: the discipline of implementing the process consistently across the whole project and the quality with which key skills are applied in practice.

A project will be able to achieve RMM Level 3 with the simple common-practice approach of using a risk register to underpin routine reviews of the implications of risks and the effectiveness and implementation of the responses designed to manage them. Although this is a simple process, there are a number of important skills involved in exploiting its potential to the full. For example, risks must be understood in a way that clarifies all relevant and significant sources of uncertainty. Failure to do this will impair the effectiveness of risk responses. Similarly, there are key skills involved in making sure that risk register contains the right risks, (and that they continue to be the right risks), that they are managed by the right risk owners, and that appropriate and sound methods are used to select and prioritise risks for review.

Although RMM Level 3 can be achieved with a simple process, application of the process must also be broad, continuous and sound. The process must actively engage all relevant members of the team and key stakeholder representatives. A key enabler of RMM Level 3 is the disciplined application of the process by risk owners. This discipline can usually only be maintained through regular risks reviews.

In practice, larger projects often have more difficulty achieving RMM Level 3 than smaller projects. Whilst they might find the process easier to initiate, issues of process application tend to be more common. Larger projects can also find it more difficult to correct issues of process design, particularly if the tools that they have invested in have insufficient flexibility. Thus, whilst smaller projects might have more difficulty initiating a risk management process, they often achieve RMM Level 3 in a relatively short period of time.

The biggest step change in the Project RMM lies in the difference between Level 3 and Level 4. Achieving Level 4 requires the risk management process to be capable of leading to 'the selection of risk-efficient strategic choices when setting project objectives and choosing between options for project solutions or delivery'. Whereas Level 3 capability requires the risk management process to support the 'achievement of project objectives', Level 4 capability makes it possible for risk management to contribute to decisions that set the project objectives in the first place. Similarly, where RMM Level 3 capability would typically identify responses to risks associated with a pre-existing project plan, Level 4 capability supports choices about the project solution; choices that can alter plans so fundamentally that they are, effectively, entirely different plans. Level 4 risk management capability therefore includes the management of risk from a project strategy perspective. Whereas RMM Level 3 supports a process designed to 'deliver the project right', Level 4 helps to provide assurance that the planned project is 'the right project'.

The step from RMM Level 3 to Level 4 requires a change of mindset and the level of management at which risk decisions are supported. The power to authorise project objectives and fundamental changes to the project solution (for example, its products, utilisation of the organisation's resources or the choice of parties to be involved) is usually vested in the project sponsor rather than the project manager. Executing the right risk responses from this level makes significant demands on both the organisation's risk management culture and the project's ability to provide relevant and realistic risk information.

Stepping up from RMM Level 3 to Level 4 usually also requires the use of more sophisticated risk management techniques. For example, at Level 4, it is necessary to quantify risk at the overall project level. Since risk management offers a wide range of techniques Level 4 capability requires people with the ability and experience to select the techniques that are appropriate to the project concerned.

One consequence of the need for different techniques is that simple techniques used to achieve Level 3 capability can prove to be too simplistic to support RMM Level 4. Temptation to over-exploit their use can thus become a barrier to achieving Level 4 capability. Perhaps the most common examples of incorrect exploitation are the Probability-Impact Matrix and the use of integrated risk register/Monte Carlo risk analysis tools. Chapter 8 (Risk Analysis, pp. 150–61) provides readers with explanations for this comment.

If the difficulties of achieving RMM Level 4 capability can be overcome, there are many benefits to be gained. An organisation with a Level 4 capability across all of its projects should find that not only more of its projects are delivered to plan, but that they are also more likely to have adopted the right project strategy when being planned. Risk management solutions will have been built into projects from the outset. Moreover, the techniques required for best practice are not always complex or time-consuming. Indeed, in the earliest stages they might be very simple (albeit not simplistic). What is required is that the right things are done by the right people at the right time.

Risk Maturity Model Questions

The Project RMM contains 50 questions, each one of which can yield information about a project's risk management process from one or more perspectives. For example, Question C2 (see Chapter 8, pp. 134–5) asks: 'How effectively do risk owners fulfil their role?' Since risk owners are responsible for managing their risks, the answer to this question will yield information about whether or not risks are properly understood (a key aspect of risk analysis) responded to effectively and whether or not the project has a good risk management culture. The model is based on a structure of six perspectives:

1. Project stakeholders,
2. risk identification,
3. risk analysis,
4. risk responses,
5. project management, and
6. risk management culture.

Each of the fifty Project RMM questions is detailed in Chapters 6 to 11. The assessor selects the level of performance being achieved by the project in respect of each question. The options for each question range from A (Level 4) through to D (Level 1). Occasionally, a question may be inapplicable to the project concerned. If the 'not applicable' option is selected, the question is disregarded in the calculation of results; in effect the question is neutralised. When answers to all 50 questions have been selected, the RMM results can be viewed in bar chart form as illustrated in Figure 1.2. The bar chart bar heights reflect the capability level from each perspective. If all answers were to be assessed as being A, all six bars would touch the top of the bar chart. In contrast, if all answers were assessed as being D, no bars would be visible since each would be calculated as being zero. The calculations use a system of weightings that reflects the relevance of each question to one or more RMM perspectives. The relative importance of questions within each perspective is also reflected in the weightings.

Assessing Overall Risk Management Capability

The overall assessment of risk management capability is equal to whichever is the weakest of the six perspectives. Figure 1.2 illustrates this approach by showing the overall assessment to be level with the top of the risk responses bar (the weakest perspective in this case).

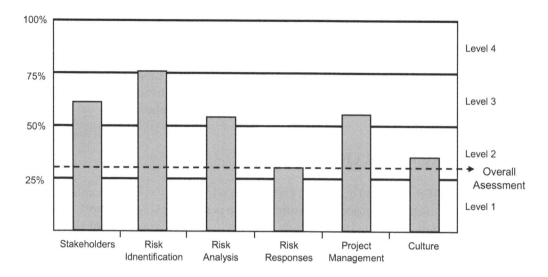

Figure 1.2   Example of the results from a Project RMM Assessment

This method used to assess overall risk management capability has two advantages. First, it resolves any ambiguity produced by results that show different levels of capability from amongst the six perspectives (something that is very common in practice). Second, it identifies where to focus the priorities for process improvement. For example, in the case of the project assessment shown in Figure 1.2, the priorities for improvement would concern risk responses. Improvements to the risk management culture would also be required to reach Level 3.

The justification for equating the overall assessment of capability with the weakest RMM perspective is based on the principle that process capability from each of the six RMM perspectives is critical to the overall risk management process. The overall process capability therefore cannot be better than the process when assessed through any of the individual perspectives. The argument that this applies to four of the six perspectives is illustrated in Figure 1.3. This figure shows the mapping of the risk identification, risk analysis, risk response and project management perspectives to an outline of the core risk management process detailed in the APM's *PRAM Guide* (2004). The *PRAM Guide* process is shown by the boxes and arrows, whilst its mapping to the RMM is shown by the regions bounded by dashed lines.

In order to function properly, the risk management process is dependent on every one of the activities shown in Figure 1.3. For example, if risk responses were never implemented, the effort spent on other aspects of the process would be wasted, even if they were performed excellently. Equivalent arguments can be made for each of the other three RMM perspectives shown in Figure 1.3. For example, if the project management process fails to initiate the risk management process appropriately or if it fails to manage it continuously (for example, through review processes), then the risk management process will be ineffective. It will be similarly ineffective if the wrong risks are identified or if risk analysis fails to create a correct understanding of the implications of risk and how it can be managed.

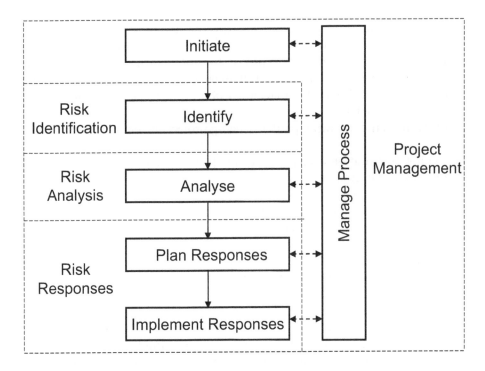

Figure 1.3 *PRAM Guide* **mapping for four of the RMM perspectives**

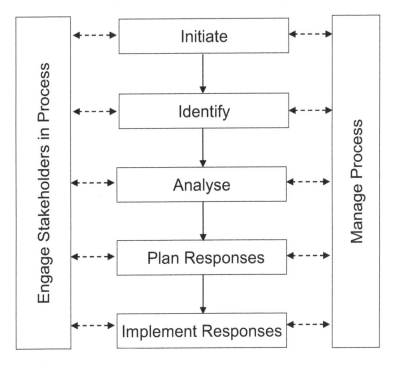

Figure 1.4 **Augmented version of the *PRAM Guide* process**

The argument that the stakeholders' perspective is critical to overall project risk management capability is illustrated in Figure 1.4. This is the same process diagram as that shown in Figure 1.3, but with the role of project stakeholders in the process differentiated explicitly from the project team's internal management of the process. The RMM thus treats the project team's internal management of a project risk management process as being not in itself sufficient.

The RMM treats the following parties as being project stakeholders:

- The owning organisation (as represented by its senior management),
- the project's lead customer,
- main (first tier) suppliers,
- other suppliers in the project hierarchy, and
- end users of the project's products.

In practice, all projects have a lead customer, even if the customer is another person (that is, the project sponsor) or another group within the same organisation. Since it is unrealistic for customers to transfer the implications of all risk to the project team, risk needs to be managed from the customer's perspective as well as that of the project team's. This does not imply that a project should manage its own customer's risk; customers should manage risks that they own. Rather, it implies that it is in a project's own interests that its customer manages risk effectively and retains, shares or transfers risk appropriately. Furthermore, the effects of many types of risk are often felt by both customers and projects. For example, schedule delay will, in different ways, affect both. There are therefore usually significant aspects of risk in which the project and customer have a mutual interest. Failing to engage the customer in the risk management process will fail to exploit this fact. It should also be remembered that customers control the agreement of project objectives. This gives them ownership of project strategy risks associated with whether or not the project's objectives are appropriate. Since projects may be in a position where they might be able to advise on and thus influence decisions related to setting objectives, this is another point on which there should be customer engagement in the risk management process.

Projects that are reliant on the delivery by suppliers of aspects of the project that involve risk are themselves customers. The arguments above concerning the need for customer engagement thus apply equally, albeit the relationships involved are reversed. There should be a strong link between risk management and contracting strategy; some of the most effective risk responses are contractual. Projects that have risk management weaknesses from the stakeholders' perspective often fail to manage this link effectively.

The argument that the risk management culture perspective is critical to overall project risk management capability lies in the observation that it may be possible for a project to convey the appearance of having an effective risk management process whilst ignoring the real implications of risk. Sometimes this might be due to unconstructive behaviour or sometimes it might be caused by a lack of understanding of what the risk management process should involve. Both are aspects of culture.

Perhaps the most obvious recent example of poor risk management culture can be seen in the behaviours of people that led to the 2007 credit crunch and the consequent recession. It now seems clear that senior executives took risks that were inappropriate, and that, for some, their organisations had sufficient information to know that this was the case. This was despite these organisations having externally audited risk management processes. In the case of one UK bank, it is alleged that the corporate risk manager lost their job after bringing management's attention to the unacceptably high risk associated with its aggressive sales strategy for mortgages. It is further alleged that their post was then filled by a sales manager! If allegations such as these are true, they demonstrate how a poor risk management culture can fundamentally undermine a risk management process.

Examples of the Project Risk Maturity Model in Practice

The following two examples are based on Project RMM assessments of real projects. They are designed to illustrate what different levels of RMM maturity look and feel like in practice. The first example (Project A) describes the case of a large civil construction engineering project that had a Level 3 risk management capability. For the project in question, this was sufficient to ensure that it achieved all its objectives. In contrast, Project B was a project that continuously underperformed against its objectives. It has been selected as a typical example of a project with a Level 1 risk management capability. Chapter 3 provides a third example (see pp. 38–59), by describing a project that achieves RMM Level 4. Comparing it to Project A illustrates the difference between RMM Level 3 and Level 4. Whereas Project A applied the risk management process after setting its objectives, the project in Chapter 3 uses risk management to shape the project solution.

Project A – An Example of Level 3 Risk Management Capability

Project A was a major renewal project on a manufacturing plant in the steel industry. Whilst the facility in question was out of commission, a number of the company's other production functions also had to be put on standby. The project timescale was therefore critical to both the company's turnover and its reputation with customers for timely delivery.

The RMM output shown in Figure 1.5 reveals a fairly even capability across the six perspectives and confirms that the project team was making good use of formal risk management practices. Risk identification and assessment produced a risk register of about 80 risks. Mapping these to a Probability-Impact Matrix (PIM) produced a reasonable priority order. A risk interviewing process led by a part-time risk manager ensured that each of these risks was reviewed on a regular basis. In addition, the top 30 risks were also reviewed at monthly project meetings, a procedure that allowed the project manager to intervene if the implementation of risk responses was inadequate. The effectiveness of this process was fostered by a good risk management culture. There was a high level of mutual respect amongst the team members that prompted constructive debate about potential difficulties. This openness of communication also extended to the project sponsor.

The approach of keeping a risk register is common practice in project risk management. Many projects do no more than this; some very simple projects don't need to. However, in the case of Project A, schedule performance was a key concern. The plant outage was scheduled for 70 days. Accordingly, a Monte Carlo schedule risk analysis was performed for the process of stripping down the old plant and then renewing it.

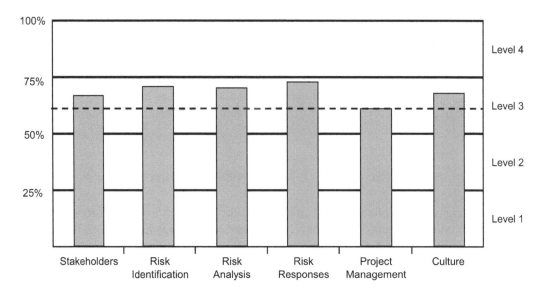

Figure 1.5   Project RMM assessment results for Project A

An early pass of this analysis suggested a probable schedule slip of 5–15 days. Lessons learned from this analysis were then used to introduce planning improvements and additional risk mitigation. Two further passes of this analysis were undertaken, after which the plan was considered to be sufficiently robust. This was an excellent example of how a schedule risk analysis should be used; the process enabled the team to rehearse the project delivery and understand how best to respond to events that could arise. During a post-project lessons learned exercise, risk management was identified as having been a major factor that enabled the project to meet its objectives.

Given the success of risk management on Project A, one could ask whether or not the Project RMM assessment should have been Level 4 rather than Level 3. The answer is that this is an example of the fact that, sometimes, a Level 3 project risk management capability is sufficient to achieve an organisation's objectives. Although Project A was large (approximately £50M), it was not particularly complex. As an internal project, it also had simple relationships with its stakeholders. Moreover, a project of this type was not new to the company concerned; it owned similar production plants and the same plant had been renewed 13 years previously. Finally, there were no incentives for members of the project team to make biased risk estimates. The sponsor had made a shrewd estimate of where to set objectives that were challenging, yet realistic and the project team knew that they would be judged by results, not forecasts.

The main reason for the risk management process falling short of Level 4 capability is that it had only a limited effect on the project strategy. For example, the schedule and cost objectives were set prior to the introduction of risk management. There was also no risk-based evidence that the project could live within its budget. For the company that sponsored Project A, these were minor issues. On more complex projects or when estimating bias or when conflicts of interest are potential causes of difficulty, a project RMM less than Level 4 would be more of a concern.

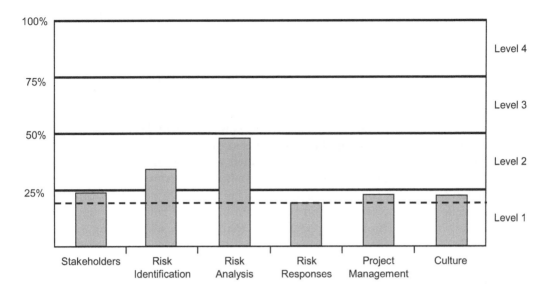

Figure 1.6   Project RMM assessment results for Project B

Project B – An Example of Level 1 Risk Management Capability

Project B was a defence equipment procurement contract, and was both larger and more complex than Project A. Figure 1.6 shows an assessment of the Prime Contractor's risk management capability towards the latter stages of development and early stages of production. A fixed price contract for these two phases had been won in a competitive tender.

The government organisation that was the Prime Contractor's customer had required a risk register to be included in the proposal. However, the submitted risk register was, in essence, a subtle part of the contractor's sales pitch. There was an emphasis on risks that competitors were more exposed to and a use of warm words and optimistic assessments to downplay any other risks that the customer could be assumed to have identified. For the first two years after contract placement, there had been no further use of risk management. However, important assumptions about the maturity of existing designs had turned out to be unfounded, and as a consequence, timescales had started to slip at an accelerating rate.

At this point, there was a change in company ownership. This resulted in at least three initiatives to make more formal use of a risk management process. First, the new finance director introduced a requirement for contingencies to be justified with calculations based on a risk register. In some circumstances, this might have prompted improved practice. However, the accepted basis for these calculations was simplistic. Moreover, the project team could quantify the board's expectations of project contingency. In practice, the project manager contrived a list of plausible risks with estimates to match these expectations.

In a second initiative, another director hired an external consultant to conduct a quantitative schedule analysis for completing the development phase. However, when the results of this analysis were published, management at all levels considered the forecasts to be so pessimistic that the modelling must be wrong. All the report's recommendations were then quietly forgotten. As it would turn out, actual schedule performance proved to be much worse.

As the condition of the project grew progressively worse, efforts were made to use the risk register to identify and manage actions for risk mitigation. Unfortunately these efforts lacked true support from the project manager. Risk reviews were invariably cancelled in favour of new emergencies. Support for the process was similarly lacking from the other organisations involved, including the customer and the major subcontractor. There was general reluctance on the part of the project leaders to tackle risks at source. To do so it would have been necessary to admit to past mistakes. Survival in project management jobs required a style that combined energetic fire fighting with the type of cunning that enables people to forecast success and then avoid blame for failure. The development phase of this project eventually slipped by more than three years: doubling the original plan.

The case of Project B illustrates a number of symptoms that may be associated with Level 1 risk management capability. Forecasts from a cost risk analysis designed to fulfil a director's expectations can be worse than useless. If the calculations are unnecessarily high, the project manager is liable to either spend unnecessarily or claim disproportionate credit for their performance. More commonly a director's expectations will be optimistic. If the risk calculations are optimistically biased in response, the owning organisation will have late notice of financial issues. In the case of Project B, the company's accountants were later forced to back trade the project's contribution to profits. But, perhaps the most important lesson to be learned from Project B is that an effective risk management process requires continuous and constructive support from managers at all levels. The project had the knowledge and resources to manage risk much more effectively, but the benefits of this were never realised.

Correlation between Project Performance and RMM Assessments

Comparing examples such as Project A and B is not untypical of experience to date when making RMM assessments. Projects with higher RMM assessments do seem to be more capable of achieving their objectives. They also tend to have relatively good reputations for being good projects to work in. Further evidence for there being a correlation between project performance and RMM assessments is discussed in Chapter 4: the UK Defence Procurement case study.

Assessing the Process as it is Applied in Practice

It is one thing to design an effective risk management process. It is another thing to carry through the process in practice. Even the best-designed process can be rendered ineffective if it is not implemented as intended. The contrast between the example projects A and B illustrates this point. By working to the process as designed, Project A was able to achieve a higher level of capability than Project B. This was despite the fact that Project B had the means to do as well, if not better.

The Project RMM has been designed to assess risk management capability as achieved in practice. This is an important factor to bear in mind when performing assessments or considering the relevance of questions. It also explains why certain issues associated with the enablement of good process that are included in some maturity models are not included explicitly in the RMM. Risk management training is an example of such an issue; there is no RMM question that asks; 'Are staff involved in the process adequately trained?' However, the availability of suitably skilled staff is essential to achieving the higher scores for many of the questions. It is the presence and application of risk management skills that is important rather than the means that has been used to make them available. The RMM is designed to assess whether the risk management process is effective as practised rather than potentially effective in principle.

2 *Scope and Context*

... because as we know, there are known knowns; there are things we know we know. We also know there are known unknowns; that is to say we know there are some things we do not know. But there are also unknown unknowns – the ones we don't know we don't know.

Donald Rumsfeld

In order to assess the capability of any process, it is necessary to understand its intended scope. What is counted in and what is counted out? It is also necessary to understand the context in which the process takes place. This chapter discusses the scope of project risk management and, hence, where the Project Risk Maturity Model (RMM) draws boundaries between risk management and other project management processes.

A number of issues concerning how the application of risk management may vary from one project to another are also discussed in this chapter. Risk management should not be a homogenous procedure to be applied identically to all projects. By definition, every project is unique; best practice risk management involves tailoring the process to the project's circumstances. In tackling this issue, this chapter also includes a discussion of a number of topical issues in risk management. As with any complex subject, there are differences of opinion between leading professionals on a number of issues. RMM users need to understand the position that has been taken.

Project Planning – Management of Known Knowns

Planning is a fundamental project management process. One cannot deliver a project without having any idea of its purposes or how to go about achieving them. Some projects may have plans worked out in more detail than others, but all projects have plans – even if the plans are only in people's minds. The disciplines required to develop project plans have therefore rightly emerged as a core component of project management.

The term 'project plan' is used here to refer to the intended course of a project as worked out using precise objectives and exact numbers. For example, a project plan will normally include a schedule of activities, intermediate milestones, end objectives and resource utilisation/cost forecasts. Project planning tools calculate and record these things deterministically, that is, with a single value. If everything that needs to be known about a project is already known and included in the plan then risk management would be a redundant process. As Donald Rumsfeld might have put it, a project plan will work well if everything that is important is a known known.

On some very simple small projects, it may be sufficient to rely solely on planning, and thus dispense with a formal risk management process. Moreover, where risk management is used, project plans provide important information and assumptions. A risk management process should therefore not be applied in isolation from planning. Also, although risk management decisions can be expected to affect plans, the process should not usurp the planning process by taking over what should be carried out by planning. Of course, poor planning practice might adversely affect risk management, but the proper solution is to correct planning process weaknesses. Accordingly, the Project RMM makes the assumption that there is a project planning process and focuses on risk management rather than planning capability.

Risk Management – Management of Known Unknowns

Despite the importance of planning, experience has shown that the development of carefully prepared project plans does not, in itself, guarantee success. Uncertainty (that is, a lack of certainty) is always a factor. On large, complex or innovative projects, uncertainty is often of critical importance. The choreographed course of a project represented by its plan can quickly unravel. Moreover, the plan may never have been the best solution in the first place. Risk management is about understanding and responding to the implications of significant sources of uncertainty that are known to exist. It can be used in conjunction with attempting to deliver a project according to its plan. It can also be used to optimise the plan before the project delivery phase commences.

Donald Rumsfeld's famous quotation about known knowns, known unknowns and unknown unknowns was the subject of fun in the press, having been awarded a 'prize' for failure to use plain English. However, close inspection shows it to be coherent and unambiguous. It is also worth remembering that Donald Rumsfeld came from a business background. Usefully, his quotation makes a point that is important to understanding the purposes of risk management. Risk management is concerned with known unknowns. This distinguishes it from deterministic project planning. Risk management will be useful to a project if there are things that are important to its success which are known to be uncertain. Of course, whether or not Donald Rumsfeld applied this understanding wisely to the management of the second Iraq war is a matter of opinion.

In the last 40 years, project risk management has been seen as becoming increasingly important. There are, perhaps two reasons. First, the number of large and complex projects has tended to increase over time. These tend to be the projects on which the implications of uncertainty are particularly important. Second, there has been evidence that the risk management process adds value. This is an important factor in a competitive world.

Despite the utility of risk management, it should be remembered that, in contrast to planning, it would be possible to deliver almost any project without consciously using a risk management process. Whilst the history of projects goes back several millennia, project risk management has only emerged as a discipline during the past few decades. Although risk management might have helped to deliver projects such as the Great Pyramids or the Suez Canal more efficiently, the absence of a formal risk management process did not prevent them from being completed. Risk management should therefore only be applied to the extent that it can be expected to add value.

Unknown Unknowns

Unknown unknowns are effects that occur as a consequence of events that could not reasonably have been anticipated. In practice this includes both events that are genuinely unidentifiable and events that are identifiable in principle, but would not be useful inputs to the risk management process. Since identification is a key step in a risk management process, the process cannot be expected to take unknown unknowns into account. It is illogical to expect that unknown unknowns will fall within its scope. Accordingly, the RMM excludes any expectation that unknown unknowns can be managed as part of the risk management process.

In principle, it would be possible to identify an infinite number of obscure risks (factory struck by meteorite and so on). However, common sense tells us that attempts to plan around these possibilities would be a distraction. Nevertheless, obscure, improbable or unexpected events can occur. Projects with long timescales, multi-ownership or that are reliant on novel technology tend to be more vulnerable than others.

The existence of unknown unknowns can also be caused by concealment. Whilst concealment can be the adverse consequence of a dysfunctional organisational culture, it can also be a legitimate management response to issues that are more important than the project. For example, if an organisation's senior management is considering plans to close or relocate a work site, there might be good reasons for not disclosing this to the project. In practice, the project has to ground its plans and risk assessment on assumptions concerning corporate objectives and organisational change. Where such assumptions are important it is good practice to record them alongside forecasts.

Thus the occurrence of unknown unknowns is a fact of life. In many organisations, provisions are made for them by dividing contingency budgets into two components: one for risk and one for unknown unknowns. The contingency fund for unknown unknowns is usually retained at a level higher than the project manager and may be pooled with similar contingencies related to other projects. Estimating provisions for unknown unknowns is often therefore a corporate responsibility.

Project Life Cycles

As time-limited enterprises, all projects go through a life cycle. There are many versions of a standard project life cycle, but all aim to reflect the way in which the purposes of project work evolves. For simplicity, this book uses just one example: the life cycle illustrated in Figure 2.1 taken from the Association for Project Management's *Body of Knowledge*.

The project risk management process should commence during the concept phase and continue up to the project closeout. After this, the management of risk should be handed over to operations. However, the sources of risks to operations may be rooted in decisions and events that occur during the project life cycle. The project risk management process should therefore cover risks that could impact across the whole of the extended life cycle.

A common failing is to focus the risk management process on just the outcomes of the current phase. The end purposes of the project need to be kept in mind at all stages. In particular, the concept and definition phases are means towards an end. Whilst it might be important to manage risks that would affect progress during the early phases, a major part of the purpose of these phases is to develop risk responses that will be

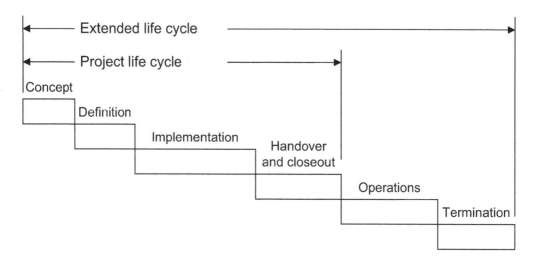

Figure 2.1   The extended project life cycle (APM *Body of Knowledge*)

effective during the implementation phase and beyond. The RMM takes this principle into account and awards poor capability assessments to projects that fail to do so.

It is sometimes argued that a project's risk management process cannot be expected to reach maturity until it has progressed through the earlier stages of concept and definition. If true, this would be most unfortunate. The implications of uncertainty can be expected to be both wider and of greater consequence in the earlier phases. Hence, it is even more important for the risk management process to be effective during these periods than during the delivery phase. An immature risk management process would represent a lost opportunity to add value at the very times when there is the greatest value to be added.

A distinction needs to be made between the idea of process maturity and the idea of project data maturity. Project estimates and assumptions can be expected to be increasingly stable as the project progresses. In contrast, the risk management process should, ideally, be at a high level of maturity from the outset. In practice, the difficulty with this is that risk management techniques that are useful during the earliest phases tend to be conceptually difficult. There is also a wide choice of advanced techniques that can be used. The Net Present Value risk modelling technique described in Chapter 3 is just one of many examples. Having the insight required to choose the most appropriate techniques is dependent upon having high levels of skill and experience. In contrast, easier techniques, based on estimating potential deviations from well-defined plans, come into their own as project data maturity increases. Whilst risk management offers a variety of approaches and techniques, the best choice of what to do is likely to change as the project goes through different phases. Making the best choices at different times is part of what constitutes a mature risk management process.

Overall Project Risk

Understanding the concept of overall project risk is an important part of understanding what is required to achieve RMM Level 4. At Level 4 a risk management process supports the management of risk associated with project strategy. Project strategy is linked with overall project performance and the implications that this has for stakeholders. A process that is fully capable of managing risk related to project strategy requires risk to be quantified at the overall project level.

The APM's *PRAM Guide* (2004), describes a concept of overall project risk. It states that 'The term "project risk" is used to describe the joint effect of risk events and other sources of uncertainty.' It defines overall project risk by stating that 'Project risk is the exposure of stakeholders to the consequences of variations in outcome.' The Project Management Institute's *Practice Standard for Project Risk Management* (2009) similarly describes overall project risk as representing 'the effect of uncertainty on the project as a whole'. It further states that 'Overall project risk is more than the sum of individual risks on a project, since it applies to the whole project rather than to individual elements or tasks.' An important implication is that it should not be assumed that overall risk can be calculated on a sum of the parts basis, for example, by adding up values for individual risks drawn from a risk register.

With regards to project performance measures such as cost and time, overall project risk can usually be conceptualised using a continuous probability distribution. The joint effects of multiple risks generate a range of potential outcomes, with the most probable outcome tending towards the centre of the range. The resulting probability distribution can be shown in graphical forms such as those illustrated in Figure 2.2.

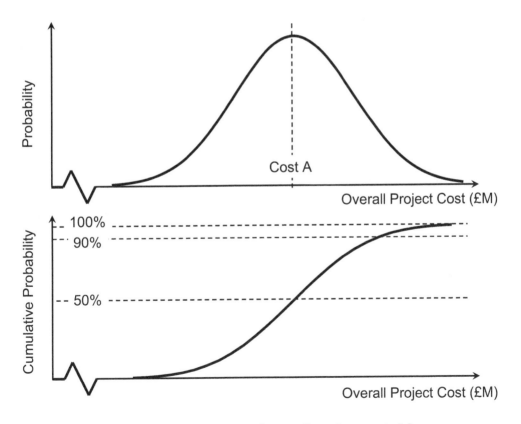

Figure 2.2   Graphical representations of overall project cost risk

The units shown on Figure 2.2 are for overall cost. However, the same formats could equally be used to show overall project performance using other measures such as completion date. The top graph illustrates the relative probability of different cost outcomes. Cost A is the most likely cost outcome and, hence, at the peak of the curve. Regions under the curve to the left of this are better outcomes and regions to the right poorer outcomes.

The bottom graph in Figure 2.2 shows precisely the same information as the top graph, but in a cumulative probability format. Its characteristic shape frequently leads to it being referred to as being the S-curve. The 50th percentile confidence value on the S-curve shows the median cost outcome. If the analysis that produces the graph is realistic, there would be a 50 per cent chance that this cost could be achieved or bettered.

Typically, the 50th percentile confidence value is similar to the value of the most likely outcome. However, there can be exceptions to this. For convenience, the curves shown in Figure 2.2 are illustrated as being smooth. Project risk forecasts can, however, produce less-smoothed shapes. For this reason, analysts often use a histogram format instead of the smooth probability distribution shown in the upper graph of Figure 2.2.

Information on overall project risk can be useful for a number of project strategy decisions, including:

- Project approval (go/no go decisions),
- setting targets and estimating contingencies, and
- choosing between project options.

A project sponsor might deem a project unacceptable if the overall level of risk was too high. A typical approach would be to consider whether or not the 90th percentile confidence outcome would be acceptable. Assuming the project was approved, the sponsor could then choose to set the project manager a target of achieving a much better outcome than this, but nevertheless allocate contingencies to provide sufficient confidence that the outcome would be acceptable. Providing a realistic basis for distinguishing between project targets, expected outcomes and commitments is an important contribution that the risk management process can make.

Project strategy decisions can also involve choosing between different project solutions. Typically such strategic choices are taken during the earliest project phases. Example 2.1 illustrates how an analysis of overall project risk can help to resolve a strategy choice.

Example 2.1 – A project strategy decision

As a consequence of a recent merger, a retail company has two major distribution centres, A and B. In order to realise some of the value added by the merger, it initiates a project to rationalise these to a single centre. During the concept phase, four options are studied:

1.   Retaining the two existing centres,
2.   transferring all operations to A,
3.   transferring all operations to B, and
4.   establishing a new enhanced distribution centre and closing both A and B.

Option 1 is to continue with the status quo. It is included in the concept phase risk analysis to provide a baseline against which the other options can be compared. Options 2 and 3 both involve risks attributable to factors such as the implications of expansion at the chosen site and the price that might be obtained by selling the other site. Option 4 is the highest cost and has the greatest level of risk. However, its potential benefits are greater since neither of the existing distribution centres are optimally located for the merged business.

During the concept phase the project team makes high level estimates of the risks involved with Options 2 to 4, taking into account the effects of risk on cost, economic benefits and timescale. This allows them to develop an assessment of the overall risk to the Net Present Value (NPV) associated with each option. The results produced by this analysis are shown in Figure 2.3.

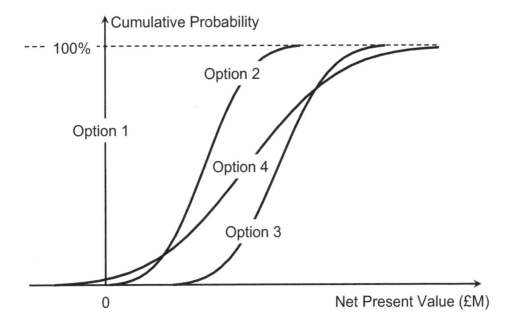

Figure 2.3   Comparison of risk forecasts for NPV

The S-curves in Figure 2.3 show the potential range of NPV associated with each option. Note that, since a positive NPV is beneficial, points on the curves towards the right indicate better outcomes than points towards the left. The S-curve for Option 4 shows that it is potentially the best option since the right most extent of the curve is better than any other option. However, the curves also confirm that Option 4 has the highest risk, since its range of possible outcomes is relatively broad. The fact that the curve reaches in to negative NVP also suggests that Option 4 might even destroy value (that is, its costs could outweigh its benefits). In comparison, Options 2 and 3 are always beneficial choices compared to the baseline. But, most importantly, the position at which the Options 3 and 4 curves cross shows that Option 3 is the more likely to produce the higher NPV.

In effect, the project team has calculated that, although Option 4 is potentially attractive, risks associated with buying the land, obtaining planning permission and ramping up a brand new facility mean that, on average, transferring operations to distribution centre B is a better choice. Based on these insights, the project sponsor instructs the project team to use the project definition phase to develop detailed plans for Option 3. However, in the meantime, the sponsor also launches a market survey of existing facilities in case an opportunity for a better version of Option 4 should present itself.

The decision making process illustrated in Example 2.1 is based on the principle of risk efficiency developed by Chapman and Ward. Option 3 is the most risk-efficient choice because it would, on average, produce the best results. The example also illustrates that risk responses can be applied at a strategy level and during the earliest phases of the project. This approach cuts out the time and effort that might be otherwise wasted developing detailed plans to compare options. The savings achieved are another contribution towards risk efficiency as explained by Chapman and Ward. As defined in Chapter 1, achieving RMM Level 4 supports '... the selection of risk-efficient strategic choices when setting project objectives and choosing between options for project solutions or delivery'. This is why the concept of overall project risk is important to understanding what is involved in achieving a Level 4 risk management capability.

Iterative Top-down Approach to Risk Management

Developing realistic forecasts for overall project risk such as those shown in Figures 2.2 and 2.3 is not an easy task. In practice, a risk analyst will need to develop a model that combines the implications of the most significant risks involved. What is required is a model that is rational in the sense that it includes all significant risk effects, takes into account how these could combine and avoids any duplication of effects. The best approach to developing a rational risk model is to do so iteratively starting from a high-level understanding of the project. The *PRAM Guide* (2004) illustration of a risk management process being delivered over time is detailed in Figure 2.4 and is based on this principle.

The core risk management process is shown on the right hand side of Figure 2.4. In practice, when this process can be maintained in a continuous steady state, many projects handle risks using a risk register. However, before reaching this steady state, the *PRAM Guide* recommends that the process should have included a series of iterative cycles in order to have managed risk from a high-level starting point. Figure 2.4 illustrates a project undertaking three iterative cycles of this process before reaching a steady state. The first cycle would be typically based on a simple, but holistic, understanding of how uncertainty could affect the purposes of the project. Each subsequent cycle would then develop an increasingly detailed understanding of the implications of risk.

The idea of starting with high-level understanding of risk and then evolving this into increasing levels of detail can be a difficult concept to grasp. However, there are many analogies that can be used. For example:

- A painter will have a concept of the whole picture before they start to put marks on the canvas. These initial marks will then often be high-level guides rather than the finished detail.

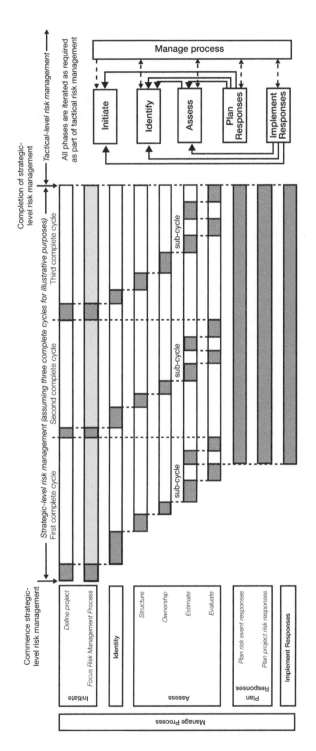

Figure 2.4 Risk management process being delivered over time (*PRAM 2004*)

- A system design engineer will establish a high-level understanding of user requirements before iteratively breaking down the design into lower levels of detail.
- The purposes of a project need to be understood before a plan is developed to deliver it. The plan is then usually developed in a top-down fashion, for example, with a product breakdown structure.

The consequences of not following a top-down process when painting a picture or designing a system can be understood readily enough. It would be naïve to do the lowest level details first and then fit them together in the hope that they would somehow combine to produce a coherent result. The same principle applies to the management of project risk. An example of a top-down approach to risk management has been included in Chapter 3 (see pp. 38–59). Reading through this should help the reader understand what can be involved.

Failure to apply the project risk management process in an initial top-down iterative fashion is very common. Much common practice is based on establishing a detailed risk register using a single-pass process. As a consequence important high-level insights into the true nature of project risk can be missed. Risk analysts are also often left in the position of trying to model overall project risk by adding up risk effects from a multitude of parts. This does not produce rational results. It also often fails to account for major sources of uncertainty that affect most or all elements of the project. The big picture needs to be understood first. It will be difficult for any project to achieve RMM Level 4 unless risk has been understood from a top-down perspective.

Risk Management or Risks (Plural) Management?

Amongst the numerous books and standards on risk management it is noticeable how many of them are focused on how to manage a collection of risks on a risk-by-risk basis. This might more properly be described as being risks (note the plural) management. This is not to say that the management of a number of individual risks will not contribute significantly towards the management of overall project risk (note the singular). It does. However, if one is to describe a process as being project risk management, there is an implication that it explicitly includes the management of overall project risk.

Managing Risks on a Risk-by-Risk Basis

The idea that risk management adds value by identifying potential problems and implementing proactive mitigation is probably the most widely understood benefit of the process. This accounts for the most widespread approach to project risk management, which is based on assigning individual risks to owners, who are then held responsible for identifying and managing actions in response. Typically, a risk register is maintained to support this process. In effect the project team manages each risk in the risk register as a potential issue in its own right. This can be described as managing risks on a risk-by-risk basis.

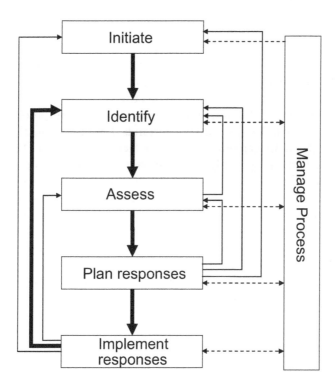

Figure 2.5   Risk management process (*PRAM* 2004)

Figure 2.5 shows the core risk management process recommended by the Association for Project Management (APM) *PRAM Guide* (2004). The interpretation of this figure (and similar figures in other project risk management guides) by many organisations is that good risk management involves:

- Writing a risk management plan tailored to the project,
- identifying risks as potentially adverse events that could impact on project objectives,
- assessing risks to prioritise them (typically using a Probability-Impact Matrix),
- planning mitigation actions designed to reduce each risk's probability and/or impact,
- implementing the actions as planned, and
- keeping all aspects of this process under continuous review,

With this simple risk-by-risk approach to risk management, risk identification, prioritisation and mitigation planning can be used as a simple decision making process. Experience has shown that, so long as the planned mitigation is actually implemented, this process can produce better results than relying solely on a deterministic project plan. Fixing potential problems before they occur has been proven to be better than allowing them to happen and dealing with the consequences.

There is thus no doubt that this simple approach of managing risks on a risk-by-risk basis can add value. Its benefits have persuaded some organisations to invest large sums of money on tools that standardise the use of risk registers across all their projects. Many of these tools map risks onto a Probability-Impact Matrix (PIM); a technique which has become a ubiquitous method for prioritising risks. The overall process is often referred to as being qualitative risk management. This can be contrasted with quantitative modelling that is used to calculate or simulate overall project risk.

However, the benefits of the simple risk-by-risk management process have led to two common misconceptions. The first misconception is that, if done to a high standard, the simple qualitative risk management process is de facto best practice. This misconception is based on an understanding that ignores the concept of overall project risk; a concept upon which some of the benefits of risk management are dependent. A register of individual risks cannot be expected to add up to the overall project risk. The second misconception is that the best methods for quantitative risk analysis are based on the use of probability and impact estimates from a detailed risk register. This bottom-up approach to calculating overall project risk has been fostered by the use of integrated risk register/ quantitative analysis tools. The fact that this can produce irrational risk models is often not well understood. The notes accompanying Question C9 in Chapter 8 (see pp. 156–61) can be read for further explanation.

The position taken by the Project RMM is that restricting the risk management process to a risk-by-risk approach will limit a project to Level 3 capability. This would not necessarily indicate an inappropriately poor process. At this capability level, the process can be still be expected to add significant value. An organisation might therefore consider this to be good enough on many of its projects, particularly if they tend to be relatively simple. However, there is still a difference between good enough and best practice, which could be better. More importantly, on large or complex projects, a Level 3 capability is often not good enough. Improving the performance of such projects may be dependent upon understanding interactions between risks, overall project risk and how these matters influence the behaviour of stakeholders. On projects where important sources of risk lie in project strategy decisions, Level 3 capability may lead to poor choices and, hence the loss of opportunities to identify the project's most risk-efficient solution.

Different Ways of Conceptualising Risks

Overall risk is the combined effect of all of a project's risks. It would therefore seem logical to describe any source of uncertainty that causes curves such as those shown in Figures 2.2 and 2.3 to become wider as being a risk. However, it has to be acknowledged that defining precisely what is meant by the term 'a risk' is a controversial subject amongst risk experts.

There are a number of standards and official guides to project risk management. Each one includes a definition of what is meant by the term 'a risk'. For example, the Project Management Institute's *Body of Knowledge (PMBOK)* states that a project risk is 'an event or condition, which, should it occur would have an effect on the project objectives'. The APM's *PRAM Guide* has a similar definition for what it describes as a risk event. One of the main areas of contention amongst risk experts is that such definitions may focus too much on the idea of risks being events. The idea behind a risk event is that the event might or might not happen; a risk event therefore has a probability of occurrence that is greater than zero but less than one (or 100 per cent).

The concept of a risk being an event lends itself easily to the use of the Probability-Impact Matrix (PIM) as a risk assessment tool. If the probability and consequence (impact) of each risk can be estimated, then risks can be mapped to a PIM for prioritisation purposes. The simplest form of project risk management is based on a process of identifying, prioritising and mitigating risks as threats. An example of a threat is: 'The contractor might use inexperienced staff, which would cause rework and delays.'.In recent years, many organisations have extended what had been threat-based risk management processes to include opportunities. Opportunities are events that, should they occur, would have benefits relative to the project objectives. Opportunities can be mapped onto a PIM in a similar way to threats, although the PIM has to be mirror-imaged, for example, as illustrated in Figure 2.6, to include a positive impact wing. The idea of the arrow of attention shown in this figure was introduced by David Hillson. It indicates the region in which the highest priority risks are mapped. This concept of opportunity management has rightly been credited with increasing the value added by risk management. It has also helped to correct the negative image of risk management being focused only on adverse consequences. Accordingly, the RMM treats both threats and opportunities as being included in the risk management process.

Threats | **Arrow of Attention** | **Opportunities**

Probability		Threats					Opportunities					Probability	
0.9	V HI	0.045	0.09	0.18	0.36	0.72	0.72	0.36	0.18	0.09	0.045	0.9	V HI
0.7	HI	0.035	0.07	0.14	0.28	0.56	0.56	0.28	0.14	0.07	0.035	0.7	HI
0.5	MED	0.025	0.05	0.10	0.20	0.40	0.40	0.20	0.10	0.05	0.025	0.5	MED
0.3	LO	0.015	0.03	0.06	0.12	0.24	0.24	0.12	0.06	0.03	0.015	0.3	LO
0.1	V LO	0.005	0.01	0.02	0.04	0.08	0.08	0.04	0.02	0.01	0.005	0.1	V LO
		V LO	LO	MED	HI	V HI	VHI	HI	MED	LO	V LO		
		0.05	0.1	0.2	0.4	0.8	0.8	0.4	0.2	0.1	0.05		
				Impact					Benefit				

Figure 2.6   Example of a PIM for prioritising threats and opportunities

Although PIMs may be a useful tool for classifying event-orientated risks such as threats and opportunities, they can prove to be a very limited way of assessing other risks that are not event orientated. In practice, many project risks are not triggered by something that may or may not happen, but, rather, are better described in other ways such as in terms of variability of effect. Example 2.2 is a case in point.

Example 2.2 – A variability risk

A project was reliant on purchasing costly equipment from a country that used a different currency. The lead time for this equipment meant that stage payments would be made over a period of three years. The project was therefore exposed to significant risk due to exchange rate variation. This was a difficult risk to map using the project's risk register, which used a tool configured to map risks to a PIM. The risk was certain to have some effect, since exchange rates would not remain constant. However, the effect was potentially either positive or negative depending upon whether the exchange rate varied either in favour or against the project.

The project manager suggested that the risk could be entered into the risk register as two separate risks: one a threat and the other an opportunity. However, the risk manager advised (correctly) that this would be a clumsy approach. In practice, the risk response amounted to a choice between accepting the risk or hedging the sums of money involved. There was no point in duplicating this choice in the risk register. Moreover, even if only the threat or the opportunity side of the risk was considered, the variability of effect was such that the impact could not be classified as falling within any particular PIM band.

Projects are often exposed to risks that are not potential events that can be mapped to a PIM. If reliance on a PIM causes a project risk management process to address only event risks (that is, threats and opportunities), then risks attributable to other sources of uncertainty may go unmanaged. Achieving the highest level of risk management capability requires all significant risks to be managed, be they of whatever type.

The common property shared by all risks is uncertainty (that is, lack of certainty). It is uncertainty that causes the spread of curves showing overall project risk. The APM's guide *Prioritising Project Risks* (Hopkinson et al. 2008) describes how a lack of certainty can lead to risks being conceptualised in a number of different ways:

- Event risk – uncertainty concerning an event, which should it occur, would have an effect on the project objectives (that is, threat or an opportunity).
- Variability risk – uncertainty concerning the eventual value of an important project variable, including those that affect duration, cost and resource requirements.
- Ambiguity risk – uncertainty concerning the underlying understanding of the project.
- Systemic risk – uncertainty concerning the combined effect of multiple interdependent factors.

In addition, the same guide identifies how risks might be further conceptualised in two ways at a higher level:

- Composite risks – uncertainty caused by the combined effect of a group of lower level risks.
- Project strategy risks – uncertainty concerning the fundamental role of the parties involved, the project objectives or factors that are critical to project success.

By way of illustration, Table 2.1 shows some examples of these various ways of conceptualising what is meant by 'a risk'.

Table 2.1   Examples of different ways of conceptualising risks

Type of risk	Example
Threat	Possibility that new equipment will prove to be unreliable.
Opportunity	Possibility that cost savings could be achieved by using an alternative subcontractor.
Variability risk	Uncertainty as to what the rework rate on a ship construction project will prove to be (knowing that all ship construction involves at least some degree of rework).
Ambiguity risk	Proceeding with work despite knowing that the associated contract specification is immature and that this has uncertain implications.
Systemic risk	A design change that could cause secondary design changes, some of which could cause further changes to the first design.
Composite risk	The overall level of uncertainty about a project's software development cost, attributable to a number of significant risks.
Strategy risk	Uncertainty about project contracting strategy choices when forming a project consortium.

Achieving a high level of Maturity with the Project RMM should involve managing all significant sources of uncertainty. Hence, if a project's risk management process is focused on only threats, or risk events, its RMM assessment will be adversely affected. This may be an important issue for projects using tools designed around the use of PIMs. For example, some projects may reject the idea that a risk can have a 100 per cent probability of occurrence and, hence, exclude variability and ambiguity risks from the process. If sources of variability and ambiguity risk are significant, this would limit the project's risk management capability. However, in practice, it may be found that workarounds have been used to include such risks in the process. The most important thing to consider is whether or not all significant sources of uncertainty are identified, assessed and responded to.

Risk Management Roles

The Project RMM assessments require that the following roles for individuals can be identified within the risk management process:

- Project sponsor,
- project manager,
- project risk manager,
- risk owners, and
- other project team members.

Project sponsors have a key role in project management. The Association for Project Management's *Directing Change: A Guide to the Governance of Project Management* (GoPM Specific Interest Group 2004) describes the project sponsor as being the person who owns the project business case. It also notes that they are the route through which project managers directly report and that they bear responsibility for providing project resources. In effect, the project sponsor is the custodian of project strategy and may be the most appropriate owner for project strategy risks. Ultimately, the project sponsor is the person who can authorise the project, stop it or change the project manager. The fact that it would be inappropriate to leave such decisions to the project manager is a key reason for needing a project sponsor.

The project manager is the person with overall responsibility for delivering the project in line with its objectives as authorised by the project sponsor. This responsibility includes leadership of the project team. The project manager should also be the person who is accountable for reviewing the effectiveness of the risk management process, although, on large projects this might be delegated.

The project risk manager is responsible for planning how the risk management process should be conducted and then ensuring that this is done. Although the term 'project risk manager' is a traditional title for this role, some organisations clarify it (correctly) using the title 'risk process manager'. Typically, the risk manager will be responsible for leading the project team's risk identification and analysis activities, although these should also be expected to involve a range of project personnel, including the project manager and, ideally, the project sponsor. Depending upon the project's size and complexity, this might be a full-time or part-time role. On very large projects, the risk manger might lead a team of risk specialists. At the other extreme, on small projects, the risk manager's role may be fulfilled as a part-time role by the project manager.

In practice, risks tend not to be managed effectively unless there is a clear ownership of responsibility for doing so. The role of risk owners is therefore very important.

The ownership of risks should be aligned with levels of responsibility and ability to influence risk outcomes. For example, a project strategy risk driven by sources of uncertainty concerning an organisation's need for the project would normally be owned by the project sponsor. In contrast, a technical risk concerned with the possibility that a particular design might not work as intended would be better owned by the project team member best placed to influence the design outcome.

Project team members who are not risk owners may still have a role to play in the risk management process. For example, they might identify risks, even if they were not assigned risk ownership responsibilities. They might also have responsibilities for implementing risk responses. The involvement of a wide variety of project team members in the process is a good sign of there being a healthy risk management culture.

Stakeholder Ownership of Risks

Whilst the ownership of risks by individuals is important, the concept of risk ownership should also be understood in terms of the implications of risk to project stakeholders (that is, the groups, organisations or companies involved). Understanding these two different levels of risk ownership together can also be very useful. Ideally, a risk that is owned by a stakeholder will be managed by an individual who properly represents that stakeholder's interests. Failure to achieve such alignment will often result in a lack of incentive to manage the risk effectively. Indeed, as illustrated in Example 2.3, it might even incentivise counterproductive behaviour.

Example 2.3 – Poor contract design

A government defence department placed a major contract for a submarine system with a large defence company. The contract included significant penalty payments for late delivery, thus transferring some of the implications of schedule risk to the company. However, development of the system was dependent upon the parallel development of a smaller communications network system to which the major system (together with weapons systems being developed by other contractors) would be connected.

The communications network system was procured under a separate contract. Delays to the communications network system project would therefore relieve the company producing the major submarine system of the risk of penalty payments. The weakness of this contracting strategy was exacerbated by the fact that both contracts had been placed with the same company. If necessary, the company could therefore escape its cost exposure to schedule risk on the major system by delaying the smaller project. Delays to the communications network project also caused the government department to default on its obligations to other contractors, thus relieving them also of the cost implications of schedule risk.

Understanding the implications of risk ownership is a major contribution that the risk management process can make to the management of projects. Work on many projects is contractually driven. Some contracts are designed with explicit reference to certain risks. However, even in the absence of this, the implications of risk ownership are implicit to contractual terms and conditions together with related specifications. There should therefore be a close relationship between the risk management process and a project team's contracting function. In practice, the absence of such a link is a common source of weakness.

In the case of internal projects, formal contracts are unlikely to be used. However, internal projects still involve making agreements between different parties within an organisation. Whilst such agreements may be subject to different degrees of formality, they all serve some of the purposes of a formal contract and thus confer risk ownership. The parties involved in internal projects often represent different interest groups; typically the project delivery team and the end product users. The concept of stakeholder ownership of risks therefore applies to both internal and external projects. This is a key reason for stakeholder engagement in the project's risk management process being assessed by the Project RMM as being one of the six perspectives of risk management capability.

Programme Management

Within the field of project management, the term 'programme' has been used in a number of different ways. What is generally agreed is that a programme includes projects that have to be co-ordinated with each other and, possibly, other related operational activities. Hence examples of the meaning of the word programme include:

- A project in its own right, for example, constructing a new airport terminal, which involves the delivery of multiple sub-projects,
- a sequence of projects, each building upon its predecessor, for example, the development of a software application through several releases,
- repeated implementation of minor variations around a particular project, for example, rebranding all shops owned by chain store, and
- maintaining or evolving operational capability by delivering related projects, for example, maintaining an aircraft in military service with obsolescence and enhancement projects.

In describing the purpose and scope of the Project RMM, it is helpful to distinguish project-related activities and operations (that is, business as usual). The Project RMM is designed to measure project risk management capability, rather than the capability of a process to manage risk associated with ongoing operations. At the programme level, the Project RMM is therefore applicable to purely project-based programmes, but not to programmes supporting ongoing operations. In the former case, the Project RMM could be used at the level of the overall programme (for example, construction of a new airport terminal) and/or at the level of any of its sub-projects. In the latter case (for example, maintaining an aircraft in military service), the Project RMM would be applicable to only the individual contributory projects.

However, it should be remembered that, where the purpose of a project is to transform the way in which operations are conducted, any risk of business as usual being disrupted as a consequence of the project should be handled by the project risk management process. Similarly, any risks to the effectiveness of the transformed state of operations when the project has been completed should also be included in the project management process since this would impact on the project's objectives. For example, a project to refit part of an airport terminal may involve risks of disruption whilst the project is being delivered and risks to the efficient operation of the terminal after project handover to operations. Failure to manage the associated risks effectively should be reflected in the RMM assessment.

Project Size and Complexity (Tailoring the Risk Management Process)

Some projects are small and simple. If uncertainty is not an important factor, a formal risk management process might not add value at all. Asking simple what-if questions when developing the project plan could be sufficient. In contrast, when undertaking a complex multi-£billion project the implications of risk will usually necessitate a range of risk management activities.

Project risk management provides a large toolkit of techniques for understanding and quantifying risk, some simple and others complex. Some techniques are appropriate to early project phases and others for controlling risk during project delivery. Simple techniques, such as the use of a risk register to manage risk on a risk-by-risk basis might be used to engage a wide range of project stakeholders and team members. Other techniques, including most quantitative approaches to analysis, require sophisticated skills or greater insight. Tailoring the process to the best interests of each project is a key risk management skill.

The RMM is designed to measure risk management capability for all projects that would benefit from the process. It therefore avoids any prescription of risk management techniques since they should vary between projects. However, achieving the highest RMM level of capability (Level 4) does depend upon the use of quantitative techniques to understand the implications of overall project risk. Using a simple qualitative approach based on managing risks on a risk-by-risk basis will therefore limit a project to having a Level 3 RMM capability at best.

3 *Starting from the Top: Using a Multi-pass Risk Management Process*

The biggest uncertainty in a risk analysis is whether we started off analysing the right thing and in the right way.

David Vose

Multi-pass Approaches to Project Risk Management

As one goes through the Project Risk Maturity Model (RMM) questions, and accompanying discussion (see Chapters 6 to 11), it should become evident that the highest scoring answers to a number of questions are dependent upon having shaped the risk management process, at least in part, with a top-down approach. However, the principle of using a top-down approach is not always followed in practice. Nor is it covered by many professional training courses or a number sources of professional guidance. Thus, many readers may be unfamiliar with what is involved. The aim of this chapter is to illustrate the importance of using a top-down approach and the multi-pass process that this implies.

Steen Lichtenberg was an early advocate of a top-down approach to risk analysis, establishing international use of his *Successive Principle* by the 1970s. A key component of this approach is 'working top down, systematically focusing only on the few most important matters during successive steps of improvement'. Chris Chapman adopted a variant which did not involve independent assumptions and integrated bottom-up analysis in a process initially developed for BP offshore North Sea projects in the late 1970s. Chapman then championed this integration of top-down and bottom-up analysis when drafting the process chapter for the first edition of the *Project Risk Analysis and Management (PRAM) Guide* (1997) published by the Association for Project Management (APM). This process chapter was then updated with minor modifications (see Figure 2.4) in the second edition of *PRAM* (2004).

The *PRAM Guide* advocates a top-down multi-pass approach to project risk management. It recommends undertaking between two and five cycles of this iterative process to ensure that the project strategy is optimised from a risk perspective. Each cycle takes the risk management process to further levels of detail. Eventually, after key strategy decisions have been taken and the project plans have reached an acceptable level of maturity, the risk management process enters something that more closely resembles a steady state. Depending upon the circumstances of the project or the policy of its owning organisation, the time at which this occurs may be at different points of the project life cycle for different projects. However it often occurs around the time of the main project approval point.

The (fictional) example of a road bridge project used in this chapter illustrates how a multi-pass process might be applied in one case. This example is used to illustrate a number of important points. In particular, it shows how insights developed during each cycle of the process are used to influence subsequent cycles. However, the example is not intended to be used as a recipe for all projects. Analysis of the most significant sources of uncertainty on another project might require the use of different techniques. A much wider range of examples, based on the same principle can be found in books by Chapman and Ward. In particular their book *Managing Project Risk and Uncertainty: A Constructively Simple Approach to Decision Making* (2002) presents ten case studies, and is highly recommended.

Use of a top-down approach helps to support a critical feature of risk analysis: one must make sure that the analysis addresses the right question. For the purposes of a first pass risk analysis, identifying the right question should start with understanding the fundamental purpose of the project. One might think that the purpose of building a road bridge would be to improve the efficiency of road transport links. However, from the perspective of the contractor, who is the subject of the example, the fundamental purpose of the project is to make money. If the first pass analysis fails to address the issue of profitability, it will fail to direct the risk management process correctly.

The quotation at the top of this chapter underlines the importance of identifying the right question. David Vose's book *Risk Analysis: A Quantitative Guide* (3rd Edition 2008) is notable for its depth of explanation of the mathematics involved in risk modelling and simulation. However, in an early chapter concerning risk analysis quality, he correctly stresses the importance of understanding what is being modelled and why. The following words taken from this chapter capture the essence of the message.

> *When we are asked to review or audit a risk analysis, the client is often surprised that our first step is not to look at the model mathematics and supporting statistical analyses, but to consider what the decision questions are, whether there were a number of assumptions, whether or not it would be possible to do the analysis a different (usually simpler, but sometimes more complex and precise) way and whether this other way would give the same answers, and to see if there are any means for comparing predictions against reality. What we are trying to do is see whether the structure and scope of analysis are correct. The biggest uncertainty in a risk analysis is whether we started off analysing the right thing and in the right way.*

The Road Bridge Project – A Worked Example

Two areas of a region are separated by the absence of a convenient road link across a river. To solve this problem, and boost the local economy, the regional government authority, with national government support, launches a competition prior to selecting an industry partner to design, construct and operate a toll bridge. It is expected that the winning company will design, construct, and operate the bridge over a period of the next 20 years and that the tolls collected will allow it to recover all costs and make a profit. The competition will be won by the company that offers best value for money in terms of traffic capacity and toll charges. However, company reputation and confidence in the competing proposals will also be taken into account.

The regional authority and government officials are aware that contractors may need further financial inducement to participate. In the event of a satisfactory project solution being identified, the government would be prepared to invest up to 40 per cent of the capital cost with an upper limit of £50million. Similar arrangements have been made for previous projects. However, since the government would prefer the project to be self-financing this has not been disclosed to competing contractors.

First Pass Risk Management – Initiation

Following the receipt of tender documents, ProSit Construction Engineering Ltd. is one of the companies considering competing for the road bridge project. The project manager and project risk manager identify immediately that they have two primary stakeholders to satisfy: their own management and the regional authority customer. The regional authority will want to see an attractive proposal with low tolls, high traffic volume and short timescales. However, to a certain extent these aspirations are at odds with the company's objective of owning a profitable project.

The ProSit project manager has been appointed by a project sponsor, a ProSit business operations director who owns a portfolio of projects and prospects. The sponsor has long experience of project forecasts and is all too familiar with the problems of the proposed business model for the road bridge project. Not only is there a tendency for infrastructure projects to be too optimistic when making cost and schedule forecasts, but revenue forecasts also tend to be too optimistic. This combination erodes profitability from two ends. What is needed is an unbiased, that is, realistic, estimate of project profitability. This can then be compared to similar estimates for other prospects, allowing the sponsor to make an early decision as to whether or not to invest money in a proposal. The key question to be addressed by the first pass of the risk management process is: given the risk involved is the project likely to be sufficiently profitable for ProSit to decide to continue with a bid?

The ProSit project risk manager recommends commencing the risk management process with a simple quantitative model. The purposes of this will be to obtain an early unbiased estimate of profitability and identify key aspects of risk that require management responses and further, more detailed, risk identification and analysis. The simplest risk model that can be developed is based on the following four variables:

1. Design and construction (capital) costs,
2. annual revenue,
3. annual operating costs, and
4. the date on which the bridge is opened.

In simple terms, the project will be profitable so long as revenue exceeds costs. However, because of the time disparity between capital expenditure and the revenue stream, the project will need to discount the value of money over time when making its financial calculations. The project manager recommends that this should be done using a Net Present Value (NPV) calculation.

Net Present Value

The calculation of NPV recognises that a sum of money has more economic value today than the same sum of money will have in the future. For example, if a business borrows £1,000 to make an investment, then it has to pay interest until such time as the loan can be repaid. Thus, if the revenue or the value of the benefit achieved from the investment is also £1,000, the business will have made a loss to the extent of the interest that has been paid in the meantime. The formula for calculating NPV is:

$$NPV = \sum_{t=0}^{n} C_t / (1 + D)^n$$

where:
C_t = the net cash flow over a period of time (typically 1 year),
t = the period of time during which that cash flow takes place,
D = the discount rate (rate of real terms loss in the value of cash expressed as a percentage - typically per annum), and
n = the number of periods of time periods (typically years) over which NPV is calculated.

The discount rate should be based on the cost of borrowing money in real terms, that is, net of inflation. Note that, when using the formula, one has to remember that a percentage represents a proportion of the number one. Hence, for example, a discount rate of 6 per cent has a value of D = 0.06.

The NPV formula calculates future values of money at today's rates, thus removing the need to consider the effects of inflation. Table 3.1 illustrates the effect of the formula. As the discount rate is increased, the value of money reduces more rapidly.

Table 3.1   Illustration of the effects of the Net Present Value calculation

Discount Rate	Net Present Value of £1,000			
	Today	After 1 year	After 5 years	After 20 years
4%	£1,000	£962	£822	£456
7%	£1,000	£935	£713	£258

In the case of the bridge project, the opening date is important because delays will reduce overall revenue during the 20-year concession period. However, the application of the NPV calculation shows it will make the importance of the opening date even more pronounced; early revenue will be calculated as having a higher relative value than later revenue when the NPV formula is applied.

First Pass Risk Management – Identification, Estimation, and Analysis

By identifying a simple structure for a risk model, the project manager has, in effect, already identified four high level risks: capital costs, revenue, operating cost and opening date. Each can be regarded as being a risk because their outcome is uncertain and the associated uncertainty is likely to be significant. However, these risks are clearly composites of lower level risks. For example, the capital costs could be driven by a number of sources of uncertainty. These include uncertainty about the precise design and location of the bridge as well as labour and material costs. In making estimates for each of the four composite risks, the project risk manger, together with the project team therefore identifies the most significant sources of uncertainty driving each one.

A review of this simple risk model with the project sponsor also identifies another significant source of uncertainty: the cost of borrowing money. The company would have a choice between funding the capital costs from its own reserves or raising finance from a third party, the latter being much the more likely option. However, since the terms of such finance are yet to be negotiated, the cost of borrowing is uncertain. Moreover, recent instability in financial markets has increased the level of uncertainty involved. Since the NPV model discount rate represents the costs of borrowing in real terms, uncertainty about the cost of finance can be included in the model by simulating variance in the discount rate.

From a risk identification perspective, the project has therefore identified risk at two levels. At a higher level there are five risks: four composite risks, plus the variability risk associated with the cost of borrowing money. Identification of these risks has been inherent to structuring the risk model. At the next level down, the company has identified the major contributing sources of uncertainty. Identification of these risks would have been informed by knowing that developing realistic risk estimates at the higher level would require this level of detail.

Table 3.2 shows the risk estimates developed for the first pass NPV risk model. Use of the uniform probability distribution at this stage reflects the simple and prudent form typical of a first pass risk model. As the model develops through subsequent cycles of the risk management process, it would be usual to utilise more sophisticated probability distributions.

Table 3.2   First pass risk estimates

Composite Risk	Lowest Value	High Value	Probability Distribution
Capital expenditure	£80M	£150M	Uniform
Annual revenue	£14M	£27M	Uniform
Annual operating costs	£2.2M	£3.0 M	Uniform
Opening date	Now + 3 years	Now + 7 years	Uniform
NPV Discount rate	4%	7%	Uniform

In order to explain the nature of four of the risk model inputs, the project risk manager produces Figure 3.1. This illustrates the cost and revenue profiles of estimates detailed in Table 3.2. In the interests of simplicity, the capital expenditure profile is based on a uniform rate of spend commencing in one year's time, by when the competition would be assumed to be over and work would have commenced. Capital expenditure is then spread over a four-year period, based on the period up to when, on average, the bridge might be opened. The risk associated with capital expenditure is illustrated by the area between the solid line for its profile (that is, the high value) and the dashed line showing its lowest value. The profiles and associated risk are shown similarly for the annual revenue and operating costs. However, since neither of these would commence until the bridge was opened, their profile slopes illustrate the effect of the way in which the implications of uncertainty in the opening date could be modelled.

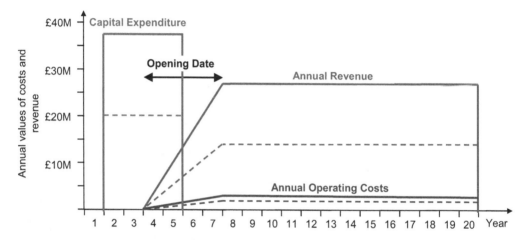

Figure 3.1   Profile of first pass bridge project estimates

The estimates detailed in Table 3.2, together with the profiles shown in Figure 3.1 are entered into a spreadsheet model for the purposes of running a Monte Carlo simulation. This model simulates the combined effects of all five risks using several thousand individual iterations. During each individual iteration, a value for each of the five risks is selected randomly from its range of potential outcomes. These are used to calculate the overall NPV. During some iterations, by chance, a favourable combination of values is simulated, thus calculating a relatively high NPV. Similarly, there are other iterations during which adverse combinations of values produce relatively low outcomes. More frequently iterations occur that produce a more likely NPV prediction, close to the average produced by the model. Figures 3.2 and 3.3 show two outputs from this modelling.

Figure 3.2 is a cumulative probability curve showing the range of NPV values that the bridge project could have. As one would expect at this first-pass stage in the risk management process, the range of possible outcomes is very broad. As more information becomes available, later passes of the process can be expected to show a reduced level of overall project risk. Overestimating the accuracy of these results should therefore be avoided. However, Figure 3.2 does indicate that there is a possibility that NPV could be negative, so this is an obvious source of concern.

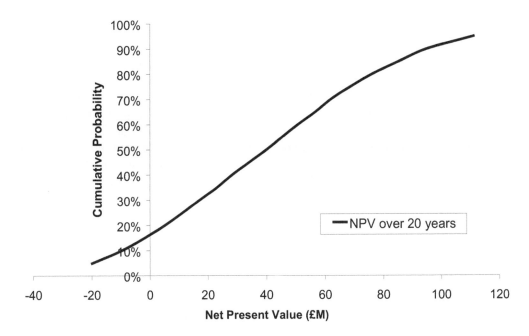

Figure 3.2   First pass NPV risk modelling results

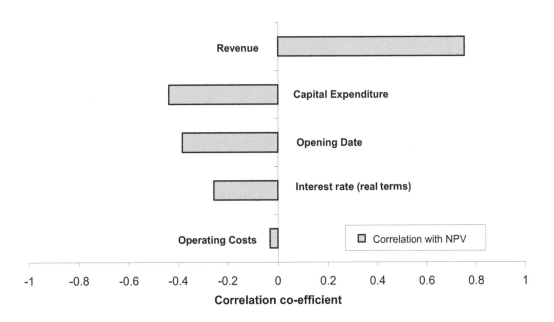

Figure 3.3   Tornado chart from the first pass modelling results

Figure 3.3 is a tornado chart that shows the correlation between each of the five risks and the overall risk to NPV. This information (often referred to as being risk cruciality results) is a product of the Monte Carlo simulation made available by the risk analysis tool. Figure 3.3 shows that there is a high positive correlation between revenue and NPV: high revenue tends to produce a high NPV. The figure also shows that there is negative correlation between the four other risks and NPV. For example, high capital expenditure or later opening dates tend to produce a low NPV. High values of correlation (either positive or negative) indicate that there is a strong relationship between a risk and the overall risk. The tornado chart therefore indicates that the risk associated with revenue has more influence on project performance than any of the other four risks.

Risk prioritisation approaches such as that illustrated by the tornado chart are useful during the earlier passes of a risk management process because they indicate where the next stage of the risk management process should be focused. There are a number of different techniques that can be used, some of which are described in the APM Guide *Prioritising Project Risks* (Hopkinson et al. 2008).

Sometimes, it is possible to identify priorities without any complex simulation. Figure 3.4 is a modified version of the cost and revenue profiles shown in Figure 3.1 and provides an example of this. It illustrates how the effect of the NPV discount factor on the value of money modifies the cost and revenue profiles. The value of the risks associated with revenue and capital expenditure is illustrated by the area between the solid and dotted lines. Examination of the relative areas bounded between the solid and dashed curves in Figure 3.4 shows that the value of revenue risk is greater than the value of capital expenditure risk. This is effectively the reason for the prioritisation order indicated by the tornado chart.

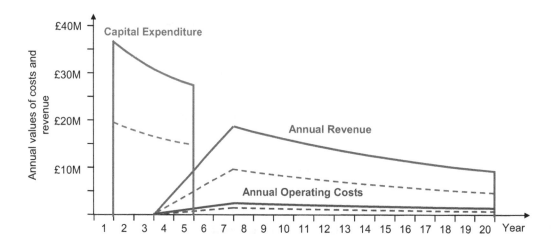

Figure 3.4   Effect of NPV discount factor on first pass modelling estimates

First Pass Risk Model Assumptions

Before presenting the first pass risk analysis results to the sponsor, the project manager and risk manager discuss and record key simplifying assumptions. These provide context without which the analysis results could easily be misinterpreted. Key assumptions made in order to simplify the analysis include:

- Operating costs will escalate at the same rate as inflation,
- traffic volumes will be constant,
- toll charges will escalate at the rate of inflation,
- capital costs will not include the purchase of land, and
- planning consent will be granted, albeit with the possibility of delays.

Some of these assumptions, such as the one concerning land ownership, identify points that need to be clarified with the customer. Others identify sources of risk that would require further investigation in a second pass risk analysis. For example, since the tornado graph in Figure 3.3 shows that revenue is the most important source of overall risk, through life variations of traffic volume could have a significant effect. Finally, when modelling risk it is often necessary to assume that certain potential show-stopping issues will not occur. The planning consent assumption is an example. Outright failure to gain planning consent would undermine the entire basis of the risk model, so it has to be excluded. However, the project sponsor and project approval bodies need to be aware that the risk does exist.

Project Sponsor's Response to the First Pass Risk Analysis

When the first pass risk analysis results are presented to the project sponsor, two questions are uppermost in their mind:

1. Should we invest in a full bid for this project?
2. If so, what does the risk analysis tell us about how to develop project strategy?

The NPV curve shown in Figure 3.2 helps to answer the first of these questions. The sponsor is concerned both about the relatively low rate of return on investment and the possibility that the project could lose money. In return for an investment that is likely to exceed £100million, the total return over 20 years would, given average luck, be less than £50million, that is, not much more than 2 per cent per annum. Furthermore, the sponsor is aware that the risk analysis does not account for unknown unknowns. Since, in their experience, the effect of unknown unknowns tends to be negative, the business case is liable to prove even weaker than currently estimated.

Given the poor prospects for achieving an acceptable rate of return, the project sponsor decides to stop the project at this point. There are other, more attractive prospects. Having thanked the project manager and risk manager for their work, the sponsor remarks that there are two ways of losing money on projects like this. 'One is to invest in the bid, only to lose the job. The other is to bid and win it!' Two days later the official responsible for running the project competition on behalf of the regional authority receives a polite letter from ProSit Construction declining the opportunity to bid. The stated basis for this position is that 'Regrettably, we judge that the return on investment may be insufficient given the level of risk involved.'

Reversal of a No-Bid Decision

Two months later, ProSit Construction receives notice of changes to the tender documentation for the road bridge project and a request to reconsider its previous no bid decision. The regional authority had experienced a disappointing response to its original tender package. The only company still intending to submit a proposal lacks sufficient credibility. On the basis of this evidence the national government was now prepared to step in with the additional funding that had previously not been disclosed. In addition, the regional authority had identified specific opportunities to enhance traffic volume. The revised tender document stated that plans were being developed to establish a large business park and a major distribution depot near the bridge. The distribution depot was estimated to generate an additional 400 lorry movements across the bridge per day.

The ProSit project sponsor quickly calculates that government funding would both reduce capital cost and raise profits, thus providing a significant uplift to the return on investment. On this basis, they re-start the project, recall the project manager and instruct them to prepare a more detailed business case.

Second Pass Risk Analysis Model

A key insight from the first pass risk model was that the most significant source of risk was revenue uncertainty. The risk manager immediately recognises that the tender changes make the importance of revenue even more pronounced. The second most significant source of uncertainty had been capital cost. However, the contractor's exposure to this source of risk has been reduced by the offer of government funding. In contrast, uncertainty about revenue has been increased. Although the tender document identifies opportunities for increased traffic volumes, there are no guarantees that they will be realised.

Somewhat to the project manager's surprise, the risk manager recommends that the next cycle of the risk management process should focus on drivers of revenue risk. The project manager had expected risk analysis to be focused on the cost and schedule risk implications of designing and building the bridge. However, the risk manager argues that this would be a mistake, since it could lead to the pursuit of cost and time savings that would have counterproductive effects on revenue, and hence the overall business case.

Having accepted that the project needs to develop a revenue risk model, the project manager buys in time to fund ProSit's traffic forecasting subject matter expert. The team then works on structuring the revenue risk model and making the associated estimates. The following factors are identified to be of importance.

- Inherent demand for use of the bridge,
- acceptable levels of toll charges from a user perspective,

- ability to maintain traffic flow (for example, avoidance of bottlenecks at junctions with existing roads and at toll payment positions),
- future national trends in traffic volume,
- whether or not the proposed new business park and transport depot materialise, and
- extent to which the existence of the bridge would influence other regional planning decisions that could impact on demand.

Most of these factors had already been considered when making the revenue estimates for the first pass risk analysis. However, more detailed consideration of the evidence available is expected to lead to more reliable forecasts and a more realistic probability distribution compared to the uniform distribution that had previously been used. The risk manager also expects to find useful connections between revenue risk and other decisions about the designs of both the bridge and the customer contract.

The structure of the revenue risk model emerges in two parts. The more complex part is concerned with the way in which local conditions will influence revenue. Evidence for this is drawn from traffic and user-opinion surveys that have been conducted by the regional authority. The ProSit traffic forecasting expert combines this evidence with learned experience from previous road bridge projects to extrapolate a probability distribution for inherent local demand and the way in which this could be affected by future planning decisions. The second part of the model reflects uncertainty in national road use trends. Actual road use will be affected by factors such as future road transport costs and national economic performance. Since regional traffic patterns are expected to follow national trends, this second part of the model effectively provides a factor that can be used to multiply values simulated by the first part of the model.

Ownership of Revenue Risk

As the revenue model is developed, it becomes clear that the most significant sources of uncertainty are beyond the control of ProSit as a contractor. Whilst it is true that the bridge design will affect traffic volume to some extent, the more significant sources of uncertainty are factors such as future economic conditions and the way in which demand could be influenced by decisions yet to be made by the regional authority. Despite this, the proposed business model transfers all revenue risk to the contractor. ProSit's traffic forecasting expert makes a telling observation. 'In my experience, if the government authorities have a financial interest in revenue, they tend to make planning decisions that enhance traffic volume. Even better, they are less inclined to argue that toll charges are too high.'

The project manager immediately realises that this has implications for optimising the contractual proposal. If the regional authority can be persuaded to contribute towards capital costs, it can be rewarded with a proportion of the future revenue. In effect revenue risk would be shared between the parties. This would have the important benefit of improving the outlook for overall revenue. It would also reduce the capital employed by ProSit. Thus, even though the absolute value of ProSit revenue would be lower, it could be expected to be higher as a proportion of capital employed. ProSit's project profitability could thus be higher whilst its risk exposure could be lower. If the regional authority could be provided with evidence that it could make money without taking unacceptable risk, this would be a win-win contracting strategy.

Identifying and quantifying the benefits of risk sharing was the type of insight that the risk manager had been hoping to achieve by focusing the risk management process through an analysis of revenue. However, there is another key question that they expect the next pass of risk analysis to answer: 'What is the best choice between alternative sites for the bridge?' Accordingly, a more thorough investigation of the potential for risk sharing is deferred to the third pass of the risk management process; it could wait for the bridge location decision to be made first.

Using the Second Pass Model to Choose Between Bridge Location Options

In its tender documentation the regional authority had identified two potential sites for the bridge. Option 1 is to construct the bridge at a site where its span would be slightly shorter than at the second site and has the further advantage of being closer to connecting roads. Option 2 would therefore require a significantly higher capital investment. However, Option 2 is closer to a major town and could be expected to save journey times for a greater number of people. This had been confirmed by the regional authority's user-opinion survey. Reading between the lines of the tender document, it seems clear to ProSit that the regional authority would prefer this option. ProSit therefore has to determine whether or not it is also the preferred option from a commercial perspective.

After considering the associated risks, the ProSit project manager agrees that it is reasonable to assume that the operating costs for each option will be similar and that each would be exposed to equivalent schedule risk. The key differentiators are thus capital expenditure and revenue. In order to compare the business case for the two options, the project risk manager suggests rerunning the NPV analysis that had been performed during the first pass assessment, but with three changes:

1. Using the revenue risk model to simulate revenue for each of the two options.
2. Making simple risk estimates for the capital expenditure of each option.
3. Assuming that maximum government funding would be available, that is, 40 per cent of capital expenditure up to a limit of £50million.

The revenue risk model for Option 1 suggests that there is a 95 per cent level of confidence that annual revenue would exceed £14million, but only a 5 per cent chance that it would exceed £24million. Overall, this is a somewhat more pessimistic estimate than the uniform distribution used for the first pass analysis (see Table 3.2). However, this reflects the first option's relatively disadvantageous location. In contrast, the revenue risk model for Option 2 suggests although the 95th percentile confidence revenue forecast is not much better, the 5th percentile is significantly larger at £31million. This is an increase compared to the best case of £27million assumed during the first pass analysis. This increase is a consequence of the analysis performed by ProSit's traffic forecasting expert, who has noticed that the regional authority's ideas for associated developments appeared to be grounded on the assumption that Option 2 would be selected.

For the purposes of estimating capital costs risk for each option the risk manager notes that the difference between the options is primarily one of scale. Other risk factors such as geology, planning risk and environmental impact are similar at each site. Since the question being addressed by risk analysis at this stage is how to differentiate between sites, the risk manager suggests using the simple estimates that were derived during the first pass analysis. Cost risk had been estimated as being £80million–£110million for Option 1 and £110million–£150million for Option 2.

Figure 3.5 shows the results produced by the second pass risk analysis. Three curves are shown: the first pass analysis results, shown by the dashed curve to the left and the NPV forecasts for Options 1 and 2. The fact that the forecasts for both options are now much more favourable than the first pass analysis is due to the assumed injection of government funding. In effect, relief on capital expenditure has shifted the curves for the two options bodily to the right.

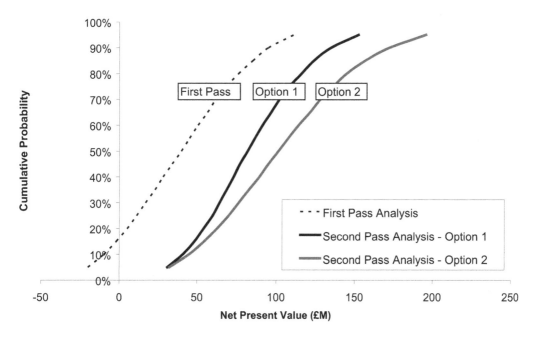

Figure 3.5   Second pass analysis NPV risk modelling results

The second pass risk analysis results confirm to the project sponsor that the business case for the bridge is now much more likely to be viable and that further work on the proposal can be justified. They also provide a sound basis for deciding between which of the two bridge options to support. Figure 3.5 shows that Option 2 provides a higher expected return on investment than Option 1. Although the slope of the NPV curve for Option 2 is shallower (indicating a greater degree of outcome variance) it is therefore the more risk-efficient commercial choice. Happily, it is also the option that the customer would prefer.

Third Pass Risk Management Analysis – Commercial Risk Ownership

Having chosen the bridge location, the project manager is now keen for the risk manager to make a more detailed risk analysis of project costs and schedule. After all, this is what a risk manager normally does. However, the risk manager persists with advice that revenue risk matters more than cost and schedule risk. In particular, they want to follow up on the insight into the importance of ownership of revenue risk that had been identified during the second pass of the risk management process.

The risk manager suggests analysing the implications of sharing revenue risk with the regional authority. In return for taking a share of the revenue, the regional authority would make a contribution to the capital cost. As a starting basis, the risk manager suggests modelling the returns offered to both parties under the following arrangements:

* Central government funds 40 per cent of the capital cost up to a maximum of £50million (as identified in the tender document),
* the regional authority provides capital funding for 50 per cent of the planned remaining costs (estimated provisionally at £40million),
* ProSit funds all remaining capital costs (also estimated provisionally at £40million),
* ProSit funds all operating costs, and
* ProSit and the regional authority share revenue on a 60:40 basis.

Under these arrangements, after accepting central government funding, ProSit would share the planned costs with the regional authority. If these were the only costs, it would then be fair to split revenue 50:50. However, since ProSit will also bear the operational costs, the ProSit share of revenue should be higher. The 60:40 is starting point for modelling (and potentially, later for negotiation).

These arrangements are a simple means of allocating risk ownership from a commercial perspective. ProSit and the regional authority share revenue risk because they have a mutual interest in achieving high traffic volumes. However, as appropriate, ProSit retains the risk associated with both construction and operating costs. The regional authority's contribution to construction costs is fixed. ProSit will therefore pay all marginal costs should they be greater than planned. In effect, ProSit is incentivised to optimise the economic trade-off between costs and revenue. This should make its proposal both competitive and credible to the customer.

Having turned attention to the commercial implications of risk ownership the risk manager also identifies another issue that had been troubling the project team. In its tender, the regional authority proposes to commence the 20-year contract period from the point at which the winning contractor is selected. This means that the contractor will be fully exposed to the risk of any delays that are caused by the planning process. Planning delays would prolong the period during which the contractor has to work alongside the regional authority during the early stages before construction commences. Funding this work for longer than planned would reduce profit. More importantly, deferring the date by which the bridge opened would delay the point at which the revenue stream would commence. Revenue losses would be much more costly than the additional effort for planning support.

Whilst obtaining planning consents for new infrastructure such as a bridge are dependent upon developing an acceptable design, the final decision is, in essence, a political one. It is therefore inappropriate for a contractor to bear the brunt of delays. Yet under the commercial arrangements described by the tender document, loss of revenue caused by planning delays will be entirely at the cost of the contractor. The project manager has previously recognised this to be undesirable. Ideally the commercial deal to be struck with the customer should be based on the 20-year concession period starting from the point when construction can commence. The contractor would then bear the burden of revenue losses due to construction delays, but not planning delays. However, the project manager needs to be able to offer an inducement to the regional authority in order to persuade it to make this change.

The risk manager adapts the second pass risk model to reflect both the risk sharing arrangements and the project manager's proposed change to the concession start date. In order to reflect removal of planning delay risk, the risk manager adjusts the capital expenditure profile, bringing it further forwards in time compared to the profile shown in Figure 3.1 and reducing the period of expenditure from four years to three. In NPV terms this increases the effect of capital expenditure. However, to compensate, the revenue profile is similarly adjusted. The probability distribution for revenue estimates is also adjusted as shown in Table 3.3.

Table 3.3   Effect of risk sharing on third pass risk estimates for revenue

Risk Estimates of Annual Revenue	Pessimistic (5th Percentile)	Median (50th Percentile)	Optimistic (95th Percentile)
2nd Pass (Option 2)	£17M	£24M	£31M
3rd Pass (Option 2 with shared revenue)	£17M	£25M	£34M

The adjustment to the revenue risk estimates consequential to revenue sharing reflect the ProSit traffic expert's prudent view of the benefit of giving the regional authority a commercial interest in promoting traffic volume. With all the adjustments completed, the risk manager uses the NPV risk model to produce revised forecasts as shown in Figure 3.6.

Figure 3.6 forecasts the return on investment to both ProSit and the regional authority and compares it to the forecast for ProSit alone (as shown by the dashed curve produced by the second pass analysis). Since the dashed curve is positioned further towards the right, in absolute terms, the return on investment to ProSit is likely to be higher if it acts alone. This could therefore still be viewed as being the preferred choice from a risk efficiency perspective. However, Figure 3.6 shows that there is a trade-off between risk-efficiency and two significant advantages of the business model underpinning the third pass analysis. First, under the risk sharing arrangements modelled by the third pass analysis, the capital employed ProSit would be halved. Despite this, the total return at the 50th percentile level of confidence is only reduced from £101million to £79million. Thus, in percentage terms, the return on investment is significantly more attractive. Second, the steeper S-curve shown produced by the third pass analysis shows that the overall risk of this approach to ProSit is lower; a further benefit of risk sharing.

Figure 3.6 also shows that the risk-sharing approach offers a third advantage; by providing an attractive business model to the customer, it could increase ProSit's chances of winning the project. Figure 3.6 predicts a positive return on investment for the local authority. The relative steepness of its S-curve is due to the fact that it is taking risk on revenue, but,

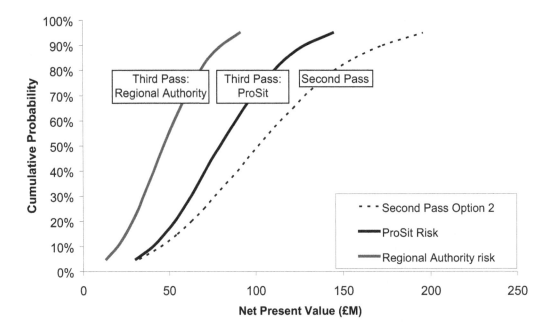

Figure 3.6   Third pass NPV risk modelling results

unlike ProSit, not on capital or operating costs. ProSit can argue that its higher average return is justified by its higher risk exposure. However, in practice, the project manager realises that ProSit may have to negotiate a slightly less favourable revenue share. This would bring the two curves closer together.

When the third pass risk analysis is reviewed with the Project Sponsor, they agree with the project manager's recommendation that the principle of risk sharing should be discussed with the customer. Now armed with evidence that the modified commercial approach to risk ownership can be expected to benefit both parties, the project manager is also finally able to broach the issue of when the 20-year concession should start.

The Customer's Response to Risk Sharing

When the project manager approaches the regional authority, they learn that other bidders have also identified the issue of when the concession period should start. In effect, the regional authority has learnt that exposing their contractor to the full implications of planning delays will be either expensive or unacceptable. Other bidders intend to caveat their proposal with an assumed latest planning consent date. Only ProSit has provided a more creative solution to the problem. ProSit's project manager thus finds that the customer is attracted to the idea of using risk ownership principles to drive contract design and share risk where appropriate. As an added inducement, the risk analysis demonstrates that the regional authority can make money from the deal.

As it happens, the regional authority had once considered financing the bridge construction itself and employing a contractor to deliver the project for a fixed price.

However this approach had, understandably, been rejected on the grounds that contractors employed in such circumstances often find reasons for significant requirement changes subsequent to the award of a fixed price contract. The resultant cost increases can be disastrous; some infrastructure projects cost several times their original estimates. ProSit's proposed solution mitigates this risk to the regional authority by accepting that construction cost risk will be transferred to industry. Having now been presented with a good business case for investment the regional authority reviews its policy on project funding and agrees, in principle, with the ProSit approach. Importantly, ProSit has also differentiated itself from the competition and fostered a climate of trust.

Effect of the First, Second and Third Pass Analysis

The first three passes of the risk management process have addressed project strategy risk. Risk identification and analysis has been designed to answer questions related to the following project strategy decisions:

- Should ProSit Construction Engineering Ltd be involved in this project?
- What is the best choice for the bridge location?
- What is the most risk-efficient contracting strategy?
- How can ProSit differentiate itself from competitors?

Now that these decisions have been made and implemented, it has become more realistic to start managing risk at a tactical level: what are the risks to bridge construction timescales and costs and what risks could affect revenue and through life costs? In the absence of a clear project strategy, attempting to identify and analyse these risks in detail would have been confusing and inefficient. Moreover, it would have failed to address key aspects of project strategy risk.

Fourth Pass Risk Analysis

To the project manager's relief, the risk manager now proposes to proceed with a more detailed identification and analysis of bridge design and construction timescales and costs. Following the bridge location decision, ProSit's design department has developed a high-level design appropriate for the purposes of planning, cost estimating and bid submission. The risk manager arranges the following meetings:

- A discussion with the project planner to understand how the project schedule should be reflected in a schedule risk analysis network,
- a discussion with the cost estimator to understand the cost breakdown structure and identify a high-level structure for cost risk analysis,
- a risk identification brainstorm session with the bid team, design staff and the traffic forecasting expert, and
- risk interviews with individuals who are likely to be responsible for risk estimates and responses.

The risk manager's primary objective is to provide realistic risk-based forecasts for the costs and timescales for delivering the bridge up to the point at which it is opened. The ProSit project sponsor needs this information for the purposes of bid approval. These forecasts will also provide improved inputs to the NPV risk model. However, the risk manager does not want the project team to lose sight of the importance of revenue. Thus a secondary objective of the fourth pass analysis is to ensure that the bridge design does not conflict with information that was used when developing the NPV risk model. Accordingly, the risk manager includes revenue and operating cost drivers on the risk identification session prompt list.

The risk identification session produces a mixture of information. Some items identified are short term issues concerned with being able to submit the bid within the required timescale. Others are of either of minor importance or based on grumbles about ProSit's management processes. However, a number of significant sources of risk also emerge. These include ambiguities (for example, interpretation of new drainage regulations), variability drivers (for example, price of steel), threats (for example, labour shortages due to other projects) and opportunities (for example, automated charging for tolls using number plate recognition). The project manager and risk manager sort through all the information generated and classify it for action. Items indicative of potentially significant risks are followed up by the risk manager through the risk interviews that have been arranged.

The risk manager now spends time developing Monte Carlo simulation cost and schedule risk models for bridge design and construction. In parallel with this they also develop a simple form of risk register, for the time being using a spreadsheet. The purposes of the risk register are to articulate significant risks, record actions to be taken during the bid process in response to individual risks and develop and record the rationale for risk estimates used in the Monte Carlo risk models.

The cost and schedule risk models are developed in sufficient detail for the purposes of making a realistic risk-based forecast of overall project risk. The risk manager observes the art of doing this by making appropriate choices about where to develop detail and where to stop the development of detail that would be irrational from a risk perspective. A more detailed discussion about the risk estimating and modelling issues involved can be found in Chapter 8. The schedule risk model includes 40 activities and 15 risk events. The cost model is based on probability distributions aligned with the high-level cost breakdown structure of ten line items augmented by significant risk events and cost variance that would be driven by schedule outcome. The outputs of this analysis are summarised in Table 3.4.

Table 3.4   Risk forecasts from fourth pass analysis

Forecasts for Design and Construction	Optimistic (10th Percentile)	Median (50th Percentile)	Pessimistic (90th Percentile)
Capital Expenditure	£107M	£128M	£152M
Schedule completion from time now	44 months	62 months	95 months
Schedule completion after planning consent	27 months	31 months	35 months

Table 3.4 shows two schedule completion forecasts. The second of these is the forecast for the time taken from the point at which planning consent is achieved to the date on which the bridge opens. In essence this is the bridge construction phase. Under the terms of its proposal, ProSit would be at risk of losing revenue should delays occur during this period. The difference between this forecast and the forecast for project completion from time now is accounted for by the competitive tendering and planning activities. The wide spread of possible outcomes (51 months between the 10th and 90th percentile confidence forecasts) is mostly attributable to ProSit's estimates of the risks associated with planning consent. This is why, in common with other bidders, ProSit is unwilling to accept the implications that this risk would have on revenue. Nevertheless, the winning contractor will bear some of the cost burden of planning delays since it will need to keep a team in place to support the planning process. This is taken into account in the cost (that is, capital expenditure) risk analysis.

The project manager and project sponsor agree to use the £128million 50th percentile confidence forecasts as the basis for the bid. As a result funding levels for each party are proposed to be:

- £50million (fixed) – central government,
- £39million (fixed) – regional authority (50 per cent of the remaining funding required), and
- £39million (nominal) – ProSit Engineering (at risk of any variance from £128million).

The capital expenditure risk forecast shows a somewhat wider range of possible outcomes compared to the cost profile used for earlier passes of risk analysis. However, when the probability distribution for costs is fed back into the NPV model, the change has a negligible effect. One reason for this is that earlier NPV modelling used a uniform probability distribution, thus providing a prudently high variance of cost.

When the results of the risk analysis are reviewed prior to bid submission, the project sponsor expresses concern about the risk associated with capital expenditure. The interval between the 50th and 90th percentile costs is £24million; almost 20 per cent above the proposed bid cost of £128million. The project sponsor is used to handling bids that require contingencies of no more than 10 per cent. Moreover, the proposed commercial approach gears ProSit's exposure to capital expenditure risk. If a risk of £24million is viewed in the context of ProSit's nominal contribution to capital expenditure of £39million, cost risk could be interpreted as being up to approximately 60 per cent. On these grounds, the sponsor argues that the risk analysis must either be wrong, or that the project is too risky to authorise. The risk manager responds to this challenge by advising the sponsor that:

- Records of similar ProSit projects show that they tend to vary in final cost by at least 20 per cent compared to bid estimates.
- Previous approaches to risk analysis used by ProSit to produce risk estimates such as 10 per cent were based on simplistic techniques now known to underestimate risk.
- Since the risk analysis addresses both the positive and negative implications of uncertainty, there would, equally, be an opportunity to reduce costs relative to the £128million underpinning the bid.

- The new estimates of capital expenditure risk have been incorporated into the NPV risk model, which continues to show results similar to those forecast earlier (Figure 3.6).

The risk manager could add that, when using gut instinct, the project sponsor, like any human being, was liable to underestimate uncertainty. This would explain why the sponsor thinks that a risk forecast showing a wide range of outcomes could be wrong. However, the final bid review is not a good opportunity for delivering a lecture on heuristics and risk estimating (see Question C7 in Chapter 8, pp. 144–9). Besides, the sponsor might take offence at the implication that they had been naïve when approving previous bids, even though this would be true. Fortunately, the project sponsor accepts the risk manager's advice and subsequently approves the bid.

Fifth Pass Risk Analysis

Three months after bid submission, ProSit Engineering is selected as the local authority's preferred contractor. The project manager, risk manager and key design staff are recalled from other duties to form a project team that will gradually grow in size, reaching a peak after the commencement of construction. New project team members, including a planner and a procurement manager are also added to the team.

The risk manager now recommends the development of a more detailed risk register, with each risk being assigned to an individual risk owner. The fifth pass risk analysis is to be focused on establishing this risk register. Risk owners are to be selected on the basis of being the person who is best able to influence the related project outcome. They will be required to review their risks on a monthly basis to ensure that the risk assessment is pertinent and that the responses are appropriate and being implemented. In addition there will be two other levels of risk review. First, the project manager will chair an internal monthly risk review based on specific risks selected by the risk manager. Second, there will be a bi-monthly risk review held jointly with the regional authority customer project team. In order to make efficient use of resources, both levels of risk review will be held as part of planned project progress reviews. A budget of one and a half hours has been provisioned for risk in each case.

The risk manager estimates that approximately ten risks can be reviewed usefully in a meeting lasting one and a half hours. Rather than repeatedly reviewing a standard 'top ten' risks, they recommend selecting out the most immediately relevant risks on the occasion of each review. On this basis, the project manager agrees that the risk manager should use their own judgement to select risks, taking into account severity (calculated using probability and impact estimates), ambiguity of risk ownership, urgency of response and whether or not the risk response is proving to be effective.

The status of each of the ten selected risks will be captured in a one-page-per-risk report generated as an output of ProSit's risk database tool. It will be important for the monthly risk reviews undertaken by risk owners to produce good quality information. An obvious reason for this is that it will help risk owners themselves to make good decisions. Another reason is that it is the risk manager's intention to make sure that the project manager's and joint risk review meetings are focused principally on the effectiveness and implementation of risk responses. The availability of good quality risk information from risk owners will avoid these risk review meetings being waylaid by unproductive arguments about risk descriptions and estimates.

The ProSit risk tool is a modern generic internet enabled database application. One of the problems that projects have experienced is that this tool supports so many fields and features that risk owners get bogged down with administration. The project risk manager plans to avoid this problem by regulating the number of risks and being selective about which fields in the tool to use. Accordingly, they write down the primary uses for risk data and select the associated database fields. This information is summarised in Table 3.5.

Table 3.5   Database fields selection

Purpose of data	Database fields
Articulate each risk so that it can be understood	Risk Title Risk description, comprising fields for: Relevant Fact(s), Source(s) of Uncertainty and Effect(s) Fallback(s)
Allocate appropriate ownership of responsibility for risk outcome	Risk owner
Develop appropriate commercial strategy for retaining, sharing or transferring risks	Risk-bearing organisation
Select risks for monthly review	Probability Impact Urgency of response
Identify, implement and monitor responses	Response Response owner Response status Planned completion date

Compared with many applications of risk management this is a minimalist selection of risk register fields. The risk manager's reasoning is that maintaining simple, but effective risk management data in the risk register will help to engage risk owners and foster the generation of good quality information. In practice, risk owners are often required to provide a greater volume of data than this. However, they frequently lack the time or understanding to do this to a high standard. For example the risk manager could have mandated the recording of three-point estimates for risk impacts in the dimensions of both cost and time. The argument for this would be that they can then be automatically incorporated into quantitative risk models. However, although the risk manager does plan to conduct quantitative schedule risk and cost analysis at strategic points during the project, they are aware of the pitfalls of the simplistic use of risk register estimates for this purpose. Hence they plan to make risk estimates for quantitative analysis separately and keep the qualitative process supported by the risk database tool as simple as possible.

Having planned the implementation of a qualitative risk management process, the risk manager arranges a team risk identification brainstorm session. The customer's project manager, planning manager and design engineer also attend. With appropriate risk sharing arrangements in place, there is little to be lost by disclosing risks and much to be gained from engaging the customer in the process. Items raised at the risk identification session, together with items identified in the bid risk spreadsheet, are restructured to form the starting basis of a revised risk register. The risk manager then follows this by holding risk interviews with each risk owner.

Some risks raised at the risk identification session are found to be customer-owned. These are risks for which the regional authority would either bear or share the financial consequences and is the party best placed to optimise the risk outcome. ProSit and the customer agree that information on these risks will be maintained on the ProSit risk database, and that the ProSit risk manager will conduct risk interviews with the relevant regional authority staff. Given their mutual interest in risk, this investment in time should be of benefit to ProSit. It will also provide ProSit with insights into customer activities that they might otherwise lack. Risks owned by the regional authority include:

- Development of business infrastructure in areas around the bridge,
- compliance with planning process requirements, and
- public acceptance during the planning process.

Whilst the other risks raised at the risk identification session are owned by ProSit Engineering, some will be retained whilst others are expected to be transferred to subcontractors. In the case of the former, the responses comprise actions designed either to reduce the level of threat or to exploit the associated opportunity. In the case of the latter, the focus for responses is expected to be on the subcontractor selection process and developing contract designs that incentivise subcontractors to act in ProSit's interest.

The risk manager recommends that two of the ProSit-retained risks should be owned by the project sponsor. These are:

- Opportunity to refinance on more advantageous terms, and
- Impact of the bridge project on company reputation.

Like other risk owners the project sponsor would be expected to review their risks on a regular basis. However, the risk manager concedes that it is unrealistic to expect the sponsor to do this formally on a monthly basis. It is therefore proposed that they should be reviewed as part of the sponsor's quarterly project progress review cycle. Nevertheless, by persuading the sponsor to be a risk owner, the risk manager hopes to engender top-down support for the risk management process as a whole.

The fifth pass of the risk management process is completed when the new risk register is fully established with risk assessments and planned responses. Initially, it comprises 35 risks. Importantly, no one has been made to feel overwhelmed by the number of risks that they own. Equally importantly, being made to articulate risks and understand their implications has influenced their choices of action. (Guidance on describing risks and developing responses based on the insights gained can be found in the discussion of Question C1 in Chapter 8 (see pp. 128–33). Whilst the number of risks can be expected to increase as new risks emerge and as more people are added to the team, risk numbers will continue to be regulated in order to focus on those risks that matter most and avoid the counterproductive effects of administrative burden. Matters of lesser importance should be handled by the routine project planning process.

The fifth pass of the risk management process has set the pattern against which the routine application of risk management will continue to be undertaken. It therefore marks the point at which the process will cease to evolve significantly. A qualitative risk management approach will be used to introduce sound judgement to decisions on a risk-by-risk basis. This should improve the outcome of the project, including its performance in the operational phase. In parallel, cost and schedule quantitative risk analysis for the project delivery phase will be conducted by the risk manager when there is a good case for doing so.

Lessons to be Drawn from the Road Bridge Project

The Road Bridge project example has been designed to illustrate a number of points. A key point is that risk management is a process that involves making and implementing decisions. Decisions are responses to questions. Hence risk identification and analysis should be shaped so that they help to answer the questions that matter most. Since the nature of questions caused by uncertainty change as one goes through different stages of the project, different tools and techniques will be required at different stages.

Another key point is that the risk management process has to engage all relevant decision makers. The risk manager helps these people make decisions. Since decision makers can be found in any of the stakeholder organisations, communication is an essential ingredient of risk management. In carrying out their work, the risk manager often develops a particularly broad understanding of the project. A good communicator in this position can often add value to the project in ways that go beyond the risk management process itself.

Further to these general points, there are a number of additional points that merit a more detailed explanation. This explanation is presented in the final four sections of this chapter below.

Using Project Benefits to Shape the Risk Management Process

Like all commercially driven projects, the viability of the road bridge project's business case is dependent upon the economic value of benefits exceeding the cost of investment. This has important implications for choosing where to prioritise attention for the purposes of risk management. Uncertainty in the value of benefits, or an organisation's ability to realise them, may be higher than the uncertainty associated with investment costs simply because the overall value at risk is higher. However, there are other reasons why uncertainty associated with benefits may be relatively high. For example, benefits are generally realised at a later time, and often over a longer period. Benefits realisation may also be outside the direct control of the project team.

Where the uncertainty associated with benefits is greater than the uncertainty associated with investment, it will normally make sense for the risk management process to be driven from the perspective of benefits in at least some of the earlier cycles of the process. Understanding this is an important improvement on forms of common practice that treat risk to time, cost and product performance as having an equivalent importance at all stages. Furthermore, assumptions made about product performance requirements may be a poor proxy for project benefits. For example, the product performance requirement for a road bridge might have been stated in terms of its traffic handling capacity.

This would have missed the point that the business case should be based upon the revenue that the bridge can attract. Capacity is only one consideration. The fact that the decision as to where to build the bridge is of greater importance to revenue would not necessarily be apparent from a description of product performance objectives.

In the case of the road bridge, use of the NPV modelling approach allows risk in the different dimensions of time, cost and performance to be translated into a common unit: economic value. This helps to clarify the trade-off between risk effects in different dimensions. In the cases of some commercial projects, the economic value of benefits may be more difficult to estimate. However, this should not dissuade the project from trying to do so, since understanding how the project's output will have value may influence the project design itself.

However, there are some projects where attributing economic value to their products ceases to make sense. Projects such as those included in the Chapter 4 case study based on UK Ministry of Defence (MoD) projects are an example (see p. 81). How can you estimate the economic value of an aircraft carrier or an air-to-air missile system? Projects such as these do not have a natural commercial basis. The same is true of many other government and charity funded projects. In these circumstances, it is unlikely that all risk effects can be resolved into a single dimension. The use of multi-dimensional techniques then becomes increasingly necessary. In practice, it may be useful to simplify the process by assuming a fixed requirement in the dimension that represents the purpose of the project: usually its product outcome.

Constructive Insubordination

Risk analysis should always be designed to answer a question. Sometimes the question is obvious, for example, which are the most significant risks? Or, how can we mitigate this risk? Sometimes, the risk analyst is just told to 'do the risk analysis'. They then have to construct the relevant question and verify that it is correct. On other occasions the risk analyst might be told to analyse a particular aspect of risk, for example, 'What is the capital expenditure risk associated with building this bridge?' Whatever the circumstances, the risk analyst might correctly identify that the risk analysis would be more valuable if the question that they are being asked to answer was changed. Putting this proposition to the relevant decision makers is described by Chapman and Ward (2002) as being constructive insubordination.

The bridge project includes two examples of constructive insubordination. The first example arises at the starting points of the second and third passes. Whilst the project manager is anxious to proceed with a cost and schedule risk analysis, the risk manager advises continuing to focus on revenue risk. The outcome is that important strategy decisions concerning the bridge location and contracting strategy are supported. The second instance of constructive insubordination arises during the final bid review. Based on the fourth pass analysis forecasts for capital expenditure, the project sponsor regards risk as being unacceptably high. The risk manager overcomes this barrier, in part, by referring to the NPV model. It is the NPV model rather than the capital expenditure forecast that addresses the question as to whether or not there is a viable business case. By focusing only on capital expenditure, the project sponsor had thus, inadvertently, addressed the wrong question.

Shaping risk analysis to the needs of the project is an essential part of best practice. The risk analyst is often the person with the best understanding of what risk analysis can achieve. Constructive insubordination can therefore be a critical enabler of best practice. However, it requires the risk analyst to have sufficient credibility to influence their superiors. It can also be uncomfortable for the people involved. Without a good risk management culture, constructive insubordination is likely to be ineffective or, even, actively discouraged.

Limitations of a Single Pass Approach to Risk Management

Many common practice approaches to risk management are based on a single pass approach. It is often expected that the process should commence with detailed identification of risks at a tactical level. In the earlier phases of a project this can often prove to be either impracticable or counterproductive. For example, one process marketed as being best practice is based purely on assumptions analysis. It requires risk practitioners to make assumptions about plans and objectives where there is a lack of clarity. If this process had been used on the bridge project the risk owner for bridge construction risks would have probably proceeded by assuming that the Option 1 site would be chosen due to its lower cost. On the other hand, the risk owner for revenue risks would have probably assumed that the Option 2 site would be chosen. Since these are mutually exclusive assumptions, the process would have become incoherent.

Even more importantly, making arbitrary assumptions undermines the value that can be added by assessing and managing risk at a project strategy level. In the case of the bridge project, choosing the Option 1 location would have been suboptimal. Introducing suboptimal assumptions for the purposes of progressing risk analysis is counterproductive. The solution is for risk management to be used to support key strategy decisions first. This is an important reason for following a multi-pass top-down process.

Supporters of single pass risk management processes can argue that the control and management of assumptions is part of their process. For example, risks can be treated as having been assessed relative to the project plan. Whilst this would address the problem of mutually exclusive assumptions, it postpones the implementation of risk management until the plan has been formed. Hence single pass approaches usually fail to manage risk at a project strategy level. In contrast the dynamic and interactive nature of a top-down multi-pass process enables it to be used during all project phases and at different levels of decision making.

Best Practice – Doing the Right Thing from the Outset

Since risk management should address the implications of uncertainty (that is, lack of certainty), and since uncertainty is usually at it greatest during the earliest stages of a project, it follows that 'best practice' risk management is needed from the outset. This has an important implication for the Project RMM.

Like many other process maturity models the RMM can trace its lineage, at least in part, from the Software Capability Maturity Model (CMM) developed at Carnegie Mellon University in the late 1980s. The CMM is based on five levels of capability, the highest of which is labelled 'Optimising'. In comparison, the Project RMM, in common with a number of other risk management process maturity models, is based on four capability levels. It is therefore worth exploring why it does not have a fifth capability level equivalent to that of the CMM. One of the answers to this question lies in the observation that best practice on projects involves doing the right thing from the outset. In contrast, the label 'Optimising' implies a state of continuous improvement. Whilst continuous improvement may be an ideal applied to honing processes from an organisational perspective, it is not an ideal state for the management of risk on a project; the ideal is that best practice is applied from the beginning. This does not mean that what is done should be complex. Rather, best practice at the outset should be based on a simple understanding of what matters most and how this can be understood and managed at a high level.

Another aspect of best practice is ensuring that each stage of the risk management process is shaped by the questions that need to be addressed. Uncertainty affects different projects in different ways. Thus best practice involves tailoring the process by selecting the techniques that are best adapted to the questions in hand. Moreover, in a top-down multi-looping process the tools and techniques used may change from one pass of the process to the next. Examples of this can be seen in the road bridge project. Best practice project risk management thus cannot be based on a homogeneous procedure that is applied identically to every project. Again, this has an important implication for the Project RMM.

Process capability maturity models often use the label 'Repeatable' to describe one of the interim capability levels. In the Project RMM, Level 3 can be attained using the simple common-practice approach of managing risks on a risk-by-risk basis supported by a risk register, typically based on a Probability-Impact Matrix approach for risk assessment. An advantage of this approach is that it can be rolled out in the form of a procedure that can be applied to all projects across an organisation. However, since best practice should be based on the selection of techniques to address key questions in hand, repeatability realised in this way can conflict with best practice. If the implications of this issue are not understood, the achievement of repeatability might even become a barrier to achieving best practice. Barriers to best practice caused by common practice are discussed in more detail in a paper by Chris Chapman (2006).

In addition to defining discrete levels of process capability, maturity models should provide a route map to process improvement. The potential for conflicts between the aims of repeatability and the aims of best practice risk management, is one reason for retaining the labels for RMM capabilities defined by Hillson (1997) rather than adopting more commonly used alternatives.

Risk Management Capability of the Bridge Project

The bridge project has been included in this book as being a good example of risk management practice. It is therefore worth considering the question: if this project's risk management process had been assessed using the Project RMM would it have achieved a Level 4 RMM capability? The answer is that during the second, third and fourth passes of the process it would have achieved Level 4, but that during the first pass it would have achieved no higher than Level 3. From the fifth pass forwards, it could have continued to achieve RMM Level 4, although there is not sufficient information in the chapter to confirm that this was sustained.

What was the weakness that constrained the project's risk management capability to RMM Level 3 during the first pass? From five of the RMM perspectives, the process would have been at Level 4. Although there were not a large number of risks identified, they were the right risks for the question that needed to be addressed by risk analysis. The risk analysis was also appropriate. Thus the risk identification and analysis perspectives would have been assessed as having been at Level 4. Likewise the risk response to the analysis results, although simple (a no-bid decision), was correct and implemented promptly. The project management and risk management culture perspectives would also have been assessed at Level 4. The risk management process was initiated in a way that was aligned to the purpose of the project. Risk was reviewed appropriately and all the people involved acted constructively in support of the process. This leaves the stakeholders' perspective as the only potential point of weakness.

It would have been the stakeholders' perspective that constrained the project risk management capability to RMM Level 3 during the first pass of the process. The reason for this result would have been low scores for questions related to the customer's involvement in the process. Not only was there a lack of active engagement with the customer on risk, but the customer's view of risk as it would affect the project was not considered at all. Instead, the first pass risk model focused solely on ProSit's own business case. ProSit, as an organisation, was, of course, a stakeholder. The other saving grace from the stakeholders' perspective is that, by understanding risks associated with traffic volumes the first pass analysis also considered the role of end users. Other potential stakeholders such as contractors would have been irrelevant at this stage. Thus the stakeholders' perspective would have produced an RMM Level 3 assessment, but due to the lack of customer engagement, not a Level 4.

There might be two views of the RMM Level 3 capability during the first pass. One view would be that the lack of customer engagement on risk represented a lost opportunity; a setback that ProSit was lucky to recover from. The project was, after all, a potential success, for reasons that ProSit would not have been aware from information contained in the invitation to tender. Another view would be that, given the fact that the road bridge was just one of many potential opportunities being considered by the company, the purpose of the risk management process was to filter out the most promising prospects. From this point of view, the project sponsor might have been satisfied that Level 3 capability was acceptable. What is clear, however, is that understanding the customer's interest in risk and then engaging the customer directly in the risk management process became fundamentally important. Smart business involves understanding the motivation of all parties involved. By taking this into account, the risk management process can help shape the project solution.

4 *The UK MoD Defence Procurement Agency: A Project Risk Maturity Model Case Study*

The Risk Maturity Model has allowed us to demonstrate the improvements that have been achieved.

MoD presentation

This chapter illustrates how the Project Risk Maturity Model (RMM) can be used within an organisation to improve risk management capability across a portfolio of projects. Whilst assessing the capability of individual projects can identify useful insights into how their risk management processes can be improved, building up a picture of project risk management capability across a portfolio can also identify key improvements that need to be taken at a corporate level. This case study also shows how linking project approvals with the assessment of risk management capability of individual projects can contribute to the corporate system for the governance of project management.

The case study is based on the UK Ministry of Defence's (MoD) equipment procurement projects. These include the development and manufacture of new military equipment for the UK's Army, Royal Navy and Royal Air Force. In common with the defence ministries and departments of all western governments, the MoD uses commercial companies to deliver the majority of this work. Hence, from the MoD's perspective, they are managed as procurement projects. Measured in terms of whole life costs, the value of the largest projects exceeds £10billion. The overall project portfolio thus represents a significant item of government expenditure.

Defence procurement projects are inherently risky. Not only are many projects very large, but many are also complex. Design aims are often driven by the need to maintain a technical capability advantage over potential combatants. For example, weapons systems need to be more accurate, have longer ranges and be faster to operate. As a result, the design of new equipment tends to push the limits of what is technologically feasible. The same principle applies to the development of aircraft, ships and vehicles, which need to be nimble and able to operate flexibly. Size and weight constraints and a need to inter-operate with other equipments are all frequent causes of design complexity. Finally, reliability and usability are very important but often difficult to achieve with new and technologically advanced designs. Risks can be attributable to all of these factors. Moreover, their combined effects are often greater than the sum of their parts.

Given the scale of its equipment procurement projects and the risk involved, the MoD has a high level of commitment to its project risk management process. For example, in order to reduce risk, the ministry invests a much higher proportion of project budgets in the earliest project phases than most other organisations. There is also a commitment from the highest levels of management to reviewing risk management effectiveness. It was as a consequence of this commitment that the Project RMM was adopted by the MoD, commencing with a pilot study in 2002.

The MoD Equipment Procurement Life cycle

When the RMM was first adopted by the MoD, its Defence Procurement Agency (DPA) was the department that led the initiative. The DPA was responsible for all new equipment projects up to the point where the equipment entered service with the armed forces, often referred to as the in-service date (ISD). When equipments had been procured and had entered service, responsibility for their maintenance was then handed over to another department, the Defence Logistics Organisation (DLO).

The standard MoD equipment procurement project life cyle is shown in Figure 4.1. Known as the CADMID (Concept, Assessment, Demonstration and Manufacture, In-service and Disposal) cycle, this standard had been formally adopted by the MoD in 1999 as part of its Smart Procurement initiative. Smart Procurement is, in essence, a governance process designed to simplify and improve project procurement across the MoD. A key feature of the CADMID cycle is the use of two gate reviews to govern executive approval of projects.

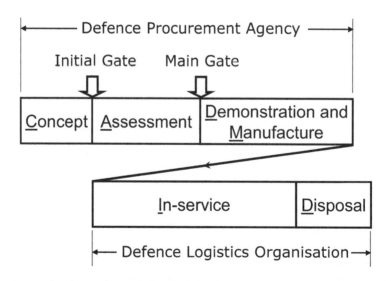

Figure 4.1   The CADMID project life cycle

The first gate review, called Initial Gate, marks the completion of the concept phase. Passing through Initial Gate releases funds for the assessment phase. The assessment phase is equivalent to the definition phase included in the APM project lifecycle (see Chapter 2, Figure 2.1, p. 20). The word assessment is used to reflect that, in addition to the risk reduction and planning definition work normally performed during this phase, the capabilities of competing contractors and equipment designs are often also being assessed. The assessment phase culminates with a business case prepared for Main Gate approval. If this approval is given the MoD allocates sufficient funding to complete the development programme, manufacture initial production quantities and carry out the logistic support activities necessary to introduce the equipment into service. Given the scale of investment involved and the implications to industry, Main Gate is a critical point in the CADMID life cycle.

The MoD's strategy for managing equipment procurement risk is to invest sufficiently in the two phases prior to Main Gate to make the risk of proceeding beyond that point quantifiable and acceptable. Smart procurement recommendations include spending 10–15 per cent of the total equipment procurement costs on these two phases. This is a figure that exceeds typical levels of investment in other industries, but which experience has proved to be necessary given the levels of risk involved in the development of defence equipment.

Following Main Gate approval, a contract is placed with the selected prime contractor, with a scope that usually covers the demonstration and manufacture phase. Since most contracts are placed on a fixed price basis, this is the point at which significant risk is transferred to industry. In principle, the prime contractor is at risk should it fail to deliver the equipment and related services to specification within its own cost estimates. In addition, the MoD also often incentivises delivery to the contracted timescales with contractual mechanisms such as break clauses and liquidated damages. Having been funded to engage in earlier phases, contractors should be in a reasonable position to accept the risk involved without needing to quote unrealistically high prices. The MoD retains risk to the extent that it might have to make contract changes. Potential causes of this include changes to performance requirements or equipment quantities and failure to meet its own contractual obligations such as the provision of technical data required by industry. Another reason for investing heavily in the concept and assessment phases is to minimise these risks.

The Equipment Procurement Risk Management Process

A key purpose of the concept and assessment phases is to reduce risk to an acceptable level prior to Main Gate approval. Risk information is included in the business case to demonstrate that this has been done. This information is usually presented in two forms. The first is a conventional register of significant risks, together with an account of how responses have already been implemented and plans for further responses to be implemented in the future. The second form of risk information is more sophisticated, being comprised of three-point confidence forecasts for the project cost and schedule outcome of the demonstration and manufacture phase. As illustrated in Figure 4.2, these are derived from S-curves produced by Monte Carlo simulation.

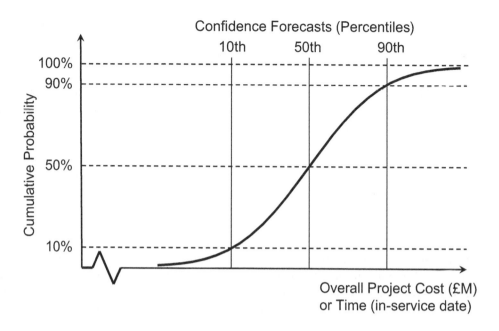

Figure 4.2   Derivation of three-point confidence forecasts

Three-point confidence forecasts are made for the 10th, 50th and 90th percentile points. For example, the 90th percentile cost point is the value that the project is 90 per cent confident that it will not exceed. Similarly, the 10th percentile point is a lower cost that the project forecasts might be achievable, but only with a 10 per cent level of confidence. The 50th percentile (that is, median) points for cost and time are effectively the project's forecasts based on an evenly balanced mixture of good and bad luck.

The three-point confidence forecasts are intended to provide the project sponsor with an estimate of the risk involved. Project sponsors are located in MoD departments outside its procurement agencies. From the perspective of equipment projects, sponsors are thus treated as being a customer stakeholder. Sponsors are responsible for achieving military capability objectives. To do this, they are allocated responsibility for funds to maintain a portfolio of projects each of which closes different military capability gaps. In order to manage their project portfolio contingencies, sponsors need to understand the extent to which they may be at risk of having to provide further unplanned funding. Thus, if, for example, a sponsor delegates funding to the project at the 50th percentile confidence point, they would expect that there was only a 50 per cent probability that the project would, in the future, need further funding. Furthermore, the gap between the 50th and 90th percentiles would provide them with an indication of how much additional funding might be involved should this happen.

The three-point confidence forecasts are effectively the way in which the MoD evaluates overall project risk. In practice, equipment procurement projects have a good record for achieving their technical objectives. National Audit Office reports for major procurement projects confirm that all fundamental technical objectives (key user requirements) are achieved by the majority of projects. However, cost and schedule overruns are more common. When taken together with the implications of major assumptions recorded in a business case, the three-point confidence forecasts indicate to approval authorities the overall risk involved.

Wide intervals of time and/or cost between the 10th and 90th percentiles indicate a relatively high degree of overall project risk. Approval authorities have to decide whether or not this risk is acceptable given the project's military capability benefits.

As one would expect, the MoD does not simply accept project business cases at face value. The larger and more complex a project is, the greater is the level of scrutiny. Large projects are approved by a central Investment Approvals Board. The largest and most strategically significant projects require formal ministerial approval. In order to provide management assurance on larger projects, independent internal scrutineers are used to evaluate the content of each business case. Their scrutiny includes an evaluation of the quality of the underlying risk analysis. In particular, scrutineers look for evidence that risk has been managed effectively and modelled realistically.

In their evaluation of risk management effectiveness, scrutineers look at the history of three-point confidence forecasts produced by the project. Three-point confidence forecasts are included in the business case at Initial Gate. By the point of Main Gate, there is therefore at least one previous forecast against which to compare. In many cases, the project would have also used quantitative risk models as part of its strategy to reduce risk during the assessment phase. Scrutineers can therefore determine whether or not the interval between the 90th and 10th percentile confidence forecasts has tended to shrink in response to risk reduction measures.

Ideally, the project will have used the risk management process to both optimise the project solution and reduce overall risk, thus producing forecasts at initial and Main Gate similar to those shown in Figure 4.3. At Initial Gate, uncertainty about what will be possible should result in a relatively shallow S curve such as that shown by the dashed line.

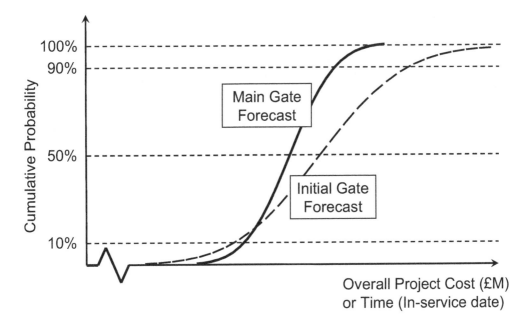

Figure 4.3   Idealised comparison of Initial Gate and Main Gate confidence forecasts

External scrutiny of the MoD's project performance is provided by the National Audit Office (NAO). The NAO's annual MoD Major Projects Report is based on the 30 top equipment procurement projects. These reports are made available to download free of charge from the NAO's web site. During any one year, the 30 top projects include a cross-section of projects in different phases from the concept phase to those that have recently entered service. For those that have passed through Initial or Main Gate, the report uses the three-point confidence forecasts from approved business cases as a basis for monitoring schedule and cost performance. To this extent, the effectiveness of the MoD's risk management process is therefore open to public scrutiny and political pressure.

Risk analysis is therefore a key tool used by the MoD to control project approvals, manage its project portfolio and provide public accountability for its performance. These are all fundamentally important aspects of its governance of project management. The MoD's project risk management process thus has corporate governance implications in addition to the more obvious purpose of improving the management of individual projects.

The Case for the Project Risk Maturity Model

In 2001, the MoD recognised that, in practice, its risk management process did not fulfil all of its purposes. For example, the majority of projects failed to meet 50th percentile forecasts and significantly more than 10 per cent of 90th percentile forecasts were exceeded. In effect, risk analysis forecasts were proving to be too optimistic. Given the significance of risk analysis to the governance of project management, this was a corporate issue. In principle, the problems could have been due to one or more of the following three causes:

1. Optimistically biased risk analysis,
2. failure to manage risk as planned subsequent to Main Gate approval, and
3. the effects of unknown unknowns.

The effect of unknown unknowns is, of course, outside the scope of risk analysis. Since the effect of unknown unknowns is usually problematic, where they are likely to be significant, one can expect the average project outcome to be poorer than 50th percentile risk forecasts. However, an independent study funded by the MoD had concluded that the majority of cost and schedule reviews could be attributed to risk that was identifiable at the project approval points. This study thus identified weaknesses in the organisation's risk management process. Referring to the Hillson risk maturity model matrix (see Appendix A) it suggested that the MoD's risk management process was generally performing at the capability Level 2. The MoD was recommended to implement a programme of process improvement. It was also recommended to invest in a tool to measure risk management capability. This would allow the effectiveness of process improvements to be monitored.

The MoD selected the Project RMM as its preferred tool to measure risk management capability. Advantages of the tool included the fact that it had been tailored to measure risk in the context of project management and that, in this form, it had already been used to measure risk management capability for a number of different clients, including some managing defence industry projects. Furthermore, the tool also enabled key areas of process weakness to be identified. Thus it was not simply a measuring tool. This was recognised to be an important factor that would help the system for process measurement to gain acceptance within the organisation. By identifying priorities for process improvement, a Project RMM assessment provides immediate and constructive feedback to projects.

Project RMM Pilot

Before committing the organisation to a full-scale Project RMM assessment programme, the MoD conducted a pilot. Its purposes were to:

- Assess the RMM's accuracy,
- assess its applicability to projects of different type and size,
- choose between alternative approaches to data collection, and
- address any assessment process issues experienced by project teams.

The pilot included the assessment of eight projects. The majority of these had procurement values in the region of between £50M and £1billion. However, a small project with a funding of £100,000 was also included. Projects were selected by the MoD to obtain a wide range of projects in terms of both previous performance and reputation for project management capability. Project scores that had been obtained using the European Foundation for Quality Management (EFQM) Excellence Model formed part of the basis for informing the latter.

The pilot confirmed that the Project RMM was a suitable tool for the MoD's purposes. Feedback from subject project teams was supportive and identified no significant issues with the assessment process. Measurement accuracy was also good, with a correct discrimination between good and poor risk management processes. Project teams also concurred with the key weaknesses that had been identified.

A further outcome of the pilot was that the MoD selected project team workshops as being its preferred method for collecting RMM assessment data. The alternative was to implement a programme of formal process audits. The relative merits of these two approaches are discussed in more detail in Chapter 5 (see pp. 87–92). However, in summary, it should be noted that whilst formal audits tend to be more accurate, team workshops have certain advantages from a risk management culture perspective.

Assessment of the MoD's 30 Major Equipment Projects

Following the pilot, the MoD's priority was to address risk management capability issues on its top 30 major projects. Project size was important for a number of reasons. First, the overall value of risk on large projects tends to be high simply because of the large budgets and long timescales involved. Furthermore, large equipment procurement projects tend to be more complex than small ones and inherently riskier. Evidence of this could be seen in the relatively poor performance of major projects in relation to their forecasts. Finally, the 30 major projects were those planned to be included in the forthcoming annual NAO Major Projects Report. Project RMM results could therefore be reviewed at a corporate level in the context of that report.

The 30 RMM assessments provided each project with a short report detailing the assessment results in the form of the RMM bar chart and overall capability level. Each report also identified a prioritised list of process improvement actions. However, interesting new insights were also obtained by combining results from across the portfolio of 30 projects. Table 4.1 summarises the number of projects found at each RMM capability level.

Table 4.1   Overall RMM Assessments for the 30 major projects

RMM Level	No. of Projects
Level 4 – Natural	3
Level 3 – Normalised	10
Level 2 – Novice	16
Level 1 – Naive	1

Table 4.1 confirms the reported observation that the MoD's risk management process had been generally performing at the RMM capability Level 2. Also, and importantly given the MoD's emphasis on quantitative risk analysis, only three projects had been found to have a Level 4 capability. Projects below this level could not be expected to produce reliable quantitative risk model forecasts. Yet this was the basis on which projects were providing business case information to approval authorities.

Identification of Risk Management Weaknesses with Corporate Significance

As explained in Chapter 1, it is the weakest of the six RMM perspectives (as shown by the shortest bar on the results bar chart) that determines the overall capability level. Figure 4.4 shows the relative number of projects for which each RMM perspective was found to be the weakest.

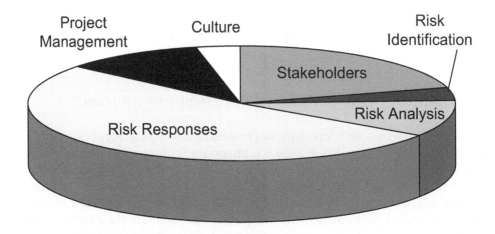

Figure 4.4   Weakest RMM perspective analysis

Figure 4.4 shows that projects displayed different weaknesses; all six of the perspectives were identified as being a key weakness for at least one project. However, there was also another clear conclusion. The most common key weakness amongst half of the projects lay in the effectiveness of their risk responses. Closer inspection of the data showed that failure to implement responses as planned (see Chapter 9 Question D6, p. 175) was a significant contributory cause for the projects affected. This was often closely coupled with a failure to review the effectiveness of risk responses on a regular basis (see Chapter 9, Question D5, p. 174). Across the world and in many organisations there is much anecdotal evidence that failure to implement risk responses is a common cause of process ineffectiveness. The Project RMM had identified that this was also an issue in MoD projects.

An analysis of average scores for individual questions also identified other common issues:

- Weaknesses in the quality of quantitative risk modelling (see Chapter 8, Questions C7 and C8, pp. 144–55 and C9, pp. 156–61 on risk estimating and modelling),
- ineffective engagement of end users in the risk management process (Chapter 6, Question A8, pp. 110–11), and
- weaknesses in the identification of fallback plans and the use of fallback decision points (Chapter 8, Question C10, pp. 162–3 and Chapter 9, Question D1, pp. 166–7).

The quality of risk estimating and modelling was of particular concern, given its significance to the MoD's governance of project management. For example, project approval bodies use this information as part of their decision making process. The effect of most risk modelling and estimating issues was to produce three-point confidence forecasts that were too optimistic. The quality of quantitative analysis was thus identified as being a direct cause of confidence forecasts being exceeded by a disproportionate number of projects.

The effect of risk estimating and modelling issues was exacerbated by failures to implement risk responses. The MoD's risk management process requires projects to use post mitigation estimates (see Chapter 9, Question D7, pp. 176–7) in risk models used to produce three-point confidence forecasts. Planned risk responses must be implemented in order for such forecasts to be realistic.

Given the combination of risk modelling and response implementation issues, the Project RMM had identified two fundamental reasons for major projects tending to overrun relative to the confidence forecasts against which they had been approved. Since one or both of these issues affected most major projects, it was appropriate to take action from a corporate level. Two steps were taken. First, all projects with a Level 1 or Level 2 risk management capability were re-assessed during the following year. The MoD identified RMM Level 3 to be a minimum level of capability that was acceptable. This provided a reasonable level of assurance that risk response weaknesses would be addressed. Second, two new guidance documents for risk modelling were developed. The first was a guide for staff tasked with developing risk models. The second provided guidance for senior managers with the aim of giving them sufficient insight into the modelling and estimation processes for them to challenge the validity of forecasts rather than accept them at face value.

Of the other two common weaknesses identified, it was the lack of user engagement that caused the most concern at a corporate level. In addition to the project sponsor, each equipment procurement project has another internal stakeholder representing users from the armed forces. Once equipment is in service, these people can literally be in the front line, dependent upon the equipment's usability and performance. Failure to engage end users in the risk management process can produce sub-optimal equipment; a fundamental flaw in the equipment procurement process.

Issues of engagement with user stakeholder groups had been a growing concern at a corporate level within the Defence Procurement Agency. The Project RMM results underlined this concern by identifying it in another context. A number of steps were taken in response. From a risk management perspective, users are now engaged more actively in the identification and management of risk. Risk process managers are also required to account for the management of risks in all lines of development relevant to users including training, personnel and interoperability. Subsequent Project RMM assessments confirmed that this aspect of risk management was improved significantly.

Joint Risk Management with Prime Contractors

Much of the risk in military equipment procurement projects is rooted in technology. The leading technology experts tend to be found in industry rather than the MoD. As a consequence, industry is usually funded to perform work on the MoD's behalf during the concept and assessment phases. Then, following Main Gate approval, industry is responsible for the management of technology risk transferred to it by contractual requirements. Significant aspects of the MoD's risk are thus managed by industry during all phases. Accordingly, the MoD expects each project to engage in a joint risk management process with its prime contractor.

A number of prime contractors on major projects assessed within the Defence Procurement Agency had sponsored independent Project RMM assessments. This provided the projects concerned with the opportunity to compare the risk management capabilities of the MoD and industry project teams. These comparisons provided additional insights to the projects concerned.

Figure 4.5 shows the RMM results for the project in which there was the greatest discrepancy between MoD and industry practice. The darker bars represent the results obtained for the MoD and the lighter bars results for the prime contractor. Not only did the MoD team's risk management exhibit a much lower level of capability, but the histogram bars also show a different pattern of relative strengths and weaknesses. Despite the existence of a joint risk management plan, practice differed markedly between the parties.

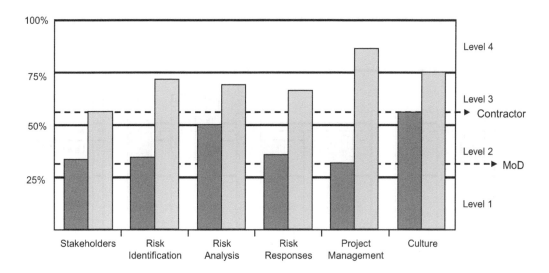

Figure 4.5   Comparison of MoD and prime contract RMM results for one project

For obvious reasons, it would not be acceptable to disclose the identity of any project with RMM results included in this book. At the time that the results shown in Figure 4.5 were obtained, in the interests of accurate data collection, the disclosure of results was also restricted within the MoD. Despite this, it was interesting to see that well-informed MoD personnel had a shrewd idea of which projects corresponded to which results. In the case of Figure 4.5, a scrutineer immediately identified the project correctly, despite it being potentially any one of 30. They had recognised it as a case in which the prime contractor had successfully exploited commercial weaknesses in the MoD's risk management process. Unsurprisingly, the stakeholders' perspective was lowest amongst the contractor's RMM results. This reflected its relationship with the MoD. In the longer term this also had adverse consequences for the contractor, for whom the project was not a commercial success.

Figure 4.6 shows the results for the project in which the MoD and industry had the best matched risk management practice. In this case, both parties' practice followed the joint risk management plan, the prime contractor doing so slightly more precisely. The relatively high values for the project management and culture perspectives reflect that this work was supported by regular joint risk reviews. The weaknesses lay in the effectiveness of risk analysis and risk responses. In practice, immature risk analysis led to risk being inadequately understood, which, in turn, impaired response effectiveness. These were technical issues with the process that could be improved relatively easily.

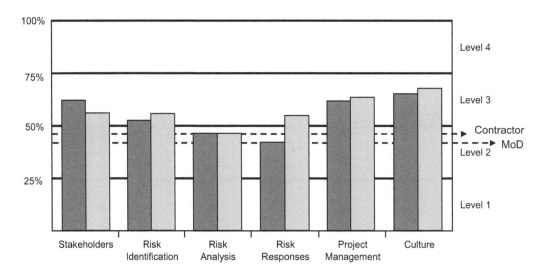

Figure 4.6   Comparison of MoD and prime contract RMM results for one project

Differences in Practice Within the Same Organisation

Although a number of common features of risk management weakness had been identified by the RMM assessment programme, it was also noticeable that there were significant variations in practice. Some projects scored well from certain perspectives but poorly in other perspectives in which their peers had scored relatively well. Figure 4.7 shows some evidence of this. It details the best, poorest and median scores amongst the 30 major projects for each of the six perspectives and for overall capability. The median overall capability was significantly lower than the median score for any of the six perspectives. This is because overall capability is determined by whichever of the six perspectives is weakest and because, other than a common weakness in risk responses, there was no consistent pattern of scoring amongst perspectives.

The MoD provides its projects with risk management guidance developed by a department tasked with advising on project management practice. In addition, the majority of the Defence Procurement Agency project teams had been co-located in a single large site. More generally, the MoD also derives key features of it process from UK government risk management guidance published in the Treasury's Orange Book. Despite all these measures, practice still varied significantly between one project and another.

One cause of variance in practice was that some risk process managers had much more specialist expertise than others. People who reach the higher levels of management in the UK Civil Service tend to be exceptionally able, and support a tradition of valuing generalists rather than specialists. Whilst this culture has undoubted benefits, it can be a disincentive to develop deep skills in any particular discipline. Instead, ambitious civil servants are inclined to move through different posts to prove their value more generally. Likewise, armed forces personnel tend not to stay in the same post for long periods. A lesson that can be learned from this case study is that risk management skills are not easy to acquire and that the risk specialist role does not suit all people, however able. An organisation aiming to achieve the highest standards in risk management needs to realise this and find constructive means of retaining its most able specialists in post.

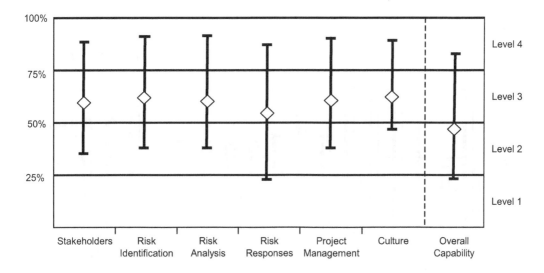

Figure 4.7   Summary of RMM results for 30 major projects

Another cause of variance of practice amongst projects was that the risk management process tends to come under particular scrutiny at certain points in the project lifecycle. In particular, risk information is treated with heightened importance in periods prior to gate reviews. In preparing business cases, projects have to respond to the concerns of the scrutineers and senior managers involved, and these were not always informed by the same understanding of risk management. A related issue was that some project managers were more supportive of risk management than others. In cases where the project manager failed to provide appropriate support, the process tended to be driven by disparate external pressures. The vigour of risk management also tended to decline when external scrutiny was relaxed.

Monitoring Risk Management Capability Improvements

During the year following the initial RMM assessment of its 30 major projects, the MoD re-assessed the 17 major projects that had failed to reach RMM Level 3. As a matter of policy, the aim was to ensure that all projects achieved this as a minimum level of risk management capability. Figure 4.8 shows the overall risk management capability results for these projects at the first and second assessments.

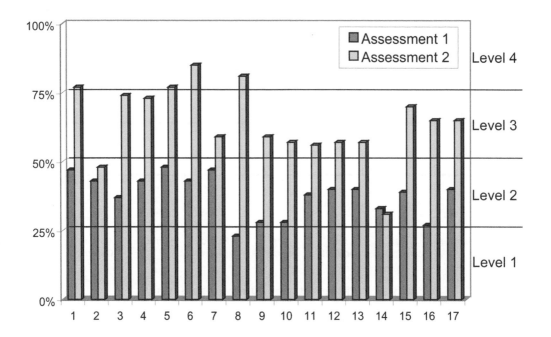

Figure 4.8   Comparison of first and second RMM assessment results

Figure 4.8 suggests that the majority of projects achieved significant process improvements. All but two achieved the minimum target and four achieved a Level 4. However to some observers the degree of improvement appeared to be too good to be true. It is therefore worth exploring some of the associated issues.

It should be remembered that significant improvement in the overall RMM score may only require corrective actions to be implemented for one of the six perspectives. The best example of this was project No. 8 in Figure 4.8 which had been raised from a Level 1 to Level 4. On the face of it, this would appear to be unrealistic. However, the very low overall score measured at the first assessment had been attributable solely to one perspective: risk responses. Scores for the other five perspectives had all been at Level 3 or above. When the neglect of risk responses was corrected, the overall RMM score was therefore lifted significantly. Furthermore, management attention on the process required to achieve this had benefited other aspects of the process sufficiently for an overall Level 4 to be just achieved.

Since each project had been provided with a prioritised list of process improvement actions following the first assessment, implementation of these was reviewed at the second assessment. In general, there was firm evidence that projects had responded well, and this explained much of the improvement measured.

Against these facts, it has to be acknowledged that there were threats to measurement accuracy during the second assessments. Unlike the first assessments, projects knew that they were under pressure to demonstrate attainment of a target. By this time, RMM results were also being disclosed more widely. Project personnel were thus incentivised to score as well as possible. These were conditions that discouraged self-criticism, particularly in the context of group discussion. As a result, it is likely that accuracy weaknesses inherent to the team workshop method of RMM data collection used for MoD assessments affected the second assessments to a greater extent.

By this stage, the MoD had built up sufficient internal expertise to operate its own RMM assessment team. Although HVR staff continued to facilitate some assessments, the MoD team now facilitated the majority. This MoD team maintained its independence from projects internally and was diligent in its efforts to achieve high standards of assessment accuracy. To this end, it continued to review any issues of measurement accuracy both internally and with HVR. Thus, although issues of measurement accuracy did exist, the greater part of measured improvements amongst the re-assessed top 30 major projects is likely to have been genuine.

Linking Risk Maturity Model Measurements with Project Approvals

Three-point confidence forecasts for cost and schedule provide one of the foundations for each project business case at the points of both Initial and Main Gate. It is therefore important for these forecasts to be realistic. However, forecasts that are the product of risk analysis conducted within a weak risk management process tend to be unrealistic. For reasons that are explained further in Chapter 8 (in particular, Questions C7, C8, and C9, pp. 150–63), immature risk analysis tends to produce forecasts that underestimate the effects of risk. Moreover, it tends to produce forecasts that are too optimistic.

Accepting the output of risk analysis at face value can be a mistake if there is uncertainty about the capability of the process that has been used. The MoD recognised this and established a policy to provide evidence of each project's risk management capability at approval points. The main focus for this was Main Gate approval; the point at which risk-based forecasts mattered most for project governance purposes. Under this policy, any project seeking funding for the Demonstration and Manufacture phase in excess of £20million was required to be assessed as having a risk management capability of RMM Level 3 or 4. Without this level of assurance it was assumed that the three-point confidence forecasts could be misleading. If assessment identified the project as having a weaker risk management process, finalisation of the business case would normally be postponed until the necessary process improvements had been made.

A minimum requirement of RMM Level 3 could be correctly criticised as providing inadequate assurance of realistic forecasts for overall project risk. However, the MoD considered that raising the requirement to Level 4 might be too great a barrier for the majority of projects. As a more pragmatic alternative, it introduced a further measure for risk estimating maturity. This measure was derived from the six Project RMM questions related most directly to quantitative risk analysis. As a minimum, projects were required to meet the Level 3 criteria in respect of all six of these questions as well as an overall Level 3 assessment.

The details of this policy are, perhaps, less important than the principle that lies behind it. If risk-based information is to be relied upon when making major project decisions, there should be a process that provides assurance to the decision makers that the information is of adequate quality. The MoD retained its policy linking Project RMM assessment to project approvals for a period of four years, ending in 2008. It was then superseded by a verification and validation process that evaluates the quality of the models used for business case forecasts. This process is undertaken by independent internal staff, supported if appropriate by independent consultants. The aim is to tackle potential project modelling accuracy issues directly.

Effect of Project RMM assessments at Main Gate approval

The MoD's policy that required projects to demonstrate a minimum risk management capability of RMM Level 3 as a precondition of achieving Main Gate approval commenced in April 2004. This book was being written in 2009. It has therefore started to become possible to compare the performance of projects approved before and after April 2004. If use of the Project RMM helped to improve the risk management capability of projects passing through Main Gate, then projects approved after April 2004 should have performed better than their predecessors when measured against the risk-based confidence forecasts provided in each business case.

The annual NAO Major Projects Report is a good source of evidence when comparing the performance of MoD equipment procurement projects. One of the measures used in this report is called risk differential consumed. This measure is illustrated in Figure 4.9. The risk differential is the interval between the 90th and 50th percentile confidence forecasts produced by a project at Main Gate approval. The risk differential consumed is calculated by dividing the change in 50th percentile confidence forecast since Main Gate by the risk differential. For example, if a project has slipped to the extent that its current 50th percentile confidence forecast for schedule completion matches the 90th percentile confidence date at approval, its risk differential consumed for time would be 1.0. Figure 4.9 illustrates a project that has suffered significant slip and has a schedule risk differential consumed of 1.2.

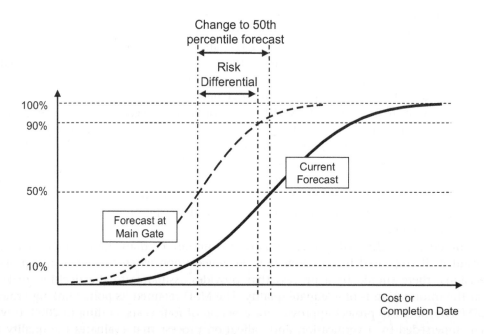

Figure 4.9   Illustration of the NAO's calculation of risk differential consumed

The chart shown in Figure 4.10 is based on data included in the NAO's Major Projects Report published in December 2008. Of the 20 of the projects covered by this report that had passed through Main Gate, 13 had disclosed values for risk differential consumed. Six of these had been approved later than April 2004. Figure 4.9 shows the risk differential consumed for all 13 projects in chronological order.

Project	Main Gate approval	Proportion of risk differential consumed
A400M	May 2000	3.40
Type 45	Jul 2000	7.00
Support Vehicle	Nov 2001	4.14
NLAW	May 2002	3.63
Terrier	Jul 2002	13.00
Soothsayer	Aug 2003	5.00
Naval EHF/SHF Sat Coms	Aug 2003	31.00
----	April 2004 ----	----
MTADS/PNVS	Sep 2004	0.33
Watchkeeper	Jul 2005	0.75
Merlin Sustainment	Mar 2006	0.00
Falcon	Mar 2006	0.00
Future Lynx	Jun 2006	0.00
Advanced Jet Trainer	Aug 2006	0.57

(x-axis: 0, 4, 8, 12, 16, 20, 24, 28, 32)

Figure 4.10 Schedule risk differential consumed for 13 major projects

Figure 4.10 shows that all seven of the projects approved before April 2004 had current forecast completion dates significantly beyond their 90th percentile confidence forecasts. In principle, unless unknown unknowns are a significant factor, only 10 per cent of projects should slip to this extent. In contrast, the six projects approved after April 2004 were forecasting completion dates before their 90th percentile confidence forecast.

The seven post-Main Gate projects for which the risk differential was not included in the 2008 NAO report are:

- Astute Class Submarine (Main Gate 1997),
- Beyond Visual Range Air-to-Air Missile (in-service date redefined),
- Future Joint Combat Aircraft (excluded from NAO analysis),
- Nimrod Maritime Reconnaissance and Attack Mk 4 (Main Gate 1996),
- Sting Ray Life Extension (in-service),
- Typhoon Fighter Aircraft (in-service), and
- Typhoon Future Capability (Main Gate 2007 – excluded on the grounds that this date is too recent to provide significant evidence in this context).

This list includes a number of older projects that have experienced lengthy delays. The Nimrod, Typhoon, Astute and the Sting Ray Life Extension projects have suffered combined post-Main Gate delays of almost 20 years. The Future Joint Combat Aircraft programme has also experienced serious delays. Hence from amongst the current population of projects approved before April 2004, it seems unlikely that any would be able to claim to have a schedule risk differential consumed of less than 1.0. In contrast every project approved after April 2004 was forecasting schedule completion within this risk tolerance. Figure 4.10 shows a marked difference between these projects and their predecessors.

It is therefore possible that the relatively good schedule performance of projects passing through Main Gate after April 2004 is significant. Of course, until these projects have been delivered, it will remain too early to make firm conclusions. The late impact of technical risks may yet cause more serious delays to recently approved projects. Nevertheless, based on the information to date, it seems not unlikely that increased risk management capability at the point of Main Gate approval has improved the predictability of subsequent schedule performance.

Figure 4.11 shows the in-year change in cost estimates for 19 of the 20 projects included in the 2008 NAO Report that have passed Main Gate. Typhoon was excluded for reasons of commercial sensitivity. The in-year cost change is calculated as the percentage by which each project's forecast of most likely cost changed during the period April 2007–March 2008. One might expect that older projects would have the more mature estimates. Figure 4.11 suggests that the cost forecasts for projects passing Main Gate after 2004 have been relatively stable. Their average cost growth has also been lower.

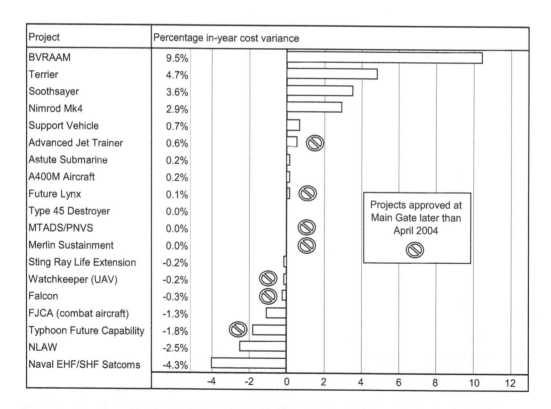

Figure 4.11 Percentage in-year cost variance for 19 major projects

The NAO report notes that procurement management issues and changed customer requirements tend to have more influence in the earlier period after Main Gate approval whereas technical issues tend to predominate from the middle period of the delivery phase. Procurement management and requirement issues can be expected to impact on MoD costs. In contrast, in a fixed price contracting environment, the cost implications of technical risk tend to impact upon contractors. From the MoD perspective, technical issues thus tend to affect schedule performance rather than costs. Given this, the relative stability in cost forecasts shown by the seven projects approved after April 2004 is encouraging.

The possibility that improved risk management capability at Main Gate approval has improved project predictability is confirmed by Figure 4.12. This shows the percentage schedule and cost variance of projects' forecasts relative to their 50th percentile forecast at Main Gate for the 13 projects included in Figure 4.10. All projects approved prior to April 2004 have a schedule variance that is greater than any of the post-April 2004 cohort by a factor of almost three. The pre-April 2004 projects also show a much greater variance in cost outcome. Moreover, although some these projects appear to have reduced their costs, some of these reductions have been due to reduced requirements.

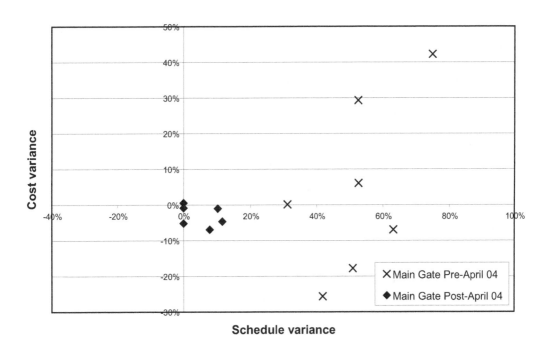

Figure 4.12 Percentage schedule and cost variance for 13 major projects

Overall the evidence from Figures 4.10, 4.11 and 4.12 suggests that making project approvals conditional on achieving a minimum level of risk management capability has been beneficial. If, when all projects involved have been completed, there is still a significant difference between projects passing Main Gate prior to and after April 2004, there will be firm evidence of this benefit. In practice, it is difficult to prove that project risk management delivers the benefits that it is designed to do. Since all projects are different, one cannot run a scientifically controlled experiment. However, when combined with other evidence, such as measured process improvements and positive user feedback, the encouraging quantitative evidence of benefits in major MoD projects provides increasing confidence that the Project RMM does what it is intended to do. Moreover this confidence has been established with a large number of high cost/high risk projects.

Management of Cost Risk across the Extended Project Life Cycle

A valid criticism of the equipment procurement process described so far in this chapter is that it fails to address cost risk over the extended project life cycle. In terms of time risk, relating risk to the in-service date is appropriate; project time risk does not impact on the in-service phase. However, constraining cost risk analysis to the demonstration and manufacture phase leaves an important gap.

Typically, maintaining military equipment for the period of its in-service life is more expensive than its initial procurement. Moreover, decisions taken during the procurement process can have a significant influence on in-service costs. This had always been recognised by the MoD; through-life cost issues were addressed during concept and assessment phases. However, by restricting three-point confidence cost forecasts to procurement, the implications of in-service cost risks were being sidelined.

An emphasis on procurement cost at the potential expense of whole life costs also reflected the division between MoD organisations. As illustrated in Figure 4.1, the Defence Procurement Agency handled initial procurement and then handed over responsibility for through-life support to the Defence Logistics Organisation. In 2007, the MoD merged the two organisations to form a new organisation: Defence Equipment and Support (DE&S). The aims of this reorganisation included smoothing out the transition from procurement to service and strengthening the linkage between procurement decisions and their whole life implications.

Under revised project approval rules, the DE&S requires cost risk analysis models at Main Gate to reflect the extended project lifecycle. Business cases are therefore based on the extended project lifecycle, thus closing the gap previously left by cost risk analysis.

Summary and Observations

The aim of this chapter has been to provide an overview of how the Project RMM can be used by a large organisation. This can be beneficial to both individual projects and to the corporate processes governing project management. This chapter also identifies some of the issues involved with implementing a programme of risk management capability assessments. Many of these are not unique to risk management; they are liable to affect any similar programme.

Compared to most organisations, the MoD sets out high standards for project risk management and pays a great deal of attention to its risk management capability. Despite being inherently difficult and risky, the MoD's projects also meet their technical performance requirements more consistently than projects owned by many if not most other organisations. Given the propensity of the news media to highlight project difficulties rather than successes, this may not be the impression that the public always gets. However, as with any organisation, the MoD's processes are not perfect. They evolve as lessons are learned and as new tools and techniques become available. The Risk Maturity Model has been part of that pattern.

5 *Risk Maturity Model Data Collection*

Like Agatha Christie's detective, Hercule Poirot, I find that nobody can spin a consistent web of deceit, so if you let them talk, they must eventually tell you the truth.

J. Rodney Turner

As with all models, results produced by the Project Risk Maturity Model (RMM) are dependent on the integrity of data input. The RMM data input comprises the answers selected in response to its 50 questions. Selecting the most appropriate answer for each question is the responsibility of the person charged with producing the assessment results: the assessor.

Before trusting RMM results, the following three questions should be asked:

1. Does the assessor know how to interpret the content of the RMM?
2. Does the assessor have sufficient knowledge of the project and its risk management process?
3. Is the assessor motivated to provide a fair assessment?

In the interests of producing consistent results, the RMM content has been designed to be objective to the extent that is realistically possible. However, there is a limit beyond which attempts to increase the model's objectivity could be counterproductive. Attempting to describe all possibilities for any project in any organisation would bury the model under a mountain of detail. Selecting the most appropriate option for each RMM question therefore requires a degree of subjective judgement. Whilst this book should help any assessor to make such judgements, there will always be cases where relevant issues are not covered explicitly. It therefore helps if the assessor has both a theoretical understanding of project risk management and first hand experience of its application.

First-hand experience of projects and project risk management is a guard against making naïve assessments. Often, staff working on the project being assessed will be hoping for a favourable result. In these circumstances, they may try to explore ways to increase the levels of answers selected. Over the years, some project representatives have proved to be particularly creative when interpreting the RMM content. In response, loopholes in the content that allowed ambiguity to be exploited have been closed by rewording. Inevitably, however, room for opportunistic interpretation still remains; there will always be a need for subjective interpretation.

Whilst assessor naïvety is, perhaps, an obvious issue, assessors can also fall into the trap of being pedantic. The purpose of an assessment should be to measure the capability of the risk management process in practice. This is not the same as measuring the completeness of the project's documentation, although the two are often correlated. Nor is it the same as considering whether or not the risk management plan is well written. The fundamental point that assessors need to consider is whether or not risk is actually being managed effectively. Coming to this judgement requires assessors to look beyond project documentation. It should be borne in mind that project risk management is a value-added process rather than a regulatory requirement. A key skill for assessors is to be able to reach a fair conclusion based on all the evidence that they have available.

To date, three different approaches have been used to gather evidence for RMM assessments:

1. Self-assessment,
2. risk management process audit, and
3. project team workshops.

All three approaches have their merits. Any of them may be considered appropriate, dependent upon the purposes of the assessment and to the nature of the project involved. However, self-assessments and project team workshops may produce results that are less accurate. This needs to be borne in mind if project RMM results are compared.

Self-Assessment

Self-assessment involves the use of the RMM by an individual or group of people to come to their own view of a project's risk management capability. In practice, this might be the most frequently used assessment approach. The usual purpose of self-assessment is to gain self-assurance about process effectiveness and identify priorities for improvement. This is a sensible use of the RMM. As we go through life, reflecting on our own performance is one of the ways in which we achieve self-improvement.

However, if RMM assessment results are published, the validity of self-assessments is likely to be compromised. For example, it would be inappropriate to use self-assessments to compare the performance of different projects. The temptation to exaggerate performance would be too strong. This would not just invalidate the scores; important insights into how each project's process could be improved might also be missed. Since the identification of process improvement actions is often the most important purpose of RMM assessments, this could be a fundamental shortfall.

Independent Assessors

If RMM assessments results are to be published, then the use of an independent assessor is advisable. Furthermore, an independent assessor is essential if a full risk management process audit is undertaken and highly advisable in the event that a project team workshop is used as an alternative.

Different organisations will have different views on how independent of the project the RMM assessor should be. Maximising independence may involve using an external contractor. However, independence from the project team might be considered sufficient, in which case the assessor could be employed by the same organisation. An internal assessor's independence is usually increased if they are employed by a different function or business in the organisation or from a different geographical base. This is one of the reasons that many organisations maintain separate audit functions.

However, there are disadvantages in using full-time risk audit specialists. Ideally, the RMM assessor should have in-depth and recent direct project risk experience. Full-time audit department personnel often fail to meet this requirement. A related problem can be attributed to the fact that people with the best insight into projects and risk management tend to like new challenges; a full-time audit job can lack appeal to the people best able to perform the role. Identifying appropriate internal independent assessors can therefore be more difficult than might, at first, be thought. It can thus be helpful to supplement internal audit effort with suitably qualified external consultants.

Repeated audits of the same project can create another difficulty. The success of an audit programme, and hence the performance of RMM assessors, will be judged, at least to some extent, on the basis of the measurement of process improvements. If repeat audits are performed by the same assessors, there will therefore be an underlying incentive for assessors to be increasingly generous with each audit. Moreover, they may fail to recognise adverse unintended consequences of process improvement actions should they occur. Against these issues, use of the same assessors for repeat audits does have advantages. RMM assessors conducting a repeat audit will start with a better understanding of the project. Also, most projects will welcome continuity of guidance and support.

Issues related to repeat audits are more likely to be important to an organisation with large projects that have long timescales. An organisation in this position should therefore think through the implications of these issues. If measurement accuracy and management assurance are of paramount importance, repeated use of the same assessors is likely to be inappropriate. However, if the primary purpose of the audit programme is to foster process improvement, then continued use of the same assessors would have some advantages.

Peer review might be considered as being an alternative to the use of specialist audit staff or external consultants. Peer group project managers or risk management specialists would provide a viewpoint that was independent of the project. They would also have the credibility that comes with being an active practitioner. However, there might be difficulties in providing them with sufficient training in the use of the RMM itself. Peers might also be less willing to be explicit about process weaknesses that they identified. In both cases, the effect of these problems might be reduced if peer assessors were selected from amongst those projects that had already been assessed as having a relatively high level of risk management capability. Thus an organisation might choose to conduct early RMM assessments with audit staff or external consultants and then selectively introduce peers to conduct the majority of assessments in the longer term.

Risk Management Process Audit

The most accurate approach to making assessments is for an independent assessor to conduct a full process audit. An audit will normally involve the following steps:

- Understand the project,
- interview the project risk manager,
- review the project's risk management documentation,
- interview the project manager and a cross-section of the project team,
- interview other stakeholder representatives, if appropriate,
- enter provisional data into the RMM,
- review the provisional RMM results with the project risk manager, and
- present the final RMM results and recommendations to the project.

The first step of understanding the project is a vital one. The assessor will need to understand the project's objectives, organisation and high-level plans. They will also need to understand key features of the project strategy such as project approval points, the roles of stakeholders and, if applicable, the contracting strategy. Important features of the risk management process cannot be assessed without understanding this context. Much of this information may be documented. However, it is usually helpful to arrange a preliminary meeting with the project manager.

Interviewing the risk manager should clarify what they believe the purposes of the risk management process to be and the roles of project personnel and stakeholders. The risk manager can also be invited to comment on the quality of risk information, including risk registers, risk models and reports. It is often a good idea to review the project's risk documentation at the same time. If this documentation includes a risk management plan, the risk process manager can be asked if it describes the process as it is actually carried out. During subsequent interviews with other project personnel it can then be interesting to see if there is a shared perception.

Interviews with the project manager and members of the project team should be carried out on a one-to-one basis. A representative cross-section of the project team should be selected so that these interviews include risk owners from different technical functions as well as the planning, commercial and financial functions. Collectively, these interviews need to address a wide range of issues, so that evidence is gathered to support all relevant RMM questions. This means that interviews do not follow a single fixed agenda. Later interviews may need to fill in gaps. For example, some risk owners might be asked about the effectiveness of reviews and risk responses, whilst others might be asked to talk through their approach to selected risk assessments and estimates.

Typically a risk audit interview lasts about 45 minutes. A key skill is to use open questions in order to avoid 'correct' answers. For example, 'Are risk reviews useful?' is an inappropriate closed question that invites the answer 'Yes'. A better question would be 'How are risk reviews useful?' Given a number of different interviews, it should also be possible to verify that people are telling a consistent story. Rodney Turner's quote beneath the heading of this chapter comes from the section on audits in his book *The Handbook of Project-based Management*. It illustrates the challenge of establishing valid information when following an audit process.

Ideally, the interviewing process should be extended to representatives of project stakeholders. For example, it can be useful to obtain the views of the project customer: do they trust the risk information disclosed by the project? Although gaining access to stakeholders can raise sensitive issues, the validity of the audit is improved if this is done. Moreover, willingness of the project to engage with stakeholders in this way tends to raise levels of trust and thus has the potential to add value in more ways than just the production of audit results and recommendations.

When the interviewing process is complete, the assessor should be able to run through the RMM questions and select provisional answers. They can then take the risk manager through each question and explain the rationale for their selections. They can also discuss the overall RMM assessment and identify priorities for improvement. There are two reasons why the risk manager needs to be re-engaged at this stage. First, for the audit is to be successful in influencing process improvement, it helps for the risk manager to concur with its results. Second, the risk manager may have reasonable grounds for altering the selection of certain answers. Usually the number of alterations will be small (two or three is typical), but the auditor should recognise that the risk manager knows more about the project than they do themselves. Having finalised the RMM input and results, the assessor can then make a final report or presentation to the project.

Project Team Workshops

Project team workshops are, in many ways, a compromise between self-assessments and full audits. The workshop is an event (lasting typically between two and three hours) in which the project manager, risk manager and a cross-section of the project team are invited to select answers to the RMM questions. This event should be facilitated by an independent assessor whose role is to help interpret the RMM content in the context of the project and foster an environment in which a realistic assessment is made. Particular attention needs to be paid to avoid the process being dominated by a subgroup or an individual. Where there are differences of opinion, the assessor should also arbitrate in the selection of answers. In general, there should be a significant majority of people in favour of a better answer in order for it to be selected.

Prior to a workshop, the assessor will need to take steps to understand the project and review the risk management documentation. Experience has shown that allowing too little time for this process leads to inaccurate assessments. Workshop attendees may have their own agenda which could introduce bias into the RMM results. An assessor who is familiar with the project's objectives, organisation and the quality of its risk management information is more likely to be successful in challenging inappropriate choices for RMM answers.

Despite the issues of assessment accuracy, workshops do have important benefits that are missing from a full audit. The first is that collective discussion about the effectiveness of the risk management process is helpful to the development of a good risk management culture. The content may also provide an indirect approach to risk training. Finally, the workshop process is faster and uses much less of the independent assessor's time. Lower costs and a rapid feedback of results and recommendations are both attractive features of this approach.

Conclusions

When an organisation adopts the Project RMM as a maturity assessment tool, it should understand its reasons for doing so before selecting its approach to collecting data input. If RMM results will be used for purposes that will have the effect of incentivising projects to achieve good results for the sake of appearance, then independent assessors will be required. The most accurate results will be produced by a full audit process. However, if the primary purpose of RMM assessments is to enable projects to identify their own priorities for process improvement, self-assessments may be a viable and more efficient alternative.

II Guide to the Project Risk Maturity Model

Our remedies oft in ourselves do lie, which we ascribe to heaven.
William Shakespeare – All's Well that Ends Well

The following chapters are a detailed guide to the content of the Project Risk Maturity Model (RMM). Inevitably, when performing RMM assessments there will be questions of interpretation that require further explanation in order to help the RMM Assessor to interpret the model correctly. To this end, this part of the book includes an explanation of each RMM question and its associated answers.

In many cases, the differentiation between criteria built into the answers to questions is based on the way in which the risk management process is applied in practice. This is an important feature of the model. RMM results should reflect the process effectiveness achieved in practice rather than what might be achieved in principle if the process was implemented as planned. In other cases, differentiation between the RMM criteria is based on the relative merits of different approaches to managing risk.

However, the differentiation built into the RMM assessment criteria will not operate correctly unless the golden rule for selecting answers to each question is followed. This golden rule is that:

> *In order to select any answer to a question, the project must meet or exceed all criteria for both that answer and all answers that correspond to lower RMM levels.*

When selecting answers to each question, the RMM Assessor should therefore consider the answers in the order (top to bottom) in which they are presented. The first consideration should be whether or not the question is applicable. Assuming that it is, the criteria used to describe the D answer (corresponding to RMM Level 1) should be considered first. Provided that the project meets or exceeds these criteria, higher level answers from C through to A can then be considered in turn. If at any stage in this process, the project is assessed as not meeting all criteria at the level being considered, the best answer that can be selected will be that at the next level below.

Part II contains six chapters which correspond to the six RMM perspectives:

- Chapter 6 – Stakeholders
- Chapter 7 – Risk Identification
- Chapter 8 – Risk Analysis
- Chapter 9 – Risk Responses
- Chapter 10 – Project Management
- Chapter 11 – Risk Management Culture

Each of these six chapters is concluded by a short section providing guidance on identifying actions for process improvement. The priority for process improvement is usually identifiable as being associated with the weakest RMM perspective. It is for this reason that the process improvement guidance has been included at the end of each chapter.

6 *Stakeholders*

The first eight questions in the Project Risk Maturity Model (RMM) concern the role of the project's stakeholders in the risk management process. When making RMM assessments, it is this section that often takes the most time to work through. However, its importance should not be underestimated. Projects do not exist in a vacuum; they exist to benefit the organisations that own them. The purposes of a project and the role of the parties involved are fundamental to project strategy and hence to its management of risk. Lack of an effective engagement with stakeholders will undermine the project's governance.

The RMM questions concern the following stakeholders:

- The owning organisation (as represented by its senior management),
- the project's lead customer,
- main (first-tier) suppliers,
- other suppliers in the project hierarchy, and
- end users of the project's products.

Of course, not all projects have this range of stakeholders. For example, internal projects using internal resources will treat questions related to suppliers as being not applicable. However, the questions related to the owning organisation and project customer will always be applicable; in the case of internal projects, the project sponsor should be regarded as being the lead customer. Lack of a sponsor who plays an effective customer role should be regarded as being a significant weakness.

Many projects exist as contracting vehicles for the delivery of change or new product on behalf of another (customer) organisation. In such cases, the way in which RMM questions are used should depend upon the positioning of the project team being assessed. For example, on a major project, the end customer's project team would regard its prime contractor as being the main contractor. Its own lead customer would be the project sponsor. However, if it was the prime contractor's project team that was being assessed, the lead customer would be the customer organisation's project manager and its main suppliers would be the next tier of contractors in the contract hierarchy.

On a hierarchical multi-organisational project, the RMM can thus be used to make separate assessments of the risk management capability of the different organisations involved. Comparing RMM assessments in such circumstances can produce interesting insights. For example, in the case of a major procurement project, the customer's project team was found to have major flaws in its risk management process as compared to its prime contractor. Thus, although it was intended that there should be a joint risk management process, this was not effective in practice. The outcome was that the contractor had been able to take commercial advantage of the customer's risk management weaknesses.

The RMM questions that follow address the role of various stakeholders, starting with the management that represents the project's owning organisation. When selecting answers, it should be remembered that all criteria should be met or exceeded in both the selected answer and all answers at a lower level of capability.

Question A1: Role of the Organisation's Senior Management

What is the nature of the senior management's involvement in risk management?	
E	Not applicable. (Never – this question should always be applicable.)
D	The organisation's senior management makes little or no use of the project's risk management process.
C	The organisation's senior management has initiated some actions concerning risk management but does not yet make full use of the process.
B	The organisation has a written policy on risk management, but practice on the project may be, to some extent, at variance with this.
A	The organisation's Executive Board has approved a written policy on risk management. The project's methodologies and risk-related decision making and reporting processes are fully consistent with the policy.
Perspectives affected: Stakeholders and Risk Management Culture	

For the purposes of this RMM question, the organisation refers to the company or organisation to which the project team is directly accountable. Most, if not all, project team members are likely to be the organisation's employees, although some might be contractors working in an equivalent capacity. The term 'organisation's senior management' refers to all relevant layers of management from the project sponsor through to the organisation's board.

The minimum requirement for selecting a C answer to this question is that someone within senior management has taken an initiative to establish risk management and that this has influenced the project's process. Such influence may be very limited. For example, it may be as simple as the project sponsor requiring simple information on risks to be included in routine internal reporting. However, the fact that senior management takes at least some interest in risk management is usually helpful.

In practice, the attitude of senior management has a major influence on project risk management capability within an organisation. The most important influence over each project's risk management capability is usually the project manager. However, the project manager generally has to live within the practices and ethos of the organisation. No matter how effectively they would like to manage risk, without overt support from senior management, they are liable to encounter difficulties with implementing best practice.

In the last ten years, risk management has become recognised as being important to corporate governance. In 1999, the Turnbull Guidance on internal control was issued to companies listed on the London Stock Exchange in order to clarify their corporate governance obligations set out in the Combined Code It was subsequently incorporated the Combined Code and then updated in 2005. The Turnbull Guidance recommends maintaining a risk-based system for internal control. In effect, it is a high-level guide to corporate risk management. In many instances private companies and government and non-government organisations have adopted its principles.

For companies listed in the USA, the Sarbanes–Oxley (SOX) Act was enacted in 2002. The primary aim of SOX is to mitigate the risk of companies misrepresenting their performance in reports to shareholders. This is a somewhat narrower aim than that of the Turnbull Guidance. However, unlike the Combined Code, SOX, together with its associated standard for auditing internal control over financial reporting, sets a legal standard with onerous penalties for directors who transgress.

Given the wider scope of the Turnbull Guidance relative to SOX, the Project RMM has been related, where relevant, to its recommendations. Question A1 is one of the RMM questions that includes a test of Turnbull compliance. The Turnbull Guidance states that a board of directors should set appropriate policies on internal control. In the case of Question A1, therefore, the minimum Turnbull compliant answer is A, which includes the statement: 'The organisation's Executive Board has approved a written policy on risk management.'

Selecting answer A also requires that the project's methodologies and risk-related decision making and reporting processes are fully consistent with the (organisation's) policy. Some organisations have risk management policies that are based on simplistic risk management processes. It is therefore possible that variance from the organisation's policy is caused by the project's risk management process being too advanced to be aligned with the organisation's process constraints. For example, a project using quantitative analysis techniques such as those described in Chapter 3 (see pp. 38–56), might find that its risk assessments cannot be easily aligned with a simple Probability-Impact Matrix (PIM) style of reporting demanded by its owning organisation's corporate risk management policy. Selecting the B answer in these circumstances would appear to be a harsh judgement on the project itself. However it would be the correct assessment from the stakeholder perspective. If the corporate risk management processes cannot accommodate the project's risk information, part of the value of the project management's risk management process will be lost.

Multi-organisational ownership is an important special case that applies to the RMM assessment of some projects. For example, two or more organisations might share ultimate control over fundamental decisions such as specifying project objectives or defining the role of other project stakeholders. Shared control over fundamental decisions distinguishes multi-owned projects from more conventional arrangements based on a hierarchical flow-down of contracts. Multi-owned projects present a particular problem for project governance for a number of reasons, including the potential for disputes related to risk. The Association for Project Management (APM) guide *Co-directing Change: A Guide to Governance of Multi-owned Projects* (GoPM Specific Interest Group, 2007) is recommended for a more detailed definition of multi-ownership and a description of the issues involved. In the case of multi-owned projects, the senior management should be considered to be the board or sponsor that oversees the project on behalf of its owning organisations.

Since governance is an issue for all organisations, Question A1 will be applicable to all projects. This is so, even if, as might be the case for all but the largest projects, the active engagement of senior management in the project's risk management process is limited to the project sponsor.

Question A2: Disclosure and Reporting Within the Owning Organisation

	How effective and efficient is the internal disclosure and reporting of risk information?
E	Not applicable. (Never – this question should always be applicable.)
D	EITHER The organisation's management makes little or no use of the project's risk management process; OR Internal communication issues suppress a realistic disclosure of risk exposure.
C	The organisation's management requires risk reports to be produced by the project, but makes less use of the information than it should do.
B	The project regularly reports relevant risk information to the organisation's management with the intention of achieving open disclosure. This is actively reviewed. However some aspects of risk that could be considered to be significant may be omitted from this process.
A	The project regularly reports realistic and relevant risk information to the organisation's management. Risks to the project are actively reviewed at the management level to which they are significant. Management also discloses relevant information to the project.
	Perspectives affected: Stakeholders and Risk Management Culture

For the purposes of this question, the organisation's management should be taken to include all people who could take management decisions that affect the project or who take decisions that might need to take account of risks attributable to the project.

Reporting and disclosure is a key component in any organisation's processes for its governance of projects. The Association for Project Management's *Directing Change: A Guide to Governance of Project Management* (GoPM Specific Interest Group 2004) includes a number of questions pertinent to the reporting of project-related risk:

- Does the board receive timely, relevant and reliable information of project forecasts, including those produced for the business case at project authorisation points?
- Does the board have sufficient information on significant project-related risks and their management?
- Are there threshold criteria that are used to escalate significant issues, risks and opportunities through the organisation to the board?
- Is the organisation able to distinguish between project forecasts based on targets, commitments and expected outcomes?
- Does the business culture encourage open and honest reporting?

In essence, these questions ask whether or not the organisation's management knows what it needs to about project-related risk. A further question in the APM guide, *Directing Change* (2004), asks: 'Do project processes reduce reporting requirements to the minimum necessary?' Hence the guide advises that management should receive as much information it needs on risk, but no more. The APM *Directing Change* guide has influenced the criteria built into the answers to this RMM question.

Selecting the A answer requires the project to report all the implications of risk relevant to the organisation's management. The primary point of contact for such reports will normally be the project sponsor. It will then be up to the project sponsor to understand how this information should be used to report project-related risk further up through the management hierarchy. This will normally require information to be filtered and/or synthesised with similar information from other projects. The art of doing this well lies in identifying what senior managers need to know and how to make the status of risk clear in this context. Failure to do this effectively may result in poor decision making at senior levels, with adverse consequences for both the organisation and the project itself.

Selecting the B answer requires the project to provide an open and honest report of risk to the project sponsor. The relationship between the project sponsor and project manager is one in which trust matters. Intent is important. In practice, risk reports may omit relevant information because of technical inadequacies in the risk management practice. However, hiding information is less forgivable since it compromises management's ability to do its job. It may also have longer term adverse consequences for both the project and the project manager.

Example 6.1 – A failure to disclose risk to senior management

The project director of a major engineering construction project provided leadership that supported a risk management process, that when judged from an internal project perspective, was exceptionally effective. However, they were also under pressure to achieve unrealistically low project cost targets. They avoided the short-term implications of this pressure by understating the project's risk exposure in their internal financial reports. When the organisation's management eventually realised the extent of cost overruns, the project director was fired. From the organisation's perspective, the risk management process had failed.

Openness and honesty are important aspects of disclosure. Without effective disclosure reports can appear to have the right data, but actually be misleading. However, whilst reporting is generally a bottom-up process it should be remembered that disclosure affects top-down communication as well. If the project sponsor should be told the truth about project related risk, the project manager also should be told the truth about organisational issues that could impact upon the project. This explains the last criterion required to select the A answer: 'Management also discloses relevant information to the project.'

On the basis that all projects involve communication between the project manager and the organisation's management, Question A2 should always be applicable.

Question A3: Relationship with the Project's External Customer

	What is the risk reporting relationship with the project's external customer?
E	Not applicable. (Internal projects.)
D	The customer does not play any part in the risk management process, although it would be in their better interests to do so.
C	The project provides the customer with risk-related information. However, this lacks some information which is significant to the customer's comprehension of risk and which is in their legitimate interest to know about.
B	The project provides the customer with all risk information requested, to the extent to which the customer has a legitimate interest. However, there may be occasions on which the customer's response has unhelpful repercussions.
A	The project provides the customer with all risk information in which they have a legitimate interest. This is supplied by the project in the knowledge that to do so is in the best interests of both parties.
	Perspectives affected: Stakeholders and Risk Management Culture

This question applies to any project funded by another organisation, that is, where there is an external lead customer. An example of this is a project run to fulfil a contractual requirement placed by another (customer) company. However, the question should also apply in the case of an order placed by another business within the same parent company. The same principle should apply to large government and other not-for-profit organisations that are divided into departments or sub-organisations. In all these cases the sources of project funding lie outside the senior management hierarchy under which the project is supervised.

An external project customer has a legitimate interest in any risk that could affect the project objectives that they provide funds to achieve. As a minimum, it is reasonable for the customer to be forewarned of potential deviations from these objectives and the extent to which deviations could impact. In practice, the project customer may also be able to respond to supplier sources of risk in ways that are in the mutual interest of both parties.

Failure to keep an external customer aware of significant risks usually leads to customer disappointment, distrust and damage to the supplier's reputation. Even on occasions when the customer's objectives are fully met, the additional knowledge that risks were managed effectively is liable to enhance the supplier's reputation. Despite this, there are often barriers to a frank disclosure of risks.

Before the customer releases funding, reasons for a supplier's project team not disclosing the full implications of risks may include:

- We need to put in a low price to get the project started,
- the customer might cancel the project, and
- the customer would probably choose another supplier.

Then, once the project has been funded and is underway, new reasons can emerge for not disclosing risks:

- We would lose the customer's trust if we disclose significant new risks following the contract placement,
- we can't give the customer an excuse to blame us for delays (for example, for commercial reasons), and
- the customer would react badly and hamper progress.

From a customer's perspective, these would seem to be unsatisfactory excuses for the supplier's failure to act ethically. However, they are often realistic concerns that place the supplier in a dilemma. They are also often a consequence of the customer's own project procurement strategy and their response to risk disclosure.

The author has seen many projects suffer from the consequences of failure to disclose risks to external stakeholders. On some projects, the denial of risk to external stakeholders is so strong that it starts to cause denial of risk within the project team, thus also impairing the internal effectiveness of the risk management process. Under these conditions, the project may go through a prolonged period of underperformance until the organisation's senior management or the customer takes radical action.

Whilst temptation to fall short of the standards of frank risk disclosure may be grounded in realistic concerns, such concerns are often dominated by relatively short-term and localised issues. In comparison, some of the consequences of failure to disclose risks have wider and longer term implications. In the author's experience, when judged by the longer term interests of their own organisation, projects teams tend to err on the side of failure to disclose risks to customers.

Selecting the B answer to Question A3 requires the project to provide a realistic assessment of risk to the customer to the extent that the customer requests. If a frank disclosure of risk is not being achieved, then the best answer that can be selected is C. Selecting the A answer requires that the lead customer receives all the risk information that they need to know. This does not have to include risks that would not affect the customer's interests. However, if the customer's own risk information requirements are weak, selecting the A answer may require the disclosure of more or better information than the customer has specified. Selecting the A answer also requires that this information is provided in the mutual interests of both parties. Whether or not this is possible may depend upon the nature of the customers' procurement strategy and the project contract.

This question should be relevant to all projects other than those whose lead customer is a project sponsor within the management hierarchy for their own organisation.

Question A4: Risk Share with Lead Customer

	What has been done to agree liabilities for bearing the impact of risk?
E	Not applicable. (Internal projects in which liabilities for risk are not an issue.)
D	EITHER The relevant formal agreements are known to be ambiguous about the implications of significant risks; OR It is not known whether or not this is the case.
C	Formal agreements define liabilities bearing the impact of risk with sufficient clarity. However one party may be exposed to significant risks that would be more appropriately borne by the other.
B	The risk management process has contributed towards defining formal agreements that align liability for risks with ability to influence risk outcomes.
A	Risk sharing arrangements have been included within relevant formal agreements as a means of reducing the overall level of project risk. For aspects of the project where risk is not shared, there is clarity as to which party would bear the risk impact.
	Perspectives affected: Stakeholders and Risk Response

In the case of internally funded projects, the lead customer will be a member of the organisation's management, typically the project sponsor. In other cases the lead customer will be external, for example, the organisation that has placed the project contract. In either case there should be clarity about how the implications of risk are borne: by the project or by the lead customer? Such clarity should be implicit in formal agreements. In this context, the term 'formal agreements' refers to the document(s) that define project deliverables, timescales and funding arrangements, and any other criteria required to define the project scope. These documents might vary from work instructions (for internal projects) to a commercial contract.

The absence of clarity in formal agreements is liable to lead to mistakes and disputes. Moreover, it would reflect fundamental uncertainties about the role of the parties involved. However, clarity is not in itself sufficient. In the interests of developing an efficient response to risk, ownership of the implications of risk impact should be aligned with ability to influence risk outcomes. If the party that is liable to bear risk impact is not able to influence the risk outcome, they can do no more than provision contingency for its effects. This is a costly approach; inappropriate risk transfer or retention leads to inefficient projects. In contrast, sound agreements create incentives to respond to risks proactively where there is value in doing so.

In practice the transfer of risk usually involves agreeing to its financial implications. Money can always be transferred from one party to another. In contrast, the customer usually bears other non-transferable consequences for failures to deliver a project's products as intended.

The simplest solution to aligning risk ownership with ability to influence outcomes is to ensure that financial liabilities for risk are clearly partitioned. This, typically, is a purpose of a conventional fixed price commercial project contract. Such contracts often have an associated hierarchy of requirement documents that define where responsibilities lie. Whilst these sometimes explicitly record the commercial treatment of each risk, the essential principle is that the commercial implications of any risk can be inferred implicitly. Equivalent, though usually less exhaustive, approaches can be used within large organisations where one element of the organisation may be responsible for delivering a project on behalf of another.

Where formal agreements are designed to partition the ownership of risk, it is good practice to test risks for the clarity and appropriateness of risk-bearing ownership. For example, if a project risk register identifies the risk owner (the individual responsible for managing a risk – see Chapter 8, Question C2, pp. 134–5) and the risk-bearing organisation, one would expect that the owner of each risk would be employed by the risk-bearing organisation. Misalignments would normally indicate that either the risk owners lack incentives to manage risks effectively or that risks are being borne by the wrong organisation. Either case would be inefficient from an overall project perspective.

However, there are limits to how precisely formal agreements can define risk-bearing responsibility. Inevitably some risks are shared. Moreover, there can be mutual interest in sharing even those risks that could be partitioned precisely. Risk sharing is a more sophisticated, and often more successful commercial approach than fixed price contracting. Sharing risk can foster a co-operative approach that makes the combined response to risk more efficient. Whereas some risks can be partitioned by making increasingly precise definitions for responsibility, shared responsibility can make this process redundant by introducing overarching responses that are more effective. Selecting answer A for Question A4 requires the project to have entered into risk-sharing arrangements to an appropriate extent.

Risk sharing usually involves the project's revenue or profitability being aligned with the project outcome. Chapter 3 (see pp. 38–53) describes an example in which a company contracted to build and operate a toll bridge receives an agreed proportion of the revenue. This allows the customer and supplier to share the risk associated with project success (as measured by traffic volume). An approach to developing successful risk-sharing arrangements is to identify key measures of project success in which a mutual interest can be exploited contractually. On this basis, project delivery cost can also form the basis for risk sharing. For example, a balanced incentive and risk-sharing (BIARS) contract establishes a price based on the expected project value, plus an agreed level of profit. If the actual costs are lower than planned, the customer and supplier then share the benefit; the customer by lower price and the supplier by increased profit. Similarly higher costs than planned result in shared pain; whilst the supplier would be paid more, this additional money would be less than the increased cost, thus reducing profitability.

Risk sharing is also likely to be a feature of any multi-owned project, where partnering organisations share elements of both costs and project benefits. In common with risk-sharing arrangements established by customer–supplier relationships, the key point to bear in mind is that the way in which risk is shared should foster mutually constructive decision making, thus reducing the overall level of project risk.

Question A4 is applicable to any project with an external customer. It may also be applicable if the customer represents a different department within the same organisation, thus creating a requirement to differentiate budgetary provisions for risk.

Question A5: Relationship with the Main Supplier(s)

How well informed is the project on risk attributable to its main supplier(s)?	
E	Not applicable. (There would be no value in requiring suppliers to disclose risk information.)
D	EITHER Suppliers do not provide risk information; OR Suppliers are reluctant to disclose any risk information that they perceive to be against their own interests.
C	Suppliers provide risk information. However this EITHER Omits significant sources of risk relevant to the project; OR Falls short of acceptable standards of frank disclosure.
B	Suppliers operate acceptably capable risk management processes and are willing to disclose relevant information. However differences in practice could lead to a loss of visibility of relevant data.
A	Suppliers operate risk management processes that are complementary with that used by the project. These processes are used routinely to inform the project with complete, relevant and timely data.
Perspective affected: Stakeholders	

This question may apply to any project that is exposed to significant sources of risk as the consequence of employing a supplier to undertake part of the project. In deciding upon the applicability of this question, the RMM Assessor will have to form a judgement as to whether or not any of the project's suppliers should have a contractual responsibility for operating a formal risk management process. When making this judgement, the key issue is whether or not requiring the project's supplier(s) to undertake a formal risk management and reporting process would add value. All project activities carry cost, and suppliers' prices can be expected to be higher if they carry contractually delegated responsibility for part of the risk management process. If this cost to the project is likely to be justified by the benefits of influencing at least one supplier's performance, behaviour and disclosure of information then this question is applicable.

The main supplier might be a prime contractor and itself be responsible for management of associated subcontracted projects. If so, Question A7 (Risk data reported through the supplier hierarchy) will also be applicable. Alternatively, there may be a number of relevant suppliers directly contracted to the project. If so, this question should address these suppliers as a group.

In many ways, Question A5 addresses the same issues as Question A3, but from a customer's rather than a supplier's perspective. In order to operate an effective risk management process, the customer needs to understand the risk to which the supplier's performance could expose it. If formal risk management relationships are appropriate, they are normally established prior to final commitment of the customer's funds. This should contribute towards the establishment of formal agreements (for example, a contract) that align responsibility for bearing risk with the ability to influence risk outcomes. Risk management information received from suppliers may also influence supplier selection. Open disclosure of supplier risk information is therefore an important factor in the customer project procurement process.

Of course, suppliers to a project know the importance of risk information all too well. If engaged in a competitive tendering process, suppliers are concerned to create the most favourable impression possible. Risk information disclosed at this stage may be limited to:

- Risks that have already been managed effectively,
- risks that reflect favourably on the supplier compared to their competitors,
- negligible risks selected to demonstrate the thoroughness of risk identification, and
- customer-sourced risks identified to protect the supplier's commercial position.

Risks that do not fall into these categories are often only disclosed if the customer has made related concerns explicit. Even then, a supplier will be tempted to provide an optimistic assessment of their implications. Customers should be wary of optimistically biased risk information provided in competitive tenders.

Equally (though less common) there can be situations in which supplier motivation inflates the implications of risk. For example, if a supplier has been awarded a cost plus contract for a programme of projects on which overruns would be deemed unacceptable, they are likely to provide risk information that supports generous contingency allowances.

When selecting the answer to Question A5, the RMM assessor should put themselves into the position of suppliers: what motivations lie behind supplier risk disclosure? If there is an imbalance between motivations that foster optimism and pessimism, what steps has the project taken to make sure that risk information is realistic?

To an extent, customers get the quality of project risk information that they deserve. One of the purposes of spending significant sums of money in early project phases, is the project should achieve a more realistic assessment of risk prior to its main authorisation point. A project that has invested resources in this way can expect to have more insight into risk managed by suppliers and hence achieve a more effective project delivery through its procurement strategy.

Question A6: Risk Share with the First-Tier Supplier(s)

	What has been done to agree liabilities for bearing the impact of risk?
E	Not applicable. (EITHER Suppliers do not have a significant influence on risk; OR They are not yet sufficiently engaged in the project to make this question relevant.)
D	Formal agreements with the first-tier supplier(s) do not adequately define liabilities for bearing risk.
C	Formal agreements with the first-tier supplier(s) have sufficient clarity to define liabilities for bearing risk. However, these agreements expose one party to significant risks that would be more appropriately owned by the other.
B	Formal agreements with the first-tier supplier(s) include terms and conditions that transfer risk in a way that is aligned with the ability of each party to influence the outcome of the risks involved.
A	Risk sharing arrangements have been included within relevant formal agreements as a means of reducing the overall level of project risk. For aspects of the project where risk is not shared, there is clarity as to which party would bear the risk impact.
	Perspective affected: Stakeholders

The issues addressed by this question are similar to those addressed by Question A4, but from the customer's rather than the supplier's perspective. First-tier suppliers in this context include those defined as being main suppliers in Question A5: suppliers with formally delegated responsibilities for operating part of the overall risk management process. If Question A5 is applicable, then this question will also be applicable. However, there may be additional first-tier suppliers who should be required to act on significant sources of risk, even if they are not required to operate a formal risk management process. This question should apply if there is any supplier responsible carrying out work that represents a significant source of project risk.

Failure to establish links between risk management and contracting strategy is a common project management weakness. Examination of a project's risk responses to supplier-sourced risks frequently reveals ineffectual or reactive measures such as closer progress monitoring. This betrays a lack of contractual incentives for the supplier to respond to risks in the customer's interest. The best opportunity for introducing such incentives is prior to a contract award; an illustration of how the window of opportunity for introducing effective responses may close a long time before risk impact could become evident.

Approaches to responding to supplier sourced risk can include:

- Engaging suppliers in the earlier stages of a project,
- investing in the management of supplier-sourced risk prior to the main project approval point for example, by paying potential suppliers to reduce specific risks,
- being clear to potential suppliers as to which risks are of greatest concern whilst competition between suppliers is ongoing,
- use of contractual penalties (such as liquidated damages) or financial incentives for achieving stretch targets,

- sharing risk using an appropriate contract structure,
- creating an opportunity budget that allows the supplier to identify contract changes in response to new risks,
- aligning suppliers' payment milestones with the delivery of high-risk objectives,
- aligning payments with the realisation of project benefits or post-project service delivery, and
- using commercial pressure related to other sources of business.

Commercial solutions to risk management should be regarded as being risk responses. If they are not employed when appropriate, the project customer is liable to retain risk unnecessarily. However, when transferring risk, care should be taken to ensure that the supplier has a proportionate influence over the associated risk outcomes. Transferring risks that the supplier cannot control will lead to either unnecessarily high supplier costs or leave the supplier vulnerable to project failure. Neither of these conditions is in the customer's best interests.

As with Question A4, answers D through to B represent different levels of quality for the clarity and appropriateness with which risk has been partitioned in the context of a conventional fixed price contract (or fixed budget, in the case of non-commercial formal agreements). Clarity is required in order to justify selection of a C answer. Appropriate risk transfer is required for a B answer.

Selection of the A answer to Question A6 requires a project to have used an effective approach to risk sharing to structure the formal agreements between customer and supplier. However, some risk sharing contract structures can themselves be a source of complexity and overhead. Thus, there will be many projects for which this would not be appropriate. Projects in this position may feel frustrated that they cannot select the A answer. Three points that can be made in response to this:

1. No project should expect to be able to select the A answer to all questions.
2. Obtaining an overall RMM Level 4 assessment does not require the A answer to all questions.
3. An organisation may reasonably regard RMM Level 3 capability to be good enough for some projects. Projects in this position should therefore not regard selecting a B answer for questions such as this as being an indication of weakness or failure.

Risk sharing arrangements are often most appropriate to complex projects where clarity of risk ownership can itself be an issue. Relatively simple projects are more likely than others to regard RMM Level 3 capability as being good enough.

Question A7: Risk Data Reported Through the Supplier Hierarchy

How confident is the project that all relevant risk data is reported and known?	
E	Not applicable. (There are no second-tier suppliers for which value would be added by their being required to operate a formal risk management process.)
D	The project has little or no confidence that it understands the implications of risks present in the second-tier suppliers or below.
C	The project has visibility of the implications of risks associated with most relevant suppliers. However, there are significant doubts about either the integrity or timeliness of risk reporting.
B	The project has visibility of the implications of risks associated with all relevant suppliers. The integrity and timeliness of this data is usually, but not always, satisfactory.
A	The project has good evidence that it is able to analyse the implications of risk data emerging from all points in the contractual hierarchy. This analysis is based on realistic data that is reported in a timely manner.
Perspective affected: Stakeholders	

This question applies to all projects with first-tier suppliers who themselves have suppliers that are (or ought to be) required to operate a formal project risk management process. In practice, most such suppliers are likely to be commercial organisations with project-based subcontracts flowed down within the context of a large or complex project. Many, if not most, smaller and medium sized projects will find that this question is not applicable.

A project managed from the top of a project-based supplier hierarchy will be aware that significant sources of risk may be attributable to the performance of lower-tier suppliers and the nature of the work contracted.

Example 6.2 – Communication of a risk through a contract hierarchy

The NASA Space Shuttle programme was severely damaged by the catastrophic explosion of Challenger shortly after launch on 28th January 1986. This event was caused by the failure of O-rings in the solid rocket boosters supplied by Morton Thiokol. The decision to launch in what were expected to be exceptionally cold conditions was taken by a four-tier decision chain in which Morton Thiokol was in the lowest level of the hierarchy. Whilst, in retrospect, this decision has been studied as a classic case in safety risk management, it could also have been handled more effectively as a programme risk. Assessing and fixing the related safety issues had programme cost and schedule implications. If the flight constraints consequent to O-ring development issues had been understood correctly, the error of launching Challenger after a freezing night might have been avoided.

There are a number of barriers that can prevent the project team at the top of a supplier hierarchy from recognising the implications of lower-tier subcontract risks. A key problem is that an analysis of risk at low levels is often not comprehended by people working at higher levels. Risk descriptions can be used as an example to illustrate this point. A good risk description will include relevant facts, thus allowing the context of the risk to be understood and linked to project objectives (See Chapter 8, Question C1, pp. 128–33). However, the objectives of lower-tier contractors are usually much narrower than the overall project objectives. This makes a risk increasingly difficult to understand if is escalated with the same description. For example, staff in a major space programme procurement team could fail to understand the full implications of a low-level software risk reported by the supplier of a communications system.

On projects with many suppliers, risk reporting requirements can also generate a large number of risks, causing distraction at the expense of insight. There are skills involved in being able to combine risk information from different sources to present a simple and coherent analysis of risk in context that makes it meaningful to personnel working at higher levels, but without losing critical insights. For qualitative risk management approaches, these skills involve synthesising up risk descriptions of associated risks into a coherent and manageable number of parent risks. For quantitative risk management approaches, the challenge lies in the analyst's ability to recognise and include the most important sources of risk in models using realistic data from all relevant suppliers.

Of course, the causes of poor visibility of lower-tier supplier risk can be simpler than technical deficiencies in risk analysis and reporting methods. Temptation to fall short of the best standards of open disclosure can affect any supplier. Suppliers may also be operating immature management processes. One response to these issues is for the project customer to require suppliers to operate within a joint risk management process. This may include a requirement to use a common risk management tool and database, thus allowing supplier risks to become visible on line. However, whilst this might appear to create a seamless approach to risk reporting, it can have significant disadvantages. Besides the costs involved, there can be significant technical problems in overcoming associated IT and security issues. But perhaps the greatest concern should be the possibility that it becomes necessary for a supplier's project to maintain parallel risk databases: one dictated by the customer and the other by its owning organisation. Since data maintained in the latter is more likely to be realistic, the customer may be better served by avoiding some temptations to be prescriptive. Obtaining good quality risk information from different organisations in a project hierarchy is not an easy task.

Questions that the RMM Assessor could ask in relation to Question A7 include:

- Do lower-tier suppliers operate a capable risk management process?
- Do lower-tier suppliers disclose the full implications of risk to their own customer?
- Are first-tier suppliers able to assimilate risk information effectively for reporting purposes?
- Is risk information meaningful to the people working at the level to which it is reported?
- Would a significant new risk identified by the lowest tier of supplier be reported promptly through the appropriate level?

Whilst Question A7 may not apply to the majority of projects, those projects to which it is applicable tend to be large and complex. Issues related to this question can cause such projects to find it particularly difficult to reach the highest levels of risk management capability.

Question A8: Role of End Users

What role do end users play in the project's risk management process?	
E	Not applicable. (End user requirements are unlikely to have significant risk implications)
D	End users have no involvement with the project's risk management process.
C	End users have visibility of the project risk data but have little or no active involvement with the project's risk management process.
B	End users have an active role in the project's risk management process. As a minimum, end users regularly contribute advice on relevant risks.
A	End users are fully engaged with the project's risk management process. As a result, end users identify relevant risks, advise on their assessment, are included in relevant reviews and contribute to risk responses.
Perspective affected: Stakeholders	

For reasons explained in Chapter 2 (see pp. 19–20), the project risk management process should cover risks that could impact across the extended project life cycle, including the operations and disposal phases. These risks will normally include effects on the end users of the project's products. If end users have more experience of the environment in which the project's products are designed they are likely to be able to make a contribution to the management of project risk. Furthermore, this contribution might be valuable from the earliest phases of the project. For example, sources of risks to operations may be rooted in decisions that are taken during the concept phase.

Example 6.3 – A project in which end users provided critical expertise

A military procurement project to develop and manufacture new equipment for soldiers maintained continuous links with a designated user group. This was drawn from a service regiment sufficiently qualified and experienced to represent the interests of the army as a whole. The end user group was able to offer critical insights into how design and testing requirements should be related to the performance of the equipment in practice. Where there was significant uncertainty about design decisions or testing processes, the related issues were managed formally as risks thus allowing end users to be engaged in the risk management process.

The RMM assessor will have to make a judgement as to whether or not this question is applicable. If the end users' experience of the project's outcome is not at significant risk, then the question would not be applicable. It would be similarly inapplicable if the end users' requirements were understood to a high level of certainty and that there was no significant risk of unplanned adverse project consequences. For example, a supermarket chain might implement a programme of changing tills to self-service checkouts on the basis of a well-researched demand from customers and a trial that had shown there to be no significant incidence of theft or customer difficulty in operating the new system.

However, if the experience of end users is significant to project risk, Question A8 should apply. This will cause more difficulty for some projects than others. For some projects, engagement of end users in the risk management process can be expected to be relatively productive and easy. Much depends upon the representativeness of the people providing end user insights and the expertise that they offer. Example 6.3 is a project on which end users were used constructively.

Unfortunately, there will be many projects for which this question is applicable but which can expect to find the active engagement of users difficult and, hence, limit the best answer that can be selected for Question A8. However, frustrating this might be, significant limitations to the engagement of end users in the risk management process should be recognised as being a constraint on overall risk management capability. Example 6.4 is an example of a project where this was the case. Whilst it is difficult to argue that the end users had nothing significant to contribute to the understanding of risk, there were natural limitations on the effectiveness on their contribution.

Example 6.4 – A project in which end users lacked important expertise

On a healthcare research project, ex-patients volunteered to be co-opted onto the project steering board. Whilst, in principle, bringing the perspectives of ex-patients to board decisions seemed to be sound, in practice, it proved to be problematic. One problem was that the self-selection process involved did not produce users who were representative of the population as a whole. Ex-patients also tended to draw from their own highly-personalised experience to make points that could distract the project board from issues with a wider importance. In effect there was a risk that the judgement of health professionals who had expertise drawn from interactions with hundreds of patients could be overridden by the views of individuals who were experts in only their own experience.

When a project introduces changes to the way in which a service is provided, end users include both service recipients and the people responsible for service delivery. Failure to include engage representatives of either group in the early stages of a project can have serious repercussions. For example, it would seem that some project teams involved in the UK National Healthcare computer system programme focused on technical solutions rather than first understanding the user environment. As a consequence, both the development and take-up rate of the programme's product have been adversely affected whilst more than one company has either withdrawn or been removed from the programme having lost significant sums of money.

End users can help to shape a project's objectives and design. In the case of some internal projects, the project sponsor may, in effect, be a manager who represents the end user's interest. In other cases, the project sponsor will need to satisfy themselves that project risk has been understood from an end user perspective. In either case the sponsor will own the business case and be accountable for the realisation of the project's benefits. A project needs a risk management process that takes this fully into account. In practice, this question should therefore apply to most projects.

Typical Actions for Improvement

This section provides guidance for the identification of process improvement actions related to the stakeholders perspective. A starting point is to identify which stakeholder or stakeholder group fared most poorly against the criteria written into the RMM questions. However, it should be noted that questions related to the project's own organisation and the lead customer tend to be particularly important and thus have relatively high weightings in the model.

Lack of clarity about what project risk information the project's own organisation needs to know is a common problem. In many instances information reported is based on what is available rather than an assessment of the decisions that senior managers make and what is required to support them. Hence actions for improvement might include:

- Improving the organisation's project risk management policy,
- focusing internal risk reports for senior management,
- appointing an owner for the organisation's risk management process,
- appointing a project sponsor,
- improvements in the quality of risk information, and
- formal reviews of escalated risks.

In the case of external projects, the lead customer will be another organisation. In the event that the priority for improvement concerns the customer relationship on risk management, actions for improvement might include:

- Compliance with customer risk management requirements,
- improving the clarity of the commercial ownership of risks,
- developing risk sharing arrangements, and
- implementing a joint risk management process.

The emphasis of these actions is to support the lead customer, in the mutual interests of both organisations. A similar, although slightly different, situation exists if it is appropriate for the project to flow down risk management requirements to subcontractors. Once contracts have been placed, subcontractors can be expected to incline towards self-interest. Of course winning follow-on business by acting in their customer's interest can be a motivating consideration. However, subcontractors can also prioritise their own internal interests (for example, cost control and the delivery of other projects) at their customer's expense of time and product quality. The art of aligning risk management with contracting policy therefore lies in being able to find means by which contractors are motivated to act in their customer's interest. Actions for improvement may therefore include:

- Improving the interface between risk management and contracts function,
- contractual flow down of risk management requirements,
- resolving issues of inappropriate commercial ownership of risks,
- assuring visibility of significant risk at all levels of the contract hierarchy,
- challenging contractors if adverse events not inherent to risk forecasts occur, and
- subcontractor Risk Management capability audits (using the RMM).

7 *Risk Identification*

Risk identification is a fundamental step in the risk management process; risks that are not identified will not be managed. No matter how effective other aspects of the risk management process are, failure to identify risks undermines the process as a whole. Given this, it is tempting to leave no stone unturned by identifying as many risks as possible. However, this can be a mistake. The art of risk identification lies in identifying the right risks at a level suitable for risk analysis.

Collectively, the right risks will:

- Represent the effects of risk throughout the project lifecycle,
- represent all significant sources of uncertainty,
- be informed by learned experience, and
- anticipate potential future effects.

The Risk Maturity Model (RMM) risk identification perspective assesses whether or not a project has identified the right risks. Causes of weakness that have often been found in practice include:

- Failure to engage all parties involved,
- failure to use a range of risk identification techniques,
- denial of risks for reasons of short-term convenience, and
- focusing on low-level issues, thus neglecting wider sources of risk.

Risks must also be identified at a level suitable for risk analysis. The number of risks identified will therefore depend upon the depth of detail to which the risk management process has reached. If using an iterative top-down approach to risk management, the number of risks identified will therefore depend upon the number of previous cycles performed. What is important is not the number of risks, but that collectively, the risks are the right risks. When a risk management process reaches a steady state in which the number of risks being managed is similar from one review to the next, the number of risks can still be an important issue. In practice, risk identification weaknesses can lead to projects having too few risks. This would be reflected in a relatively low RMM score for the risk identification perspective. At the other extreme, a problem experienced by some projects is that they identify too many separate risks. The burden that this imposes on resources and administration can lead to ineffective risk assessment and weak responses. Managing large numbers of low level risks can also cause neglect of broader sources of uncertainty and push responsibilities for risk away from the most senior levels of management. This may produce a poor risk management culture. Although projects that have identified too many separate risks may achieve a reasonable RMM score for risk identification, they tend to score poorly for risk analysis, risk responses and risk management culture. Where this occurs, it should be recognised that the roots of the problem lie, at least partly, in risk identification.

Question B1: Top-down Risk Identification

	In what ways have risk identification processes been driven from the top down?
E	Not applicable. (Never – this question should always be applicable.)
D	The risk identification processes have only focused on individual risks to be managed at lower levels within the project team.
C	The Project Manager and senior members of the project team have been actively engaged in the risk management process.
B	At least one formal risk identification approach has been structured to identify risks associated with the project's purposes. The implications of some risks require them to be managed at the most senior levels of the project team.
A	The risk identification processes have been driven by a top-down approach related to project purpose and strategy. The approach used has either actively engaged the project sponsor or received their explicit endorsement.
	Perspectives affected: Risk Identification, Project Management and Culture

Projects that lack a top-down element to their risk identification process will often find that they have identified a large number of potential low-level problems, but neglected some of the most important and overarching sources of uncertainty. Whilst tackling low-level problems is likely to be helpful, neglecting overarching sources of uncertainty limits the overall effectiveness of risk management. It also makes it more difficult to engage senior decision makers in the process.

Understanding the project strategy is a good starting point from which to start identifying risks. Project strategy is primarily in the hands of the project sponsor. The sponsor should own the business case and be accountable for the realisation of benefits. Project strategy therefore includes defining the purpose of the project and the fundamental roles of the parties involved. Uncertainties associated with the project purpose or with the fundamental role of the parties involved can be regarded as being project strategy risks. The project sponsor should also ensure that critical project enablers (for example, resources and key decisions) are provided by the organisation. Such enablers are often referred to as critical success factors.

An example of a top-down approach to risk identification is to use project strategy risks, critical success criteria and critical success factors as prompts to support risk identification techniques such as brainstorming. Not only does this help to identify risks from a broad perspective, but it also helps produce information that will be seen to be relevant by the sponsor.

Example 7.1 – Risk identification driven by understanding the project purpose

On an industry infrastructure renewal project, the project sponsor regarded the facility outage time to be a key project strategy risk. This was due to the effect that delays would have on turnover and customer retention. A conclusion reached during the early passes of the risk management process was that minimising these effects should be regarded as being part of the project's purpose. On this basis, risk to schedule performance became recognised to be more important than risk to capital expenditure.

The project manager therefore focused the next cycle of the risk management process on schedule risk, identifying at least 40 individual risks that could cause delays and incorporating their effects into a schedule risk model. The forecasts from this model, together with information on escalated schedule risks became the most important elements of the project's reports on risk to the sponsor.

Example 7.1 provides a simple example of risk breakdown. Where the sponsor owned one risk, the project manager and their team owned many. Both views were appropriate since they were tailored to the level at which the individuals were making decisions. The link between high-level and lower-level risks are often described as being parent–child relationships. An advantage of a top-down approach to risk identification is that these relationships can be seen with greater clarity.

The Risk Breakdown Structure (RBS) was introduced as a risk management technique by David Hillson (2002). It is a source-orientated approach to organising risk information into a hierarchical structure of parent–child risks starting with overall project risk at the highest level. The RBS can therefore be regarded as providing a top-down approach to risk identification.

Two further top-down approaches to top-down risk identification are:

1. Identification of relevant sources of uncertainty when assessing composite risks as part of a constructively simple risk model (for example, as illustrated in Chapter 3).
2. Use of a knowledge-based model designed to assess overall levels of project risk exposure (risk being identified as being the questions or criteria to which the project is most sensitive).

Selecting the A answer to Question B1 requires the project to have driven risk identification primarily from an understanding of the project strategy and to have gained the support or active engagement of the project sponsor when doing so. If the project falls short of these criteria, the RMM Assessor will have to consider whether or not there has been any explicit use of a top-down risk identification technique. This may enable the B answer to be selected. However, as with all RMM questions, the B answer should only be selected if the criteria for the D and C answers are met or exceeded. Hence, there would also need to be evidence that the risk identification approach had not drilled down to such low levels that the Project Manager and senior members of the project team had delegated the ownership of all risks.

This question should be applicable to all projects. Even small and simple projects will benefit from being clear about the link between their risks and the project's purpose.

Question B2: Combination of Risk Identification Techniques

How appropriate is the combination of risk identification techniques?	
E	Not applicable. (Never – this question should always be applicable.)
D	The risk identification process does not make use of any recognised techniques.
C	The risk identification process makes use of at least one recognised technique.
B	The risk identification process makes use of a combination of risk techniques that support both initial and ongoing risk identification. These techniques include measures designed to reduce barriers to risk identification.
A	Risk identification is conducted in the context of a top-down iterative risk management process that addresses all significant sources of uncertainty.
Perspectives affected: Risk Identification	

There are many different techniques that may be suitable for risk identification. For example, the *PRAM Guide* (2004) describes the following techniques:

- Assumptions and Constraints analysis,
- checklists,
- prompt lists,
- brainstorming,
- risk interviews,
- stakeholder analysis,
- strengths, weakness, opportunities and threats (SWOT) analysis,
- project progress monitoring,
- nominal group technique,
- Delphi technique,
- technology readiness levels (TRLs), and
- peer review.

This is not an exhaustive list; other techniques may offer their own advantages. However, whilst any such technique may be useful, no single technique can be expected to resolve all the issues of risk identification. For example, some of the above techniques are effective in terms of stimulating lateral thinking and thus help to anticipate future events. Brainstorming is a good example of this. However, other techniques, such as checklists and peer review are more effective in terms of using learned experience. Identifying the right risks is dependent upon anticipating risks from both a future and a historical perspective. Effective risk identification is therefore dependent upon using a combination of techniques.

A second reason for using a combination of risk identification techniques is that, whilst some people naturally identify threats or dangers by impact, others prefer to search for risks more systematically by source. Assumptions and constraints analysis and project progress reviewing are techniques that appeal to the latter.

Third, as the project progresses or as the risk management process addresses lower levels of detail, new risks can be expected to emerge. However, group techniques such as brainstorming can be difficult or time-consuming to repeat. As a project matures such techniques therefore often need to be supplemented with others such as project monitoring or risk interviewing.

Finally, it should be remembered that criticism can be a barrier to risk identification, particularly if such criticism comes from senior levels. Some risk identification techniques are designed to take this into account. For example, risk brainstorming sessions should be facilitated in a way that avoids criticism. The nominal group technique and Dephi technique take this a stage further by introducing different degrees of anonymity to the process. Peer review offers a different solution to the same problem by sidestepping the perception of insubordination that might otherwise be felt by managers on the receiving end of risks identified by people over whom they have line management responsibility.

If the project does not use any formal risk identification techniques, it will be reliant on an ad hoc collection of ideas that occurred to the people involved, possibly at just one point in time. This will usually lead to a number of shortfalls, which the following later RMM risk identification questions are designed to detect.

- Question B4 – Breadth of risk identification,
- Question B5 – Identification of new risks,
- Question B6 – Identification of risks from progress monitoring,
- Question B7 – Use of learned experience for risk identification and assessment, and
- Question B8 – Breadth of responsibility for risk identification.

Question B2 should therefore be applicable to any project. Selecting the C answer requires the project to have made proper use at least one formal risk technique. Selecting a better answer than this requires the project to use an appropriate combination of risk identification techniques. If this is achieved in the context of a top-down iterative approach to the overall risk management process, then the A answer can be selected. However, if the risk management process is based on a single pass approach that commences with the identification of low level risks, the best answer that can be selected will be B.

Question B3: Identification of Non-compliance Risks

	How effectively does the project identify risks associated with compliance?
E	Not applicable.
D	Risks associated with compliance have not been identified, even though they may exist.
C	Some aspects of compliance have been considered for the purposes of risk identification, but only on an ad hoc basis.
B	The identification of compliance risks has been addressed, but this process may have omitted some significant risks that are relevant.
A	Responsibilities for risk identification have been allocated through the project team to ensure that all sources of compliance risk have been addressed systematically.
	Perspectives affected: Risk Identification

All projects have to comply with relevant legal or regulatory requirements. For example, it is hard to conceive of a project that would not be affected by one or more of the following:

- Employment legislation,
- health and safety at work legislation,
- product safety legislation,
- building regulations,
- accounting standards, and
- information security requirements.

Most organisations have risk-based controls assurance processes in place to handle these and similar compliance requirements. It would be a mistake for the project risk management process to duplicate these other processes. Routine compliance risks would therefore not normally be handled by the project risk management process. However, compliance can still have implications that could affect a project's objectives and, hence, lead to the identification of project-specific risks. For example, a project might involve employees working in an unstable foreign country and, hence, raise novel health and safely at work issues. Other risks might be consequential to future changes in legislation.

Example 7.2 – Security requirements risks

The specification for a major government IT infrastructure project included stringent security requirements. The project team identified three significant sources of security requirements risk. The first concerned uncertainty as to whether or not the design would actually meet all requirements as they were understood. Given the terms of the contract, this risk was owned by the contractor. The second was an ambiguity risk; final approval of certain aspects of system design was at the discretion of another government authority which could prove to have a different interpretation of the security requirements. In practice, this was a shared risk between the government project team and its contractor. Finally, the project was also exposed to the risk of changes to government legislation. This was a regulatory compliance risk retained by the customer.

In addition to legal and regulatory requirements, many projects are affected by compliance with commercial agreements. These may include:

- Contractual terms and conditions,
- commercial confidentiality arrangements,
- conditions of guarantee attached to procured materiel,
- conditions of insurance, and
- accounting practices (for example, for open book contracts).

These sources of risk are more likely to be project-specific than legal or regulatory. In most cases, sensible management and normal working practices might be expected to handle their implications without managing them formally within the risk management process. However, some project contracts may be based on particularly onerous conditions; or even worse have unlimited implications. In these circumstances, the consequence of contract compliance risks can be disastrous. The risk management process would be seriously flawed if such risks were not identified.

Example 7.3 – Onerous terms and conditions

A computer systems company that specialised in defence products expanded its business by winning several projects in the offshore industry. Unlike its defence contracts, the contractual terms and conditions negotiated with its offshore clients included exceptionally heavy penalties for late delivery. These reflected the clients' costs of lost production. In the event of delays, the offshore project clients also reserved the power to intervene in the deployment of the supplier's resources, thus affecting its defence projects. The full implications were not recognised until offshore project delays caused a crisis that threatened the computer system company's business future.

Question B3 is applicable to all projects. The A answer should only be selected if there is evidence that the project has identified all relevant compliance requirements and has then used this information to identify significant project-specific risks systematically. Selecting the B answer implies that the project has considered various sources of compliance risk as part of its risk identification process. This would normally require the use of an appropriate technique such as a checklist. A more ad hoc approach should limit the project to selecting an answer no better than C.

Question B4: Breadth of Risk Identification

Does the project identify risks from a broad perspective?	
E	Not applicable. (Never – this question should always be applicable.)
D	Risk identification does not follow any recognised process or guidance.
C	Risk identification tends to be concentrated on specific areas such as technical or cost risk.
B	Risk identification addresses most of the following sources of uncertainty to the extent that they might be relevant: Project scope and strategy, Financial, Technical, Resource, Schedule, Benefits realisation, Operational performance, Management, Commercial, Environmental, Political and External.
A	The context of risk identification is sufficiently broad to capture risks in all relevant project phases and from all significant sources of uncertainty.
Perspectives affected: Risk Identification	

A project may be subject to a wide variety of sources of uncertainty. It may also be appropriate to identify risks across the extended project life cycle, that is, including the operations and termination phases. Despite this, a common failing is to focus risk identification on the risks that are short-term, easy to estimate or easy to manage with simple actions. Often these are the technical risks that project team members are most confident with being able to handle. The other common area of focus is on risks that have direct cost implications that are relatively easy to estimate. Often, this is the consequence of projects being required to justify contingency funding using risk information held in a risk register.

The idea of risk identification having breadth therefore covers two questions:

1. Have all significant sources of uncertainty have been included?
2. Have all relevant phases of the project been included?

Failure to achieve a good breadth of risk identification in respect of either of these questions will cause significant risks to be omitted from the process. Selecting the A answer to Question B4 would be based on a judgement that this had not occurred. This can be a difficult standard to achieve.

There may be two approaches to making sure that major sources of uncertainty are included. One is to use a combination of risk identification techniques, for example, from amongst the techniques listed in the text under Question B2. The other is to start the risk management process at the highest level. Good estimates for the composite risks involved will then necessitate the exploration of a wide range of sources. Example 7.4 illustrates the second of these approaches, although in practice, risk identification was also assisted by the application of formal techniques. Example 7.4 also shows that by considering factors such as benefits realisation and effects on operations, risks can be identified across the extended project life cycle.

Example 7.4 – A railways infrastructure renewals project

A project owned by a national railways organisation aimed to increase the efficiency with which it implemented its programme of track renewals. During the concept and definition phases, various solutions were considered each of which involved using different renewals methods and contracting strategies. A risk model was built to compare the relative merits of each solution from a long-term economic perspective. In effect, the risk model compared the capital expenditure required to introduce each solution with the economic benefits that would be enabled.

Working from this high level concept, detail was added iteratively to reflect the effects of major sources of uncertainty. These included uncertainties about the performance of renewal methods, their implications for track possession time, the ability of the railways' organisation to identify a stable work bank and the degree to which costs could be controlled through competition. A number of these sources of risk were inter-related. There were also project strategy risks concerned with changes to stakeholder objectives.

Working from a high level concept of how its overall project risk could be measured in terms of economic value forced the project team to identify risks from a wide range of sources. It also focused attention on the project benefits: the reduction of routine renewals costs. Thus, although some risks were concerned with costs of project delivery, others were concerned with the project's effects on operations subsequent to the selected new renewals method having been introduced. The risk management process therefore covered the extended project life cycle.

Example 7.4 shows that achieving breadth in risk identification does not necessarily imply identifying a large number of risks. However, as the project progresses, the number of risks will tend to increase as the risk management process develops an understanding of risk at lower levels of detail. Continued use of a combination of risk identification techniques will help to ensure that the risk management process retains appropriate breadth.

This question is applicable to all projects.

Question B5: Identification of New Risks

How promptly are new risks identified?	
E	Not applicable. (The project is using a minimal number of risks as part of an early cycle of a top-down risk management process.)
D	New risks are often not identified until their effects start to occur.
C	New risks are identified during reviews. However the frequency of such reviews is not sufficient to avoid unacceptable delays to risk identification.
B	The lead time to identify new risks is usually, but not always, acceptable.
A	New risks are consistently identified in a timely manner to the appropriate person.
Perspectives affected: Risk Identification and Risk Management Culture	

As a project progresses, new risks can be expected to become identifiable. As they do so, the best opportunity to respond effectively may be earlier rather than later. Risks are sometimes described as having a risk impact window (the period during which their effects occur) and a response window (the period during which the best response could be implemented if it is to be effective). In some cases there can be a significant gap between these windows. For example, the best response to risks attributable to a subcontractor's performance may be a commercial solution that would need to be negotiated before the contract award date. Delays to identifying risks can therefore result in failure to manage them effectively.

To a certain extent, delays to risk identification can be reduced by including risk identification in routine risk reviews or other project reviews. These would need to be held regularly for this to be effective. Selecting the B answer to this question would reflect a project that uses this approach. If the reviews are insufficiently regular, the RMM assessor should select an answer that is no better than C.

Ideally, the project team should be able to augment its use of reviews by fostering a risk management culture that encourages people to identify news risks as and when they are first recognised. Achieving this requires a team ethic of open disclosure within the team and a culture that prompts people to help each other by communicating new information. If this can be achieved, it would not only reflect a good risk management culture, but a healthy project team culture in all respects. Selecting the A answer would depend upon the project team's culture being of this nature.

Unfortunately the condition described in the D answer is not uncommon. A symptom of weak risk management is that the process becomes one that warns of risk effects that have become more or less inevitable. Whilst this may help people to deal with personal accountability issues, it does little or nothing to add real value.

This question is applicable to all projects.

Question B6: Identification of Risks from Progress Monitoring

Are new risks identified from monitoring the project's progress performance?	
E	Not applicable. (The risk management process is, appropriately, focused on plans for later phases.)
D	EITHER Project performance is not adequately monitored; OR Significant shortfalls in performance are tolerated without emerging risks being identified as appropriate.
C	Project progress is monitored regularly. However, although such monitoring sometimes identifies new risks to which the risk management process is alerted, it often fails to do so.
B	Project progress is monitored regularly against well-defined plans. Although this often identifies potential risks that the risk management process then handles appropriately, it sometimes fails to do so.
A	The disciplined application of project monitoring consistently results in the early identification of risks identifiable from shortfalls in project performance. These risks are then handled appropriately by the risk management process.
Perspectives affected: Risk Identification and Project Management	

In order to select the answer to this question, the RMM Assessor will have to take into account the quality of the project's planning process. The question is primarily applicable to projects that are in the implementation phase of the project lifecycle. However for projects with long concept or definition phases, the RMM assessor might consider this question relevant to those phases as well. When entering its implementation phase, a project should have well-defined plans against which risks can be meaningfully assessed and managed at a lower level than would be rational during the concept and definition phases. However, it would be unreasonable to assume that all significant implementation phase risks can be identified before that phase starts. Some emerging risks may therefore only become apparent from the project's monitoring of its progress performance. For example, a trend of delays in one area of the project schedule may suggest that it could later become critical.

Selecting answers A or B to Question B6 is dependent upon the project having well-defined plans. A distinction should be made between the idea of plans being well-defined and plans being detailed. Use of the term 'well-defined' is intended to indicate clarity. Very detailed plans often lack clarity. A well-defined plan will clarify what will be produced, by whom and with what resources (and hence cost). A well-defined plan will be characterised by lack of ambiguity and a clear link to the project objectives. For the purposes of risk management, the level of planning detail only needs to be sufficient to make progress monitoring meaningful.

In recent years there has been an increasing interest in the use of Earned Value (EV) for project progress monitoring. The validity of EV is dependent upon planning clarity; ambiguous activities make its results spurious. The proponents of EV therefore rightly regard it as a means of improving the quality of plans. If the EV approach is carried out well, its results provide an effective means of identifying emerging risk. For example, if the Schedule Performance Index (SPI) is significantly lower than 1.0, the underlying causes can be investigated as a potential source of risk.

Question B7: Use of Learned Experience for Risk Identification and Assessment

	What use does the project make of learned experience?
E	Not applicable.
D	Despite the existence of significant gaps in the project team's experience, risk identification is reliant on the experiences of people working on the project.
C	Learned experience has contributed significantly to the risk management process. However, significant opportunities for improved use of learned experience may have been lost.
B	The project has made much good use of learned experience for risk management purposes, including the use of formal links (for example, records or debriefs) with at least one similar project.
A	Formal and informal methods are used to exploit learned experience for risk management purposes. These are supported by a) an ongoing and productive process of communication with other projects, and b) relevant quantitative historical data.
	Perspectives affected: Risk Identification and Risk Analysis

Risk management is all about what could happen in the future. A cardinal error in risk management is to assume that the future will be precisely like the past; the future is more uncertain than that. However, in project risk management, lessons from previous projects are often the best guide that we have. Inevitably, therefore, learned experience has a major contribution to make towards the risk management process.

A project team is a temporary organisation. One of the pleasures of working on projects is that each one represents a new start. From a learned experience perspective this can be both an opportunity and a problem. Whilst a new start allows team members to respond to previous experience by adopting new ideas, it can also allow them to become too confident that 'things will be different this time'.

One approach to making use of lessons learned is to select project teams on the basis of experience. Of course, the drawback to this approach is that it can create entry barriers for other people and thus lead to organisational inertia. However, if the project team has appropriate experience and if this has been applied to the risk management process, the RMM Assessor should select an answer to Question B7 that is C or better.

In order to select the B answer, the project should have used a formal means of reaching beyond the project team's direct experience. This might involve looking through the organisation's records for previous projects. Such records could include project closure reviews, risk registers or risk identification checklists. Alternatively, face-to-face debriefs might be used. These would give the project the opportunity to assess its own risks in more depth.

Selecting the A answer is dependent upon the project maintaining regular links with similar projects. It is also dependent upon the organisation being able to provide a quantitative knowledge-based approach to risk identification and analysis. Techniques that support this include the development of high-level (or top-down) risk models and the application of historic trends analysis.

Question B8: Breadth of Responsibility for Risk Identification

What is the range of the organisation's personnel who consider project risk identification to be part of their responsibility?	
E	Not applicable. (The project is either very small or is using a minimal number of risks as part of an early cycle of a top-down risk management process.)
D	EITHER The Risk Manager or Project Manager working in isolation; OR No specific responsibility for risk identification at all.
C	EITHER The Project Manager and project management team; OR A subset of the project team that has taken part in formal risk identification exercises.
B	All personnel with a role in the technical or line management of project team members.
A	All people involved in the project who might plausibly be in a position to identify risks, up to and including the project sponsor.
Perspectives affected: Risk Identification and Risk Management Culture	

A project team will include people with different skills, experience, and personalities. One of the arts of building a project team is to recruit a productive blend of people who can make different contributions. Project team synergy is not best achieved by selecting people with similar characteristics. Establishing a good risk management culture is similarly dependent upon understanding different points of view. Although Question B8 is primarily about risk identification its answer will also provide evidence as to whether or not there is a good risk management culture. Conversely, a good risk management culture will be an invaluable aid to risk identification.

This question will apply to most projects. However, there are exceptions. If the project is in the earliest cycles of a top-down risk management process such as recommended by the *PRAM Guide* (see Chapter 2, pp. 24–6 and Chapter 3, pp. 37–8) then one would expect to be dealing with a limited number of high-level risks. In these circumstances it may not be practicable or even desirable to engage all team members in the risk identification process. It might be more appropriate to involve a limited number of subject matter experts. The other exception would be the special case of a single-person project team. Applying this question in this circumstance would be unfair.

Relying on a single person from a project team to identify risks should result in the D answer being selected for Question B8. Selecting the C answer requires that, as a minimum, both the project manager and other team members have been involved. The term 'project management team' used in this answer refers to the people who provide direct support to the project management function. The project team is usually a wider group than this since it includes all people involved in the project delivery.

Selecting the B answer is dependent upon all project team members with management responsibility to be accountable for risk identification. This does not mean that each one must have identified at least one risk, but rather that each would do so if appropriate. Selecting the A answer is dependent upon this principle being extended to all project team members with a potential role to play in the risk management process. This would include people with technical or delivery roles, but would usually exclude those with more general supporting roles, for example, a secretary.

Typical Actions for Improvement

This section provides guidance for the identification of process improvement actions related to the risk identification perspective. A starting point is to identify problems associated with the RMM questions for which the lower answers were selected. Typical problems include failure to identify risks from a sufficiently broad perspective or the related problem of failure to identify risks pertinent to all project phases. Both problems stifle risk management by narrowing its scope to only a subset of the sources of uncertainty to which project performance is exposed. Usually the root cause lies in a lack of understanding of the scope of risk management or technical failures to make good use of risk identification techniques. Corrective actions can therefore include:

- Extending the scope of risk identification to the extended project life cycle.
- identifying risks with a top-down approach such as a Risk Breakdown Structure,
- engagement of the sponsor or lead customer in risk identification,
- training that includes the use of different risk identification techniques,
- formal use of a combination of risk identification techniques,
- providing prompt lists and/or check lists as a centralised resource, and
- management of learned experience to provide guidance to projects.

A further practical problem in practice is that risk information can become stale. As new risks emerge, they may prove to be more significant than risks that were already being managed. If the root of risk management weakness is that risk identification has framed the process in a way that no longer seems as relevant as it once was, then corrective actions might include:

- Using risk reviews and risk interviews to identify emerging risks,
- use of Earned Value data from the planning process to identify emerging risks,
- closure of relatively insignificant older risks, and
- refreshing the risk information, for example, by holding a team workshop and rationalising the output of this with previously held information.

Whilst technical actions may correct risk identification issues in many instances, there are, unfortunately, circumstances in which the underlying problem is more intractable. Occasionally, risk identification is suppressed by cultural barriers. In the worst cases this can amount to the exercise of power by individuals for whom acknowledging certain risks would be inconvenient. Projects that have been authorised on the basis of optimistic forecasts are often vulnerable; acknowledgement of risks can involve the exposure of previous omissions to identify what should have been disclosed. 'Must-win' projects approaching a major approval point may be similarly vulnerable. Corrective action in these circumstances is difficult. However, the following can be considered:

- Development of a learned experience model to calibrate project uncertainty forecasts,
- introduction of or publicity in support of a whistle-blowing procedure,
- independent scrutiny of the risk management process, and
- use of consultancy support to identify and quantify key risks.

8 *Risk Analysis*

A common, but limited, understanding of project risk analysis is that its purpose is to produce a rank-order list of risks prioritised by importance. The Probability-Impact Matrix (PIM) is a popular technique used for this purpose, with many risk database tools having been designed around its use. However, focusing simply on risk prioritisation results in other important purposes of risk analysis being overlooked.

The purpose of risk analysis is to enable a project and its owning organisation to optimise their response to risk. This is more than a matter of focusing management resources on what might appear to be the most important individual risks. Effective responses to individual risks can only be developed if the risks are well understood. Moreover, many of the most effective responses can only be identified when the implications of risks are understood in combination. Understanding the sources of uncertainty that influence risks, their implications and how these things combine is therefore a fundamentally important part of risk analysis.

The idea of risk responses should also be seen in the wider context of the overall project. For example, risk responses may affect stakeholder behaviour, contracting strategy or choices to be made between different options for project delivery. From a strategic perspective, risk responses also include authorisation decisions and sizing contingencies to differentiate between targets and commitments. Projects that limit risk analysis to risk prioritisation may either overlook such responses or fail to understand how their outcomes are affected by risk.

Risk analysis methods are often categorised as being either qualitative risk assessment or quantitative risk analysis. Qualitative risk assessment is based on developing descriptive understandings of risks and then sizing risks using approximations for properties such as probability, impact and manageability. Quantitative risk analysis is based on the development of models that combine the implications of risks up to and including the level of overall project risk. This categorisation can be criticised as being simplistic. For example, descriptive understandings are a necessary part of estimating risks for quantitative modelling purposes. Likewise, risk modelling can also produce insights that aid description. However, for ease of explanation, this book uses the terms qualitative and quantitative analysis as described above. Of particular importance for Risk Maturity Model (RMM) assessment purposes, it should be noted that:

- A purely qualitative risk assessment approach will not support a risk management capability greater than RMM Level 3.
- RMM Level 4 is dependent upon using quantitative analysis to model overall project risk and using this modelling to influence both strategic and tactical responses.
- It may be possible to achieve a capability of RMM Level 4 with a quantitative approach that does not have a risk register typical of qualitative risk analysis.

The ten Project Risk Maturity Model (RMM) questions that follow are designed to test whether or not a project's risk analysis is capable of producing a sound understanding of risk when selecting risk responses.

Question C1: Risk Descriptions (Understanding of Risks)

	How well are the project's risks described?
E	Not applicable. (Never – this question should always be applicable.)
D	Risks descriptions tend to be impact orientated, and thus lack context and/or an identification of the relevant sources of uncertainty.
C	Risk information usually includes an indication of the source of each risk (for example, sources of uncertainty can be inferred from risk titles or simple or formulaic risk descriptions).
B	Risks are understood and described with sufficient depth to provide a consistent basis for the identification of appropriate risk ownership and the development of effective risk responses.
A	Risks are understood and described with sufficient depth to provide a consistent basis for risk estimating, allocation of risk ownership, understanding relationships with other risks and the development of effective responses.
	Perspectives affected: Risk Analysis and Risk Responses

This question is a key component of the RMM assessment of risk analysis. If a project does not understand its risks it is difficult to see how other aspects of its risk management process can be sound. For example, a risk must be understood before:

- Its ownership can be identified correctly,
- estimates can be made for properties such as probability and impact,
- relationships with other risks can be understood, and
- effective responses can be developed.

The effects of the issues raised by Question C1 thus ripple through to a large number of other RMM questions. For example, a poor understanding of risks will constrain the answers that can be selected to all of the other questions related to risk analysis. Likewise it will affect the choice of answers to questions on matters such as the selection of risk responses, stakeholder engagement (where risk ownership is also an issue) and a number of aspects of risk management culture.

Despite the importance of understanding risks, examination of a typical project's risk information often betrays the fact that its risks are not well described. Yet risk descriptions typically provide the best available evidence that there is a good level of understanding of each risk and that this understanding is shared by everyone concerned. Hence it is worth dwelling on the question as to what constitutes a good risk description in some detail.

The value of using descriptive techniques to understand risks has received increasing attention in recent years. Examples include Hillson's risk meta-language and the Association for Project Management (APM) *Project Risk Analysis and Management (PRAM) Guide* (2004). The APM's guide *Prioritising Project Risks* (Hopkinson et al. 2008) builds upon these references, emphasising the need to describe risks before prioritising them and identifying three key features that should be present in the description of any risk:

1. Facts that explain the context of the risk,
2. The source(s) of uncertainty (or risks), and
3. The risk's effects.

There are a number of methods that can be used to capture these three features of a risk description. Perhaps the most common method is that employed by many risk register tools: the use of three fields for recording risk descriptions. A typical combination of field names is 'Cause' (which can be used to capture context), 'Description' (which can be used to capture relevant source of uncertainty) and 'Effects'. The worked examples 8.1, 8.2 and 8.3 below illustrate how this structure can be used in practice.

However, before examining the three worked examples, it should be noted that there are alternative approaches to risk analysis that do not necessarily involve maintaining a risk register, but that can nevertheless achieve a high risk management capability. In general these are approaches in which risk analysis is based on quantitative modelling. Examples of such approaches are included in two books by Chapman and Ward (2002 and 2003), whose approaches are based on a top-down, risk-efficient process for understanding risk effects that can be linked directly to decision making. In the context of Question C1, a key feature of these approaches is that clarity is required when constructing risk models and developing risk estimates. This clarity ensures that there is a good understanding of the risks involved, including both sources of uncertainty and the associated relevant facts that explain context. Without this clarity, the analysis cannot be linked to the decisions it is designed to support.

In general, any form of quantitative risk modelling requires clarity that differentiates between context, sources of uncertainty and risk effects. For example, in a Monte Carlo schedule risk model, the activities and dependencies that form the risk network are based on what can be assumed to be known about the project, whereas the estimates of probability and/or variance of outcome can only be made if the associated sources of uncertainty have been identified and understood. The effects of this combination of beliefs about facts and sources of uncertainty are, of course, simulated by the overall model. Similar observations can be made when looking at the basis of other forms of quantitative risk model including Bayesian belief networks, decision trees and Monte Carlo risk models for cost or Net Present Value (NPV). Whilst there may be different approaches to project risk analysis, any effective approach will be underpinned by a sound understanding of risks. This is the essence of what Question C1 is about.

For processes that are based on using a risk register to manage risks on a case-by-case basis, a common problem is that little thought is put into exploring relevant sources of uncertainty. Impact-orientated risk descriptions that simply invert the non-occurrence of a risk are a symptom of this problem for example:

• There is a risk that the computer hardware will cost more than planned,
• there is risk that the supplier's price could be higher than estimated, and
• there is a risk of failing the system acceptance trial.

Impact-orientated risk descriptions provide no insight into how the risk could be managed proactively. Examples 8.1, 8.2 and 8.3 illustrate how such descriptions can be improved with a well-structured approach.

Example 8.1 – Description of a risk event

Example 8.1 is an example of a risk event: something that may or may not occur, but which, if it did, would have an effect on the project objectives. The occurrence of a risk event results in a step change to the project outcome. In this case, the event is that the software developed for a computer might exceed its sizing estimates and thus require upgraded hardware compared to that assumed for project costing purposes. This could be described as follows:

The computer system hardware cost has been estimated on the basis of the minimum hardware capability required to be adequate for the software based on current software sizing estimates. These estimates could prove be too low as a consequence of either inefficient software design or changes to the software specification. Should this occur, the hardware specification would have to be changed, thus increasing hardware costs.

It should be noted that the risk description has three sentences. The first is a factual statement of context, the second identifies sources of uncertainty and the third describes the impact of risk occurrence. More detail can be added to this description, but this would make it more difficult to read. However, breaking the more detailed description down into its three components, as shown in Figure 8.1, improves its clarity. This is why risk register tools often have three fields to capture risk descriptions.

Risk Title: Effect of software margins on hardware choice		
Context (Relevant Facts)	**Sources of uncertainty**	**Effect(s)/Impact**
Based on current software estimates, the hardware provides only 20% margin for RAM utilisation and 15% margin for processor performance. Exceeding these limits would slow system performance to unacceptable levels.	The software design could exceed current sizing estimates due to a number of factors including: 1. Inefficient coding caused by inexperienced team members or time pressures, 2. changes to the high level design.	1. Immediate upgrade to hardware specification would cost £20K. 2. Later hardware upgrade decision, if necessary, would cost £80K unless original hardware could be sold on, and would incur project delay of up to 3 months.

Figure 8.1 A risk description broken into three components

A number of points can be noted from the description in Figure 8.1. First, capturing relevant facts provides a context against which risk estimates can be developed. The software growth potential values are low, thus indicating that the risk's probability of occurrence is relatively high. If the relevant facts change, then so should the risk analysis. If another pass of the software sizing process changed the relevant estimates, then the risk would need to be re-assessed.

Second, a detailed exploration of the sources of uncertainty involved provides a basis for identifying potential risk mitigation responses. Proactive mitigation of this risk might involve choosing to resource the project with the organisation's best software staff. However, the implications of taking actions such as these might be unacceptable. Hence it is useful to know, from the risk effects, that an alternative course of action is to make an early commitment to spending £20K on higher specification hardware in order to avoid the potentially more serious consequences of delaying this decision. Overall the risk description shows that an early decision is required either to avoid the risk by spending

£20K or to accept the risk and manage it by intervening in the plans for software design. Making this decision should be seen as being a risk response in its own right.

Example 8.2 – Description of a variability risk

Example 8.2 is an example of a variability risk; a risk characterised by uncertainty as to where, within a continuous range of possible outcomes, the actual outcome will prove to be. In this case the outcome at risk is the cost of a subcontract that is planned to be placed in connection with a railway infrastructure project.

Risk Title: Signalling contract price varies from project estimate		
Context (Relevant Facts)	Sources of uncertainty	Effect(s)/Impact
The project budget for the design, installation and testing of new signalling equipment is £10,560,000. The preferred contractor has yet to be selected.	1. Contract prices could be affected by wage inflation caused by key skills shortages. 2. Contractors could identify gaps in the basis for project estimates. 3. The effectiveness of competitive tendering could vary.	The final agreed contract price could range from £9,000,000 to £14,500,000 with a most likely value estimated to be £11,000,000.

Figure 8.2   Variability risk described using three components

In this case, the first source of uncertainty would be beyond the project's control. However, it would be relevant to making estimates for the risk's effects. In contrast, the second source of uncertainty could be responded to proactively. However, the most effective approach to reducing the overall level of risk would be to tackle the third source of uncertainty; effectiveness of competition. Thus, the best risk response would probably be to maintain the competition process through to final negotiations with at least two potential contractors.

Variability risks can be quantified using a continuous probability distribution function. Some project risk management processes treat variability risks as being uncertainties for quantitative modelling processes, but fail to identify explicit management responses. If a project risk register is maintained in order to help manage responses, excluding significant variability risks can be mistake.

It can be noted that Example 8.2 might also be treated as a being a composite risk. Composite risks provide an approach to conceptualising risks in a simple way at a high level but with the knowledge that they can be broken down into lower levels of detail if this should later prove to be useful. The idea of using composite risks is particularly helpful during the early iterations of multi-pass risk analysis approach.

Example 8.3 – Description of an ambiguity risk

Example 8.3 is an ambiguity risk. Ambiguity risks describe circumstances in which there is known to be uncertainty about the meaning of something that is important to the project definition. Ambiguity risks tend to be more prevalent in the earlier stages of a project. The process of developing more detail to support the project's plans and requirements then reduces their number and importance as the project matures. Ambiguity risks may be a particularly important focus for concern leading up to the point of bid submission or the authorisation of the project's main delivery phase.

Example 8.3 is a risk owned by a contractor and concerns its risk exposure to the successful completion of final acceptance trials.

Risk Title: Interpretation of acceptance trials requirements		
Context (Relevant Facts)	**Sources of uncertainty**	**Effect(s)/Impact**
Customer design acceptance is dependent upon the demonstration of system capability during the final trials.	The scope of final trials is uncertain. The key points are whether or not trials must: 1. Include integration with other systems, 2. require the system to be exercised under extreme conditions (requiring the use of overseas trials sites).	1. Risk of failure to achieve acceptance for reasons attributable to incorrect interface requirements or faults in other equipments. 2. Additional cost and schedule implications of overseas trial.

Figure 8.3   Ambiguity risk described using three components

In the case of Example 8.3, there are two sources of uncertainly, each of which has a distinct effect. Dependent upon circumstances, there might therefore be good reason to use this risk to spawn two child risks, particularly if the two child risks were separately owned. However, it should be noted that the combined implications of the risk's effects might be worse than the sum of the two parts ,that is, the risk of having to do repeat trials as a consequence of interfacing issues could be exacerbated by the need to do such trials overseas. The advantages of splitting the risk into two would thus have to be weighed against the resultant loss of management and risk estimating information.

Example 8.3 is a risk that would need to be addressed contractually. Failure to do this prior to contract acceptance would be liable to foster distrust between the parties and would expose one or both to inappropriate exposure to risk that they were unable to influence.

A Common Approach to Describing Risks in Risk Registers

The three risk descriptions provided by Examples 8.1–8.3 share a number of important common features:

- They are written using the same combination of three components.
- They help to identify effective risk responses.
- Clarification of sources of uncertainty and risk effects aids risk estimation.
- They can be related to issues of risk ownership.

Figure 8.4 is based on a structure identified by the APM guide *Prioritising Project Risks* (Hopkinson et al. 2008) that can be used for risk descriptions in the context of maintaining risk information in a risk register. In essence, this figure has the same three-component structure that is shared by Examples 8.1–8.3, although it uses the term 'risk(s)' to refer to sources of uncertainty. In effect, use of the term risk(s) shows that several related sources of uncertainty (or risks) can be identified within the same risk, thus leading to either a richer understanding of the risk or the identification of parent–child risk relationships. In principle almost any risk can be broken down further into child risks; one of the arts of maintaining good risk information lies in knowing when to stop!

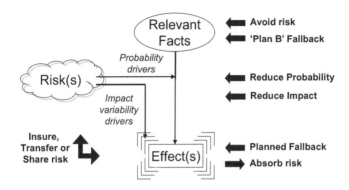

Figure 8.4   Relationship between a risk description and types of risk response

Figure 8.4 also illustrates the relationship between risk descriptions and common approaches to the identification of risk responses. For example, in order to avoid a risk, one has to change the facts about a project in a way that precludes the possibility that the risk could occur. However, since such changes are often not possible or acceptable the project is more usually in a position whereby it has to respond to risks at source by tackling sources of uncertainty associated with risk probability or impact variability drivers. Thus a key point shown by Figure 8.4 is that well-structured risk descriptions lend themselves to the identification of effective risk responses.

Selecting the Appropriate Answer for Question C1

Selecting the D answer to Question C1 would indicate that the understanding of risks is taken no further than risk identification prior to other risk analysis activities. As a minimum, selecting the C answer is dependent upon the project having some information on sources of its risks. This might be achieved by the routine application of a formulaic combination of words, for example, 'there is a risk that (the risk and its effects) could be caused by (the source of uncertainty)'. However, risk descriptions based on a single formula generally fail to explore risks in the manner that they deserve. Often, their effect is to atomise risk into low-level components that cause the project to lose sight of interrelationships between risks, thus impairing the project's understanding of risk at higher levels.

Selecting the B answer to Question C1 requires that risks are consistently understood to the extent that is useful for qualitative risk analysis purposes. Support for an A answer requires that risks are also adequately understood for the purposes of estimating input data in support of quantitative analysis.

Question C1 is of fundamental importance when assessing any project risk management process. It is one of the most heavily weighted questions in the calculation of RMM results. There should be no circumstances in which it is not applicable.

Question C2: Effectiveness of Risk Owners

How effectively do risk owners fulfil their role?	
E	Not applicable. (Never – this question should always be applicable.)
D	The risk management process makes little or no use of the role of risk owners.
C	Most risks have a nominated risk owner. However, EITHER Risk owners are not sufficiently engaged in the risk management process; OR Some may have insufficient authority to manage the risk responses.
B	All risks have a nominated risk owner. However, there are some risks for which the risk owners do not or cannot fulfil the full role of risk ownership.
A	All risks have a nominated risk owner. All risk owners accept responsibility for risk assessments and have sufficient authority to oversee any action required.
Perspectives affected: Risk Analysis, Risk Responses and Risk Management Culture	

Things tend not to get done unless responsibility for getting them done is assigned to individuals. For the purposes of Question C2, risk owners are the individuals who are assigned responsibility for the management of risks. This role can be confused with others. For example, a project often has a Risk Manager: a team member responsible for operating the overall risk management process. Some projects also distinguish between risk owners and risk response owners. If so, the RMM assessor will need to clarify which of these roles fulfils the risk ownership responsibilities identified below. In some cases, these responsibilities might be shared; a potential source of process weakness if communication between the individuals involved is less than excellent.

The role of the risk owner should be considered to have two components:

1. The risk owner is responsible for the quality of the project's understanding of the risk and related risk estimates.
2. The risk owner is responsible for selecting and directing appropriate risk responses.

The first of these components is important to the capability of risk analysis. The second underpins the effectiveness of risk responses. The risk owner's role also includes communication on risk, and is hence important to risk management culture.

Principles concerning the selection of risk owners are a frequent cause of discussion on projects. Some people advocate that the project manager should be the owner of all its risks. In certain circumstances this might be appropriate. For example, when conducting the early passes of a quantitative top-down risk management process, individual risks may continue to be assessed at a relatively high level, that is, directly related to key questions of project design. However, on large projects and when the number of risks has increased in response to more detailed analysis, a project manager should consider delegating the ownership of most risks.

With delegated risk ownership, some people argue that the risk owner should be the person who feels most affected by the risk's effects. The basis for this argument is that it allocates risks to the people most motivated to manage them. The problem, however, is that the sources of risks and their effects often have different ownership. Thus, risk owners might lack the authority to act preventatively. They may also lack insight into what preventative action could be effective. One outcome can be that risk owners become inclined to focus on provisions for the consequences of problems outside their control. In the extreme this can fuel the development of self-serving lists of pre-emptive excuses to account for the causes of poor performance. This can be a serious weakness on large or complex projects.

A more pragmatic approach is that the risk owner should be the individual who has the most influence over the risk outcome. However, application of this principle requires subjective judgement. A balance is often required between the ideal of identifying the person who best understands the risk and the need to ensure that the risk owner has sufficient authority to direct responses. If authority is a key issue, this can escalate risk ownership up the management hierarchy to a level at which a risk owner's technical understanding of what should be done is relatively weak. In this circumstance, the risk owner may need to call upon other people to provide the expertise required to understand and estimate the risk. In practice, ensuring that the communication necessary to manage each risk is effective is a key aspect of the Risk Manager's role.

Team culture and communication weaknesses are often an issue on large projects. Achieving a high level answer to Question C2 may therefore be more difficult on larger projects. Selecting the C answer requires that risk ownership responsibilities are, in most cases, defined clearly. However, this may not be sufficient to make the management of risks effective. If risk owners are not sufficiently accountable or are not empowered to direct responses, a B answer can be discounted.

Selecting either the A or B answers requires all risks to have a nominated owner. If delegated risk ownership would not add value, then it is correct for the project manager to be the only risk owner. In such circumstances, the project manager should be personally engaged in the whole risk analysis process. Differentiation between answers A and B is based on the consistency with which each risk owner carries out their responsibilities for both risk assessment and directing risk responses.

The risk owner's role should always be relevant to a project whether there is one risk owner or many. Question C2 should therefore always be applicable. An RMM assessor may also find that the effectiveness of risk owners has an effect on the answers selected for other questions.

Question C3: Assessment of Risk Impacts (Effects)

	How well are the impacts (or effects) of risks assessed?
E	Not applicable. (Never – this question should always be applicable.)
D	The assessment of risk impacts does not play an explicit part in the risk assessment process.
C	Impact assessments are made for all risks. However they may lack the rigour required to consistently achieve the standards required for answer B.
B	Impact assessments a) capture all types of impact relevant to the overall project objectives and b) produce realistic value comparisons between impact types. The basis for such value comparisons is agreed with all stakeholders who are engaged in the risk management process.
A	Impact assessments are based on an understanding of how sources of uncertainty influence the extent and variability of risk effects.
	Perspectives affected: Risk Analysis and Stakeholders

All risks have an effect or potential effect. The term impact as used in this question is intended to mean the equivalent of effect; impact is still, perhaps, the most common term in use. Another similar word, consequences, is also used in some standards. In practice, the effects of a risk should be both significant and relevant to the project objectives. Loading the risk management process with insignificant risks is a distraction and can also undermine the project's core planning process.

Risk impacts can usually affect one or more of at least three dimensions against which project performance objectives are specified: time, cost and product. In some cases, there may be additional dimensions. For example, a project involving a manufacturing facility outage may include the objective of preserving customer relationships during the period in which production is halted. To be relevant, it must be possible to relate the dimension in which any impact is estimated to a key project objective.

On some projects it may be possible to translate impacts into the single dimension of economic value (measured in the same units as cost). This would involve being able to calculate the economic value of project benefits by relating them to product performance and the periods in time over which benefits would be realised. The value of benefits can then be compared to the project costs to calculate overall economic value. Many organisations take the additional step of calculating the phasing implications of costs and benefits, for example, by calculating Net Present Value (NPV). Using a single impact dimension such as NPV makes risk effects relatively easy to compare. It also enables the development of quantitative risk models that clarify the implications of risk decisions.

On many projects, however, impacts cannot be meaningfully translated into a single dimension. Government funded projects are an obvious example. It is difficult, if not meaningless, to attach an economic value to projects such as a social housing development or the procurement of an aircraft carrier. In order to compare risk impacts, and hence trade risk implications when developing responses, projects in this position have to make subjective judgements about the equivalence of risk impacts. The basis of this judgement should be agreed with the stakeholders with a legitimate interest in the decisions that could be affected. A common-practice method for recording points of impact equivalence is to develop a risk impact criteria table associated with the use of a Probability-Impact Matrix (PIM).

Selecting the B answer for Question C3 requires the project to take account of all relevant dimensions of risk impact and to agree the basis of risk impact comparisons with relevant stakeholders. This can be done in the context of using the common-practice method of developing a risk criteria table for prioritising risks using a PIM.

Selecting the A answer for Question C3 requires that the project should also take into account impact variability when making risk assessments. This is particularly important if the project is using quantitative risk analysis methods. The ways in which sources of uncertainty can affect impact variability are discussed earlier in the context of Question C1 (Risk descriptions). For the purposes of this question the RMM assessor should consider whether sources of uncertainty that affect impact variability are understood appropriately when making impact estimates.

If a quantitative approach is being taken to risk analysis, it should be possible to relate risk descriptions to estimates of effect expressed in the form of probability density functions. By way of example, Figure 8.5 illustrates two different types of probability density function. For non-event orientated risks such as variability and ambiguity risks, the area bounded by these distributions would be 1.0. For impacts conditional on the occurrence of events, the area bounded by each distribution would be equal to the probability of occurrence.

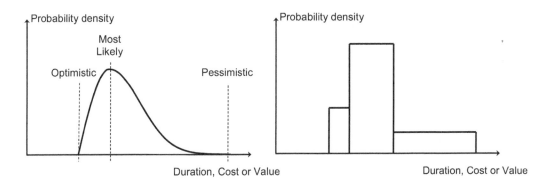

Figure 8.5   Examples of risk probability distributions

Since all risks have effects or potential effects, this question is applicable to all projects.

Question C4: Analysis of Secondary Effects

	How does the analysis of impact include the consideration of secondary effects?
E	Not applicable. (The project is sufficiently simple for secondary effects to be minor.)
D	Risk impacts are not assessed.
C	The assessment of risk impact is usually restricted to the consideration of immediate or direct effects.
B	Consideration is given to secondary effects when making risk assessments. In doing so, risk owners usually seek the advice of the other parties (internal or external to the project team) who would be affected.
A	Appropriate quantitative analysis techniques are used to evaluate overall project risk in a way that includes the implications of secondary effects whilst avoiding their duplication.
Perspectives affected: Risk Analysis	

In many cases, the effects of risks can extend beyond the immediate risk impact. There can be additional, and often, wider consequences. The term 'secondary effect' refers to the occurrence of such additional consequences. Understanding and estimating the implications of secondary effects can be very important, particularly on complex projects. The following are examples of secondary effects:

- Project management team costs driven by delays attributable to technical risks,
- retrofits to products already delivered caused by design changes, and
- lost opportunities due to budgets being consumed by the effects of other risks.

Secondary effects can also contribute to the occurrence of systemic risks. A systemic risk occurs when the implications of one risk exacerbate another, which in turn feeds back to affect the first risk. The overall level of risk may be much more than the sum of the parts. This is an important aspect of risk for some projects which is explored in depth by Williams (2002). Complex projects in which design involves trade-offs within tight constraints (for example, time, weight or space) are particularly vulnerable to systemic risk. Williams recommends the use of techniques such as influence diagrams and system dynamics to analyse risks of this nature.

Dealing with the implications of secondary effects can be difficult for a project that approaches the problem by combining risks using a bottom-up process. As an example, a project that maintains risk data in a flat risk register of discrete risks could find itself in the dilemma illustrated by Figure 8.6.

The example illustrated in Figure 8.6 shows the secondary effect on costs of five risks. In assessing impacts the project may choose to estimate just the direct effects for each risk. If so, it may underestimate the importance of risks that contribute significantly to secondary effects. If it also uses the risk register data as the exclusive basis for a quantitative cost risk analysis, the secondary effects would be omitted. An alternative approach would be to include the secondary effects in the assessment of every risk. However, this would have the effect of duplicating secondary effects in the quantitative analysis.

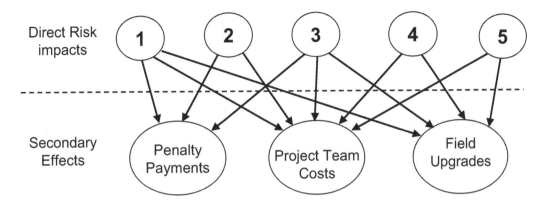

Figure 8.6   Example of the relationships between direct and secondary risk effects

In the author's experience, most projects that pull through estimates from a risk register for the purposes of quantitative analysis fail to handle the implications of secondary effects in a rational way. Such projects are liable to produce spurious forecasts for overall project risk. The solution is to use an iterative top-down approach for the development of quantitative models; a topic covered in more detail under Questions C8 and C9.

A sound iterative top-down approach to risk modelling helps to ensure that secondary effects are accommodated within the analysis as a matter of course. Significant secondary effects of lower level risks should be identified during passes of the risk management process that precede the identification of most of the lower-level risks themselves. In the absence of this type of approach, it is most unlikely that a project will be able to select the A answer to Question C4.

Communication can be another barrier to a project's analysis of secondary effects. There can be a separation between the responsibilities of a risk owner and responsibility for managing the implications of secondary effects. If a risk owner has been selected on a source-orientated basis, they may need to consult other interested parties to understand the wider risk implications. These parties could be other project team members or representatives of affected stakeholders. Failure to do this is liable to cause sub-optimal risk response decisions. Selecting an answer better than C to Question C4 is dependent upon interested parties being engaged as part of the risk analysis process.

The difficulty and importance of handling the implications of secondary risk effects is thus affected by both project team size and project complexity. These factors need to be taken into account by the RMM assessor when deciding whether or not this question is applicable. For many small and simple projects it may be reasonable to treat the question as being not inapplicable. In contrast, on a complex project the significance of secondary effects might be a factor that shapes the design of the risk management process itself.

Question C5: Estimation of Probabilities

What is the quality of risk probability estimates?	
E	Not applicable.
D	EITHER Probability estimation does not form part of the risk analysis process; OR Probability estimates are biased (for example, by being altered to adjust the outcome of risk analysis).
C	Probabilities are estimated. However EITHER The accuracy of probability estimation is generally weak; OR Probabilities are estimated in ill-defined ways that undermine comparisons that are made between risks.
B	Estimates of risk probabilities are generally as realistic as possible given the information available. However, some risks estimated as having a probability <100 per cent may be events that are, in practice, inevitable.
A	Risk probabilities are estimated realistically by evaluating sources of uncertainty associated with risk occurrence. (The implications of risk probabilities might be included in estimates for composite risks.) Risks with a High probability <100 per cent are, realistically, events that might not occur.
Perspectives affected: Risk Analysis	

The probability of a risk is a prediction of the likelihood that its effects will occur. All risks have a probability greater than zero or they would be irrelevant. The highest probability that a risk can have is 100 per cent (that is, a probability of one) signifying that the risk's effect is certain to occur. Variability and ambiguity risks have probabilities of 100 per cent; the uncertainties involved only drive variability of effect, not probability. Composite risks arising from complex sources of uncertainty and developed for quantitative modelling purposes could also have an overall probability of 100 per cent. Discrete event-orientated risks have a probability between zero and one; they include sources of uncertainty that are linked to risk occurrence.

Probability estimates are the most common method for predicting the likelihood of occurrence for project risks. However, frequency of occurrence is an alternative that is occasionally more appropriate. Where this is the case, Question C5 should be interpreted by substituting the term 'probability' with the terms 'frequency' or 'rate of occurrence'. Frequency or rate of occurrence is estimated as being a number of occurrences per unit time, for example, twice per year.

Probability estimates can be an important factor in both risk prioritisation and quantitative risk modelling processes. However, weak probability estimating is very common. This has a serious effect on the integrity of analysis. The problem tends to have three sources:

1. A lack of attention to understanding how sources of uncertainty affect risk occurrence. Weak risk descriptions lead inexorably to weak estimates.
2. Mathematical perception difficulties amongst some people who find even simple probability estimates hard to conceptualise.
3. Bias fostered by the project environment or a poor risk management culture.

The first two of these sources of poor probability estimating can be managed with assistance from a person with risk management expertise, for example, the Risk Manager. However bias can prove to be a more intractable problem. Moreover, estimating bias has the potential to undermine the purpose of the risk analysis process. If there is systematic bias present in risk estimates (for example, in order to produce a desired risk analysis outcome) then the answer to this question should be no higher than D.

When the primary purpose of making probability estimates is to provide inputs to a risk prioritisation process (for example, using a Probability-Impact Matrix), weak estimates may be the consequence of using ill-defined terms such as Low, Medium or High without any explanation of how they are aligned with a numerical probability scale. Equally, some probability scales that appear to be numerical may not actually represent probabilities at all. For example, the author has seen projects using a probability scale of 1, 2, 3, 4 and 5 with no guidance as to what these numbers mean in terms of probability. The best that such schemes might achieve is to differentiate between risks owned by one individual; comparisons of risks assessed by different individuals would be invalid. If risk owners find a numerical probability scale difficult to use, a scale based on descriptive terms such as 'very unlikely', 'less than 50/50', '50/50', 'more likely than not' and 'almost certain' might be more appropriate.

A more sophisticated approach to probability estimation might involve the use of subjective probabilities. This approach recognises that there could be uncertainty about the accuracy of each probability estimate. This may be particularly important if the estimate is only supported by weak evidence or subjective opinion. In these circumstances (which are common on projects) it can be best practice to estimate probabilities as being subjective. A probability might therefore be estimated as being somewhere in the range of 10 per cent – 30 per cent rather than being estimated at single representative point such as 20 per cent. However, although this is something that risk practitioners should bear in mind, selecting the A answer to this question is not conditional on the use of subjective probability. It should also be noted that the idea of subjective probability should not be confused with the idea of using prescribed probability classification ranges such as those used in conjunction with a Probability-Impact Matrix.

Since all risks have a probability, Question C5 would appear to be applicable to all RMM assessments even if all probabilities are correctly estimated to be 100 per cent. A possible exception might occur whilst a project uses a high-level knowledge-based tool to perform risk analysis as part of its first pass of the risk management process.

Question C6: Risk Prioritisation

How effective are the risk prioritisation processes?	
E	Not applicable. (Never – this question should always be applicable.)
D	Much more use should be made of risk prioritisation.
C	Risks are usually ranked in priority order when appropriate. However there may be significant faults in the techniques employed.
B	Risks are prioritised using a valid method that is applied correctly. This data is used to focus management effort on responding, as a priority, to the most important risks.
A	Appropriate risk prioritisation techniques are routinely used to influence both management responses to risk *and* the iterative development of quantitative risk models.
Perspectives affected: Risk Analysis and Project Management	

Risk prioritisation is often treated as a simple problem that can be solved with the application of a Probability-Impact Matrix (PIM). The PIM tends to be regarded as being a simple technique that can be taught quickly and introduced into computerised risk database tools. However, careful consideration of risk prioritisation issues reveals the PIM to have significant limitations. Furthermore, PIMs are often applied incorrectly.

The APM's guide *Prioritising Project Risks* (Hopkinson et al. 2008) identifies a wide range of prioritisation techniques of which the PIM is only one. The APM guide also identifies why risk prioritisation can serve different purposes, dependent upon the question that the analysis is intended to address. To take but one example, the following two questions can be contrasted:

1. Which risks should be prioritised for escalation purposes (to stakeholders or senior management)?
2. Which risks should be prioritised from a project resources perspective?

It makes sense to escalate risks if the most effective responses are outside the direct control of the project team. Uncontrollable risks might also have to be escalated to warn stakeholders of their implications. In contrast, prioritising risks for the project team to act on should focus it on controllable risks where responses would deliver the best value. This example illustrates that, before prioritising risks, it is necessary to understand the purpose of prioritisation. It also shows that probability and impact are not the only risk attributes that should be taken into account. *Prioritising Project Risks* identifies the following list of attributes that could be relevant to prioritisation, depending upon the purpose of prioritisation and the circumstances of the project:

- Probability,
- impact,
- variability (for example, as evaluated by standard deviation),
- urgency (time by which responses would have to be implemented),
- risk impact proximity,
- propinquity (perception of risk acuteness by an individual or group),

- controllability,
- response effectiveness,
- manageability,
- relatedness (to other risks), and
- ownership ambiguity.

One limitation of the PIM is that it only takes into account the first two attributes on this list. However, whilst it is easy to be critical of the PIM as a technique, there is no single alternative that is the best technique to use in all circumstances. The art of risk prioritisation lies in choosing the simplest technique that returns acceptable and relevant results.

Risk prioritisation is always an important aspect of the risk management process, so Question C6 will always be applicable. Selecting the answer C requires that active use is made of risk prioritisation although the prioritisation technique may not be as good as it could be. The most common instance of a project in this position is likely to be one that uses a PIM but with one or more of the following faults:

- Inappropriate comparisons between different impact dimensions built into the scoring scheme (for example, cost implications exaggerated in comparison to time),
- adding up PIM scores for different impact dimensions,
- use of linear indices for impact and/or probability scoring, when the scoring scheme is non-linear (a fault that often produces a symmetrical PIM that treats probability and impact bands as having identical significance), and
- use of the scheme by risk owners to manage reported information (for example, reverse-engineering estimates to make risks go red, amber or green).

Correct application of a PIM or other qualitative risk prioritisation techniques would enable a project to select the B answer, provided that the technique was valid in the circumstances in which it was being used. The test for validity should be: is this the simplest technique that would produce realistic results and would support the decisions that need to be made?

Treating risk prioritisation as being a process to produce a rank order of discrete risks will limit a project to the B answer to Question C6. Selecting the A answer requires a project to have used risk prioritisation for a further fundamental purpose; to direct choices made when developing risk models. The importance of this purpose of risk prioritisation should become more apparent when reading the discussion of Questions C8 and C9 which concern quantitative analysis. However, to summarise at this point, assurance that a project's quantitative risk models are both rational and realistic requires an iterative top-down approach to their development. There is an art to doing this well. Much of the art lies in making appropriate choices when structuring models. The choices made should reflect the relative importance of different sources of uncertainty; choices that should be influenced by risk prioritisation.

It should be remembered that achieving Level 4 RMM risk management capability is dependent upon the project being able to make risk-efficient strategic choices. This is dependent upon developing realistic quantitative models to analyse overall project risk.

Question C7: Risk Estimating

	How good are estimates of risks likely to be?
E	Not applicable .(Never – this question should always be applicable.)
D	EITHER Risk estimates are haphazard and tend not to be supported by scrutiny; OR Risk estimates are likely to be subject to significant bias due to the project environment or to risk estimating processes.
C	Most risk estimates are performed diligently, but some may be subject to modification for the purpose of influencing management decisions.
B	The right people are responsible for risk estimating and can draw upon some experience in the areas concerned. They provide estimates that are as realistic as possible. The basis of estimates is well understood.
A	The people responsible for risk estimating can draw upon long-standing experience in the areas concerned and use well-structured processes to make risk estimates that are as realistic as possible. When risk estimates affect a strategic project decision, they are subject to peer or independent review as appropriate.
	Perspectives affected: Risk Analysis and Risk Management Culture

Risk estimates are a critical input to risk analysis. Even qualitative risk assessment techniques require estimates to evaluate the implications of risk attributes such as probability, impact and urgency. If the application of these techniques is based on poor quality estimates, they will provide misleading results. For example, the importance of some risks may be exaggerated relative to others. However, the quality of risk estimates provided as inputs to quantitative risk models is usually an even more significant issue, particularly if its results are used to make strategic decisions, such as whether or not a project should proceed. As with any form of mathematical modelling, the results from quantitative risk analysis are critically dependent upon the input data. If this data is of poor quality, the misleading nature of risk analysis results can make the process worse than useless.

Many projects operate a risk management process that mixes both qualitative and quantitative risk analysis techniques. Given the importance of risk estimating to quantitative analysis results, such projects should address Question C7 in the context of their quantitative models. Projects that employ only qualitative techniques should address this question in that context only. In practice, this may make it easier for the latter to select a relatively favourable answer to this question. They will also find that Questions C8 and C9 are not applicable. However, treating Question 9 as being not applicable will limit their RMM assessment result to a maximum of Level 3.

Selecting the answer C to Question C7 requires, as a minimum, that risk estimates do tend to stand up to scrutiny. This implies that the basis of each estimate can be traced to a recorded understanding of the risk. A common cause of haphazard risk estimates is that the risks have not been adequately understood. The RMM assessor therefore should also consider the evidence used to select the answer to Question C1 (Risk Descriptions) when assessing the quality of risk estimates.

Developing risk estimates in an appropriate environment and using a process that avoids significant bias is also a precondition to selecting the answer C to Question C7.

Bias distorts the results of risk analysis. Exposure to bias should be considered significant if serious mistakes could be made as a consequence. Bias can be conscious or unconscious. It can be caused by the project's circumstances and environment or technical factors in the estimating process. The RMM assessor needs to be able to judge if bias could be a significant issue and ask the right questions to find out whether or not it is.

The most damaging sources of bias are often attributable to the project environment. Typically, these are organisational pressures to support a preferred forecast for project costs and objectives. An obvious example is pressure that prevails during the period prior to a project approval decision. This pressure often produces an optimistic bias, with risk estimates produced by a project team anxious to proceed with the project and thus motivated to forecast outcomes acceptable to the sponsor. However, approval point pressure can also produce a pessimistic bias in an environment in which subsequent failure to meet targets would have serious consequences for the individuals involved.

Example 8.4 – Optimistic bias at project approval

A defence company specialised in the design and manufacture of a particular type of equipment. The UK Ministry of Defence held a competitive tendering process for the design, manufacture and logistic support of the most comprehensive and sophisticated equipment of this type yet developed. Everyone involved knew that this was a make or break contract; failure to win would threaten the future of the company itself.

The bid submitted to the MoD was successful. However, whilst competitive pressure had generated useful innovation, project delivery proved to be much more difficult than forecast. Adherence to the plans was problematic from the start, often for reasons that were unsurprising to the design staff involved. The development programme eventually slipped by several years and the project became a financial burden to the parent business.

Example 8.5 – Pessimistic bias at project approval

An organisation responsible for the maintenance of public infrastructure had a rolling programme of infrastructure renewals. A work bank of renewal projects was approved each year and aligned to the organisation's budgets. Managers were expected to meet the renewals profile within budget. They also know that their delegated budget set the context against which future work would be planned. In practice, managers therefore sought to justify as much funding as they could defend. In order to develop sufficient evidence to satisfy the scrutiny of senior management, they asked contractors to help generate detailed plans for each project. When the project work bank had been approved, the same contractors then delivered the planned projects on a cost-plus basis; another factor that encouraged pessimism bias. In practice, this system was protected by a further factor: public outcry and political pressure in the event of a disruptive renewal overrun. Overall, this system delivered predictable project outcomes, but at the cost of economic efficiency.

In any project there is likely to be a mixture of incentives and disincentives to be optimistic. In their book *Megaprojects and Risk*, Flyvbjerg et al. (2003) make a disarmingly simple observation about bias: if the incentives to be optimistic outweigh the disincentives, then project forecasts will be optimistic. Although authorisation pressure in smaller projects may be less extreme than it is on megaprojects (in which people's careers can be dependent upon the decision), this observation will still usually hold. The RMM assessor should be able to find out how risk estimates are used and the implication that related decisions have on the individuals and groups involved. Figure 8.7 shows a simple model for detecting vulnerability to bias.

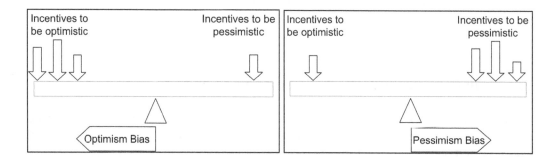

Figure 8.7   Simple model for detecting vulnerability to estimating bias

In the event that the project environment could engender significant risk estimating bias, it should only be possible to select a more favourable answer than D to Question C7 if explicit steps have been taken to curtail its effects. These steps might include:

- The use of previous similar projects as comparators, and
- independent review of the estimates and estimating processes.

Bias can also be introduced inadvertently by technical factors in the risk estimating process. In practice, risk estimates can be affected by several heuristics: estimating short cuts that people use intuitively. This subject is covered in a number of sources on project risk management including Hillson and Murray-Webster (2005) and Vose (2008).

A consequence of heuristics is that risk variability tends to be underestimated. Thus, probability density functions estimated for risks are typically too narrow. This is often caused by the adjustment heuristic: a shortcut to risk estimating that starts with an estimate of a midpoint and then proceeds to estimations of extremes. A fault with this approach is that the extremes are often attributable to a combination of different sources of uncertainty; starting with a midpoint scenario does not lend itself to understanding what the extremes could be. The resultant narrowness of risk estimates is often referred to as anchoring bias.

The simplistic use of baseline project plans for risk modelling purposes can foster anchoring bias. It is, for example, common to see the planned (single) values for activity costs or duration pulled across from plans to be used as the de facto most likely point for the associated probability density function. Doing this as a matter of routine invites anchoring bias. Moreover, any bias inherent to the plan is pulled across into risk estimates. This is a common form of immature practice that has been enabled by the design of several popular risk tools.

Example 8.6 – Poor estimating practice built in as a default into a risk tool

A popular tool for Monte Carlo schedule risk analysis allowed activity networks to be imported from planning tools such as Microsoft Project. In its default setup, the Monte Carlo tool auto-created probability density functions, with the Most Likely (mode) point estimates defaulting to planned duration and the extremes calculated on the basis of default percentage adjustments from the mode. The company that sold this tool had been advised that its design could foster poor practice. However, its position was that so many of its customers liked the feature that changing the default setup would cause confusion.

Auto-creation of risk estimates anchored around planned values is a common clue that the risk estimates will not bear serious scrutiny. If this is how all estimates have been made for the purposes of quantitative analysis, then it is likely that a D answer should be selected for Question C7. The effect that such an approach could have on bias should also influence the answers to Question C7 and C8.

The availability heuristic is another shortcut that can produce poor risk estimates. People are inclined to overrate the significance of information that is closest to hand. This can often be the information that is most recent. For example, risk estimates could be distorted by the outcome of a recent project. The availability heuristic can also combine with another error known as the confirmation trap. People considering different sources of information are inclined to overrate the significance of evidence that confirms their preferred view. Filtering by the confirmation trap can produce seemingly objective evidence that supports biased forecasts. Group behaviour can accentuate this error, as has been documented in research that identified phenomena such as the risky shift and groupthink. More detailed explanations of these issues can be found in two books on understanding and managing risk attitude by Hillson and Murray-Webster (2005 and 2008).

Matthew Leitch (2008) uses the term 'uncertainty suppression' to describe bias that results from the selective use of information. On projects, uncertainty suppression can be the result of group behaviour combined with the effects of heuristics on estimates produced by both individuals and groups. Figure 8.8 illustrates how uncertainty suppression can produce risk estimates that are both too narrow and optimistically biased. The top of the figure illustrates an environment that fosters optimism bias. This environment then influences the effects of heuristics and group behaviour to produce a risk estimate that is both biased and unrealistically narrow.

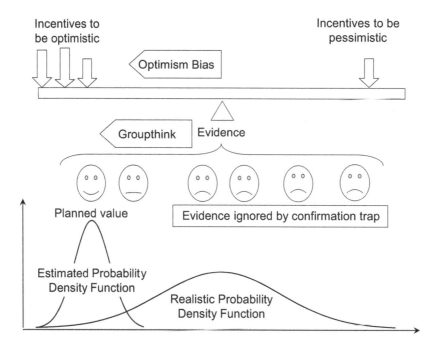

Figure 8.8   Illustration of the process of uncertainty suppression

Example 8.7 – Uncertainty suppression

A subject matter expert (SME), a cost analyst and a senior manager participated in a project cost estimating review. The project involved the development of a major new defence equipment (platform) planned to be in service in ten years time, and the organisation to which the participants belonged was competing to be selected for the implementation phase. The SME provided a range of potential costs for procurement of the platform's data network. The lowest end of the range was based on the production cost of a network design already in service. The highest end of the range was based on the forecasts for the costs of another design in current development.

Even a network design in current development would be obsolete in ten years time and there was a historical trend in cost escalation for developments of this nature. The senior manager and cost analyst could therefore have pointed out that the costs could easily be higher than anywhere within the range identified by the SME. Instead, they suppressed the uncertainty involved by electing to use the lowest estimating point in the interests of setting a low target cost. The SME protested that they could be certain that a design currently in service would not be accepted for a new platform ten years hence. However, he was overruled and instructed to 'make it happen'.

It should be noted that, dependent upon how estimates are built up, estimating error produced by uncertainty suppression can produce compound effects. For example, if one estimate is built up by multiplying two independently estimated variables, the overall error will be similarly multiplied.

Example 8.8 – Compound effect of two risks

The labour estimates for building a sports stadium is built up by multiplying an estimate of the cost of contracted labour in man-days by an estimate for labour productivity rates. Both rates reflect best case values from previous projects. During the project, labour shortages occur due to other major construction projects in the region. The consequence is that average labour rates are 20 per cent higher than planned and that productivity falls by 30 per cent compared to the values assumed. The overall cost of labour thus becomes 71 per cent (that is, $1 - (1.2/0.7)$ expressed as a percentage) higher than planned.

The fact that risk can impact in a compound fashion is an important factor to take into account when making risk estimates. One cause of unrealistically narrow risk estimates is failure to take into account the combined effects of multiple sources of uncertainty. Relating these uncertainties to estimates also requires an understanding of how estimates have been derived. Making realistic risk estimates therefore requires the combined skills of the people who are most knowledgeable about the issues involved and people who have appropriate risk estimating expertise. Selecting the B answer for Question C7 is dependent upon the right people being involved.

Selecting the A answer to question C7 is dependent upon the people involved in risk estimating having long-standing experience in the estimating issues involved. They should also be supported by people with sufficient risk estimating expertise to ensure that there is an appropriately structured approach to estimating the effects of all significant sources of uncertainty. Finally, where the estimates contribute to project strategy decisions they should be subject to appropriate review. If the project environment could engender bias, the review of risk analysis should be by an independent party.

Although much of the above discussion concerns risk estimates made in the context of quantitative risk analysis, it is hard to identify a situation in which Question C7 would be not applicable. A possibility might be the case of a project that was using a high-level knowledge based model for risk analysis during the first pass of the risk management process. Even then, information about the project would have to be estimated to match its scope and circumstances to the knowledge base.

Question C8: Quantitative Schedule Risk Analysis

	How effective is the project's use of quantitative schedule risk analysis?
E	Not applicable. (The use of resources required to conduct schedule risk analysis cannot be justified by its potential benefits.)
D	Quantitative schedule risk analysis is not used.
C	EITHER Quantitative schedule risk analysis is carried out, but the modelling has significant deficiencies liable to result in bias; OR Very little action is taken in response to the analysis.
B	Quantitative schedule risk analysis is used to support decisions made at strategic points in the programme. The risk model(s) simulate both the effects of activity variance and the implications of risk events. Although acceptably free from bias, the model(s) may have weaknesses that can cause forecast for the overall variance of outcome to be unrealistic.
A	Quantitative schedule risk analysis is used whenever it would add value to decision making or the strategic review of plans. Risk models are based on data aligned with a sound planning process and use best practice techniques for building risk models and making realistic forecasts.
	Perspectives affected: Risk Analysis and Project Management

Typically, project schedule risk analysis is conducted using a Monte Carlo simulation of a schedule risk network with features similar to those illustrated in Figure 8.9. Such analysis can be very useful, particularly for larger projects with parallel streams of work. It should also be noted that the cost (or economic performance) of many projects is affected by schedule outcome. Thus, besides being of value in itself, a forecast of overall schedule risk may be an important input to other quantitative risk models.

Figure 8.9 illustrates how schedule risk modelling may differentiate between risks that influence the variance of activity durations (for example, variability risks) and event risks (which may or may not occur). Many organisations use the term 'uncertainty' to describe the former. The use of language is unimportant so long as all sources of uncertainty are simulated appropriately using realistic risk estimates.

In addition to providing forecasts, schedule risk analysis can provide insights to help manage the response to schedule risk. For example, a schedule risk model can be used to test the relative merits of options for project delivery. Also, the relative importance of different elements of the schedule can be determined using metrics derived from statistical outputs of the Monte Carlo process. Examples of such metrics include criticality, cruciality and schedule sensitivity index (APM guide, *Prioritising Project Risks* – Hopkinson et al. 2008).

However, despite the benefits of schedule risk analysis, some projects will make a correct judgement that the benefits do not justify the effort involved. Schedule risk analysis is only worthwhile if it is done to a high standard. This requires more time, resources and skill than is often understood to be the case. A recent book on the subject by Hulett (2009) provides an in-depth exploration of the issues involved.

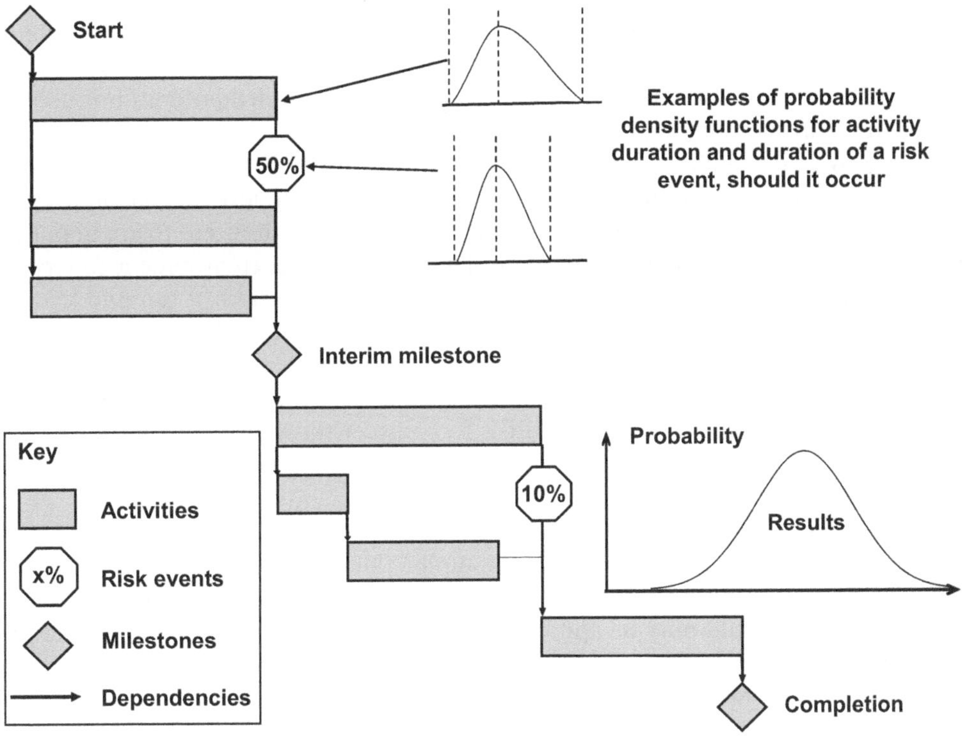

Figure 8.9 Typical features of a Monte Carlo schedule risk analysis model

Projects for which Question C8 is not applicable will fall into one or both of the following categories:

1. Projects with a completion date that would not be allowed to slip under any circumstances.
2. Small or simple projects that can reasonably expect to manage schedule risk with conventional project planning processes supported by a risk register.

Example 8.9 – A completion date that could not be allowed to slip

A project team conducted a Monte Carlo analysis for completing a two-month bid process. However, the customer had specified a precise date and time for receipt of proposals; late receipt would invalidate any proposal from the tendering process. Working back from this deadline also dictated dates for internal bid approval reviews. The Monte Carlo schedule risk analysis forecast was therefore redundant. However, given the complex nature of the project being bid for, a Monte Carlo analysis for the post-contract award project implementation phase would have been useful. In particular, it would have helped the project's owning organistaion to quantify risk being accepted by submitting the proposal.

The RMM assessor will have to make a judgement as to whether or not Question C8 is applicable. If a project would, in principle, benefit from using schedule risk analysis properly, then the question should be applicable. If the project then does not use such analysis the D answer should be selected.

The C answer to Question C8 is representative of two conditions that often affect schedule risk analysis. The first condition is that poor quality modelling produces biased forecasts. The second is that the people to whom the analysis results are given disregard them. In practice, these two conditions are often linked, particularly if the project environment fosters bias. A risk analyst who has gone to great trouble to provide realistic forecasts can find that they are disbelieved by the recipient. The easy, but ill-advised, way out of this difficulty is for the analyst to be less diligent and produce forecasts that are more palatable.

The RMM assessor therefore needs to be capable of distinguishing between realistic and naïve analysis. A good starting point is to consider the evidence collected prior to answering Question C7 (Risk Estimating). If risk estimates are biased, then so too will forecasts from schedule risk analysis.

Schedule risk analysis results can also be undermined by inappropriately structured models. The most common cause of this is a model that contains inappropriate levels of detail. The *PRAM Guide* (2004) recommends using a maximum of 250 activities and risks. Even this number would only be appropriate to a very large and complex (for example, multi-£billion) project in an advanced state of project definition. Usually an appropriate number of activities and risk is very much lower than 250. Despite this, many projects treat their detailed schedule (with hundreds, if not thousands of activities) as being the risk network.

Inspection of a project's detailed schedule can reveal significant faults. Thus, unless the project's planning process has produced a good quality schedule, it is an error to base schedule risk analysis on the assumption that the schedule is correct. There are also a number of other practical reasons why it is usually inappropriate to pull across a detailed schedule for risk analysis purposes. They include:

* Copying logic that invalidates risk analysis (for example, Start-Start dependencies with lags),
* copying constraint dates that would override the Monte Carlo process, and
* creating an unrealistic risk estimating burden that, in practice, is resolved by making poor quality estimates.

Although less well understood, there are further technical reasons why the detailed schedules are an inappropriate form of risk network. One is that detail can undermine the principle that risk analysis should model uncertainty. The reality of almost all detailed schedules is that they represent only one of many possible ways in which the project will be delivered. In practice, as the project progresses, this single detailed view will change as new activities are added and dependencies changed. In contrast, a simple Monte Carlo schedule risk analysis model treats activity dependencies as being 100 per cent valid. By including detailed level activities in schedule risk networks, analysts can inadvertently embed unreliable assumptions in the model. Thus, whilst the presence of low-level activities creates an impression that the model is objective, it is nevertheless irrational. The effect is to subvert the fundamental purpose of the analysis which is to model the implications of uncertainty.

Simulation of covariance between activity and risk outcomes is another technical factor that affects the quality of schedule risk analysis. The underlying causes of covariance between project activities and risks can include:

- The effect of low-level interactivity relationships that are not captured by the risk model,
- the common effect of overarching issues that influence the project, and
- systematic effects of a risk that affects multiple activities.

Typically, the effects of covariance are simulated using a correlation function built into the Monte Carlo simulation tool. A positive correlation between two variables will simulate a trend between the two in which higher or lower values tend to coincide. Figure 8.10 illustrates a correlation of 0.5 between two variables with Beta Pert probability density functions.

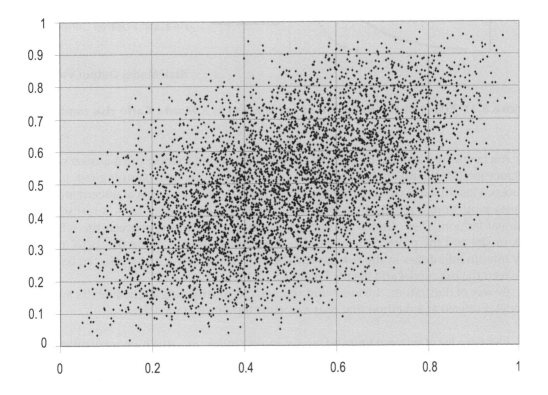

Figure 8.10 Scatter diagram: correlation of 0.5 between two Beta Pert distributions

The effect on risk analysis results of simulating correlation between elements in a risk model is illustrated in Figure 8.11. In effect, recognising the reality of activity/risk covariance increases the forecast variance of overall project performance. Thus, unless the schedule risk model is very simple, and the outcome of its various elements independent, any schedule risk analysis that omits correlation should not allow the selection of an answer better than B to Question C8.

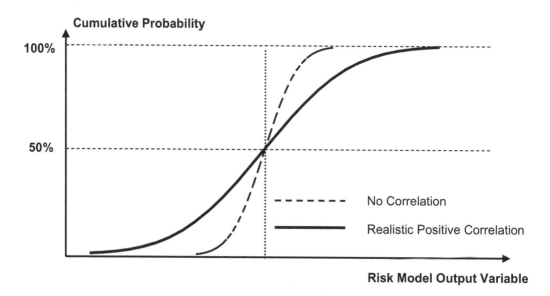

Figure 8.11 Effect of the inclusion of correlation in a Monte Carlo risk model

A schedule risk analysis model that is sufficiently sound to meet the A answer criteria to Question C8 will usually have been developed using a top-down planning/risk analysis process. This will have ensured that the model simulates those sources of uncertainty that matter most from a schedule performance perspective and it does so in a realistic and rational fashion. There should also be key points of comparison between the schedule risk model and the project's detailed plan. An effective way of doing this is to include key interim milestones in the risk model. This will ensure that sense checks can be made between the risk model and detailed plan.

By way of illustration, the following approach to constructing a schedule risk analysis model is offered as a method that uses a suitable top-down approach.

1. Identify a list of between four and ten key project milestones (the number of milestones is likely to reflect the complexity of the project). These milestones should be chosen on the basis that they, a) represent points at which different paths within the project schedule converge, b) can be associated with well-defined products or events, c) are spread relatively evenly across time and d) are of significant interest to the senior managers and stakeholders.
2. Working with a minimal number of (high-level) activities, establish a first-pass schedule network to show how the above milestones could be driven by aspects of the project delivery that are potentially time-critical.
3. Identify those areas of the above network that would benefit from a greater degree of activity/dependency detail. Increased detail may be justified where, a) certain areas of the schedule are of interest because they are particularly exposed to risk, or b) it would produce

more precise activity or dependency definition that would improve the modelling of risk events, the integrity of the risk estimates or the validity of the schedule analysis. Judgment as to which areas of the schedule are at risk may be based on a Monte Carlo analysis using the first-pass network and/or inspection of the risk register.

4. Compare and contrast the deterministic version of the schedule risk network with the project plans using key dates and the flow of activity. Errors in either may be detected and corrected at this stage. Managers and stakeholders are more likely to be persuaded of the risk analysis integrity if the deterministic version of the risk model can be aligned with the project's detailed schedule. However, it should also be appreciated that an advantage of developing an independent schedule risk model is that it provides an integrity health check of the project plan itself.

5. Estimate probability density functions for each activity in the final network. These estimates should be made using a structured method that ensures that all sources of risk are considered other than those responsible for event risks. A typical fault found in Monte Carlo models is that the estimates of uncertainty are unrealistically narrow. By focusing narrowly on each activity at a time, estimators can forget the wider influence of the project environment and the effect that sources of variability and ambiguity risk can have, particularly when they combine.

6. Introduce any event risks that are not already inherent to the model. In doing so, take care to avoid introducing risks that are either already simulated by the network logic or incorporated into composite risks represented by activity probability density functions. The risks introduced in this step should be linked into the activity network as events that, should the risk occur, would effectively create new activities, extend the activity to which they are linked or alter the logical dependencies between activities.

7. Introduce correlation to model the behaviour of groups of activities and/or risks whose outcome is likely to be affected by common underlying factors. A top-down identification of strategic and systemic risks may help to identify where correlation groups exist.

8. Run the schedule risk model with the purposes of, a) making risk-based forecasts of the major milestone selected in the first step, and b) identifying which areas of the project are likely to be the most important causes of schedule slip.

9. Report the results produced in Step 8, together with any recommendations for risk responses. This report should also clarify key simplifying assumptions that have been made for the purposes of analysis. These might include assumptions that 'show-stopper' risks would not occur; risks sometimes have to be excluded on the basis that their occurrence would fundamentally invalidate the model. The target audience would need to be aware that the analysis validity was limited by such conditions.

The above process requires a significant degree of skill and judgement on the part of the risk analyst. The level of commitment required means most projects are unlikely to undertake such analysis on a very frequent basis; tactical control of the schedule therefore remains in the domain of the core project planning process. However, experience has shown an investment in well-structured quantitative risk models can produce realistic forecasts and a sound basis for strategic project control. In contrast, bottom-up approaches to quantitative risk modelling tend to produce unrealistic forecasts that may lead to poor management decisions. The answer to Question C8 should be selected with these facts in mind.

Question C9: Quantitative Risk Analysis for Overall Project Economic (or Financial) Performance

	In what ways is the overall risk to the project's economic performance modelled?
E	Not applicable. (Variance of the project's economic performance is not a sufficiently important issue to justify quantitative risk analysis.) **Note** – Selection of this option will restrict the assessment of the risk analysis perspective to being no better than RMM Level 3.
D	EITHER There is no analysis of overall economic performance risk; OR The integrity of risk modelling is undermined by bias fostered by the project's circumstances or environment.
C	The approach to risk modelling for the project's economic outcome has significant weaknesses that could introduce bias to the forecasts produced.
B	Risk modelling for the project's economic outcome can be expected to forecast a realistic average value, but may have weaknesses that result in an unrealistic forecast of overall variance.
A	Best practice is used to build model(s) that produce a realistic forecast for overall risk to the project's economic outcome in terms of costs, or business case value (for example, NPV or profit) as appropriate.
	Perspectives affected: Risk Analysis and Project Management

Question C9 is a key question in the Risk Maturity Model. Selecting the E (not applicable) answer will, by default, limit the RMM assessment of the risk analysis perspective to a maximum of Level 3. Since the overall assessment of risk management capability is equal to whichever of the six RMM perspectives is the weakest, the overall assessment would be likewise limited to this level. Question C9 is unique in this respect. The Level 3 default, which is programmed into the RMM software, is not repeated for any other question. The reason for this approach is that the management of risk to a project's overall value can always be expected to be of importance to project strategy decisions; and this requires a sound quantitative approach. Whilst a simple process based on managing risks on a case-by-case basis might be beneficial, it cannot be relied on to handle the management of risk to the overall project value in a rational way. The examples presented later in the discussion of this question explain why this is the case.

In some cases, Question C9 can be interpreted in terms of the project's cost risk analysis capability. However, in many cases this would be an inadequate approach to the risk management of economic value. The RMM assessor should therefore understand the purposes of the project and interpret the question accordingly. The following notes should help to resolve this issue.

In the commercial world all projects should have an economic basis that can be used to justify their existence; the value of a project's benefits should exceed its costs. In the case of a project delivered under contract to a customer, the most obvious measure of benefit will be invoiced output. Although there might be other benefits, in most cases, profit would be the primary measure of economic performance. In the case of internal projects, benefits may be more difficult to measure. If benefits can be measured reliably in cost terms, the project's net value (value of benefits minus costs) could be used as an economic measure. If the costs and benefits are phased over different periods, a more satisfactory measure would be Net Present Value (NPV). Finally, in some cases the trade-off between cost and benefits may have to be based on the subjective judgement of the project sponsor. Delivering the project's product by the time planned would effectively be deemed worth the authorised cost. In such cases, cost would therefore be a reasonable proxy for economic value.

To summarise, the planned economic performance of a project should always be a key objective. Dependent upon circumstances it could be measured in terms of:

- Profit,
- net value,
- Net Present Value, or
- cost.

The position for government organisations, charities and not-for-profit organisations is similar. However such organisations are more likely to own projects that lack any commercial basis. For example, governments may fund infrastructure and social service projects without any expectation of financial return. Within such organisations cost, related to the value for money, will be more often the primary measure used to judge economic performance.

Cost risk analysis will lie at the core of any analysis of risk to economic performance. Perhaps the most frequent use of cost risk analysis, in practice is to calculate appropriate values for financial contingencies. Issues that affect risk analysis for other measures of economic performance are similar. Hence, for ease of explanation, the majority of examples below are based on cost risk analysis. A common-practice method for performing this task is illustrated in Figure 8.12.

	Risk title	Probability	Impact (£K)	Risk value (£K)
1	Rework following testing	30%	300	90
2	Supplier price higher than expected	60%	600	360
3	Exchange rate worse than assumed	50%	300	150
4	Price of steel increases	40%	100	40
5	Late delivery of design to supplier	20%	60	12
	Expected value total of 16 other risks			59
			Total:	711

Figure 8.12 Example of a faulty common-practice cost risk model

Figure 8.12 shows a contingency budget calculation for a train operating company's £10million project to procure new railway carriages from an overseas supplier. The risk values in the last column are calculated as the product of probability and impact. The overall total is the sum of the risk values from individual risks.

The calculation shown by Figure 8.12 has numerous faults. The first fault to note is that the total is not actually a calculation of overall risk. The concept of overall risk is based on variance of overall outcome. In contrast, the total shown in Figure 8.12 is but one single value from a range of possible outcomes that could realistically occur. Figure 8.13 includes a cumulative frequency distribution (S-curve) to illustrate the extent by which the project cost might realistically vary compared to the simplistic risk calculation of £711K shown in Figure 8.12.

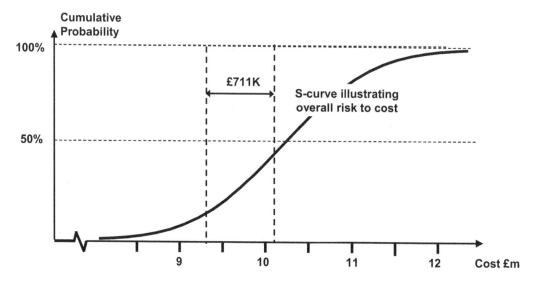

Figure 8.13 Overall cost risk shown as a distribution of possible outcomes

The RMM assessor should consider whether or not variance of overall outcome is a sufficiently significant issue to merit a quantitative analysis of overall risk in order to produce a forecast equivalent to that shown in Figure 8.12. In the case of some simple projects, it may be reasonable to conclude not. Question C9 would then be deemed to be not applicable. By default, this would imply that the RMM assessment results would be limited to Level 3, but this might be considered to be good enough for the project concerned. However, if the variance of economic outcome is a significant issue to the project sponsor, the question would be applicable. In the latter case, if a project calculates cost or economic performance risk to produce a single value, the D answer should be selected.

A common approach to analysing overall project cost risk as shown by the S-curve in Figure 8.13 is to use a Monte Carlo model using the same structure as shown in Figure 8.12 but with estimates defining probability density functions for each risk impact. For example, the railway carriages procurement project might have produced a model using the data shown in Figure 8.14.

Risk title	Probability	Minimum Impact (£K)	Most Likely Impact (£K)	Maximum Impact (£K)	Simulated value (£K)
1 Rework following testing	30%	150	300	500	
2 Supplier price higher than expected	60%	300	500	900	
3 Exchange rate worse than assumed	50%	0	200	900	
4 Price of steel increases	40%	20	80	230	
5 Late delivery of design to supplier	20%	40	60	90	
16 other risks similarly simulated					
				Total:	Simulated sum

Figure 8.14 Example of a faulty common-practice Monte Carlo cost risk model

Although the model shown in Figure 8.14 will support a Monte Carlo simulation, it retains many of the faults of the earlier single figure calculation. For example, inspection of the risks involved shows that they could include an element of duplication. If the supplier buys the steel required, the steel price inflation risk could be a component of the supplier price risk. Another deficiency is that the estimates do not reflect the positive side of some of the risks involved. For example, exchange rates might change in favour of the project. The exchange rate risk is also the source of incorrect calculation of effect; if the supplier's price increases and exchange rates move against the project, this produces a multiplicative, not an additive effect. (Example 8.8 is based on a similar fault.) Failure to understand the multiplicative effects of combined risks usually results in the underestimation of overall risk.

The example shown in Figure 8.14 illustrates a number of mistakes that can be made in quantitative risk analysis. They are typical of errors produced by assuming that overall risk can be modelled as being the sum of the parts of a detailed risk register. The result is usually an underestimation of overall risk, although overestimation of risk is also a possibility. The main point to note is that summing risks from a risk register cannot be relied upon to produce a rationally structured risk model. Analysis based on this, or similar practice, is therefore likely to make it difficult to select an answer better than C for Question C9.

Structuring a rational model for a project's economic performance requires the analyst to start with a clear high-level understanding of how economic value can be calculated, the most important sources of uncertainty involved and the relationships between them. It should then become more evident as to how risk analysis should be structured before moving to lower levels of detail. This approach, which is recommended by the *PRAM Guide* (2004), provides assurance that overall risk continues to be analysed on a rational basis through successive iterations of the process. This is an important concept for risk analysts to grasp. Risk management offers a selection of tools and techniques. Risk analysts need to understand how these can be adapted to the needs of each project.

For the purposes of this book the railway carriages procurement project can be used as a brief example of a sound top-down risk analysis. The train operating company would be procuring the new carriages to enhance or protect its passenger revenues. This purpose could be translated readily into estimates for financial benefit. However, this benefit would only start to accumulate after the procurement costs had been borne. It would therefore be appropriate to discount the value of benefits on a Net Present Value basis. Accordingly, the risk analyst would start quantitative analysis by constructing a simple NPV risk model.

The calculation of NPV would depend upon costs, revenue and their profiles across time. A first-pass NPV model might involve developing estimates for a simple probability distribution for procurement costs at current rates. For revenue modelling purposes it might use a flat profile commencing from the availability date for carriages, but with uncertainty associated with the revenue rate. Sensitivity testing with this simple model would then show whether the most significant sources of risk were due to revenue or procurement cost uncertainty. The significance of other factors might also be clarified by adding them to the simple model. For example, uncertainty about through-life maintenance costs might prove to be more important than procurement costs. Responses to the risks involved with either revenue or through-life cost might also, if understood early enough, be used to influence carriage design and procurement. The relationship between design issues and risk becomes clearer with a simple well-structured risk model.

With a sound simple starting basis, risk analysis could then be focused on the sources of uncertainty that matter most. If procurement cost is still an important focus of interest, then a start can be made on refining that part of the NPV risk model. The major source of risk at this stage would probably be identified as being uncertainty about payment to the supplier. The associated estimates could be developed in the form of a composite risk that includes the implications of steel prices, design decisions (driven by maintenance costs and revenue considerations) and exchange rates. The threat of potential rework following testing might also be included in the model as a separate risk. Developing risk estimates for cost in this way avoids potential duplication of effects and ensures that all major sources of uncertainty are included. This can be contrasted with simplistic bottom-up (sum of the parts) approaches such as that illustrated in Figure 8.14.

Selecting an answer better than C to Question C9 will normally be dependent upon following a top-down process to structure the risk model(s) used to analyse overall risk to the project's economic performance. In the case of a large or complex project where secondary effects are significant (for example, Figure 8.6), a top-down approach will be essential. It is possible that some simple projects can realistically model overall risk by summing individual lower-level risks. However this would only be valid if the effects of each risk were independent of the others.

Assuming that the project has an appropriately structured risk model and estimates that are not liable to bias, either the B or the A answer could be selected for Question C9. Differentiation between these answers should be based on a judgement as to whether or not the analysis is likely to have forecast a realistic variance of outcome: is the range covering best-case to worst-case outcomes realistically wide? In practice, most risk analysis underestimates overall risk, producing an unrealistically narrow forecast of possible outcomes. The most common causes of this are:

- Unrealistically narrow input estimates, and
- failure to simulate the effects of co-variance.

The RMM assessor should consider the answer selected to Question C7 (Risk Estimating) before selecting the answer to this question. If the risk estimates are known to be potentially biased then the answer to this question should be no better than C. Similarly, if the estimates have average values that are realistic, but boundaries that are unrealistically narrow, the answer to this question should be no better than B.

The importance of simulating the effects of covariance was explained earlier in the discussion under Question C8. This can be an even more important issue in cost/ economic performance modelling. Whilst schedule risk models include dependencies between components, many economic performance models do not. Failure to simulate statistical dependencies between the components of an economic performance model can therefore have a more pronounced effect. Despite this, with a model structured along the lines shown by Figure 8.14, it is common to find that each probability and impact value is simulated independently of the others. The averaging out effect this generates produces results that are unrealistically narrow.

Example 8.10 – Omission of correlation from a risk model for a major national project

On a project of national importance, the risk model used to simulate net value subdivided the project costs and benefits into a breakdown of approximately 30 line items. Three point estimates had been made for each of these at the 10th, 50th and 90th percentile levels of confidence. A Monte Carlo analysis on this data led to the conclusion that the interval between the 10th and 90th percentile points for the overall project net value was £0.5 billion. This became the basis on which the project was authorised to continue.

However, in the absence of correlation inputs, each line item in the net value risk model had been simulated as being independent. When a realistic degree of correlation was subsequently introduced to the model, the interval between the 10th and 90th percentile points for overall project cost grew to £1.5 billion.

Selecting the A answer to Question C9 will normally depend upon correlation being included in the risk model. In a simple risk model, all components might be correlated with others. As models grow in detail and complexity, a limited number of correlation groups might be identified to simulate covariance amongst model components affected by common sources of uncertainty. An example of this is practice based on Lichtenberg's (1989) successive principle, which combined the use of correlation groups with a top-down (successive) approach to risk modelling.

In summary, selecting the answer to Question C9 involves a number of issues that are critical to producing realistic forecasts of overall project risk. Weaknesses in either risk models or the input estimates can undermine the validity of quantitative risk analysis results. The results of biased or naïve risk analysis can be positively misleading.

Question C10: Maintenance of Fallback Plans

To what extent are fallback plans maintained by the project?	
E	Not applicable. (The project is sufficiently small or simple for it to be likely that value would not be added by maintaining fallback plans.)
D	There are no fallback plans.
C	Fallbacks have been identified, but these are brief descriptions of possibilities that, if implemented, might expose the project to significant consequences that are inadequately understood.
B	Some fallback plans are developed appropriately, but others lack sufficient detail to provide an acceptable basis for decision making.
A	For all risks to which they apply, fallback plans are developed to the level of detail that is economically justified by the status of the risk.
Perspectives affected: Risk Analysis and Project Management	

Risk fallbacks tend to be one of two types:

1. What could be done to alleviate the effects of a risk should it occur.
2. A planned risk avoidance that could be implemented if deemed appropriate at some future date (the fallback decision point).

The purpose of developing the first type of fallback plan would be to have thought through the response to risk occurrence before it happens. Development of the fallback is therefore a pro-active means of mitigating risk impact. The alternative would be to react to the risk's consequences as and when they occur. The development of fallbacks of this type is a sign that the project has thought through its plans in contexts other than the assumption that the plans will work perfectly.

Example 8.11 – A fallback prepared to mitigate a risk should it occur

A steel manufacturing company had to rebuild the interior of its largest blast furnace. The first step in this rebuild was to drain the furnace, a procedure which involved driving through a new hole below the level of regular tap holes. Ideally, this new hole would break though precisely at the bottom of the molten iron. However, attrition in the furnace hearth meant that there was uncertainty as to where this point would be. In practice, therefore, the procedure would leave some iron behind. This iron would quickly form a solid mass (called the bear).

After draining and opening up the furnace, the next activity was to remove the bear. The preferred method for doing this was excavation using mining machinery. However there was a high likelihood that the bear would be too large to enable this work to be completed on schedule. Accordingly, the company employed an explosives expert to plan the removal of the bear and be on standby so that explosives could be used if necessary. In the event, explosives did have to be used. The project was completed on time.

This type of fallback can be related directly to a risk's effects. It is for this reason that Question C10 is positioned within risk analysis. However, planned fallbacks are also a risk response strategy. Hence Question C10 is also positioned immediately before the response questions detailed in the next chapter.

Fallbacks that are of the planned risk avoidance type are also relevant to Question C10. Unlike the first type of fallback, they are also relevant to Question D1 (Use of fallback decision points). The following is an example:

Example 8.12 – A planned risk avoidance

Two companies were in competition to win the prime contract role on a defence sonar system project. The government customer for this project funded both companies to deliver a programme of technical risk reduction trials prior to final selection. The potential prime contractors had each formed an industrial team of subcontracted companies. However, for one part of the sonar, the same subcontractor was being used by both parties.

One of the potential prime contractors identified the risk that the shared subcontractor would take commercial advantage of its position. It therefore developed a fallback to avoid this risk by using an alternative contractor. This was not a preferred solution. Whilst the alternative contractor had the necessary technical capability, it was a foreign supplier and lacked defence experience. As the project progressed, it became apparent that the shared contractor was likely to preclude promising design options by imposing its own solutions. As the risk to the prime contractor's own position had become too high, the fallback contractor was employed. In the event, increased competition for this part of the sonar proved to be very beneficial. The company that employed the fallback won the prime contract role.

Risk register tools often make provision for identifying and recording fallback plans. Whilst this is generally a good thing, it should be borne in mind that fallbacks will not exist for all risks. Moreover, some fallback plans deserve much more detailed attention that others. Projects maintaining a risk register can fall into the trap of slavishly filling in the fallback box without discriminating between what is important and what is not. It is not uncommon to see the quality of risk registers being judged on completeness rather than a more intelligent subjective judgement based on value added. The RMM assessor should bear this in mind when selecting the answer to Question C10.

The C answer to Question C10 would be typical of a project that records fallback plans for the sake of completeness. A typical symptom is the recording of simple generic statements that are the first reasonable idea that occurs to the person involved. Selecting the B answer requires the project to develop some fallback plans that, as a minimum, allow the implications to be quantified. Selection of the A answer would confirm that the project develops all fallback plans to an appropriate extent.

Typical Actions for Improvement

This section provides guidance for the identification of process improvement actions related to the risk analysis perspective. The identification of improvement actions will be affected by whether or not the project is using a quantitative or qualitative analysis approach or a combination of the two.

In practice, a lot of quantitative risk analysis is performed to a poor standard. It is not sufficient just to be able to operate a risk analysis tool, although this is how many practitioners receive their training. The issues may involve structuring models or making realistic estimates. More often than not, both issues need attention. Hence actions for improvement may include:

- Training practitioners how to structure risk models using a multi-pass process,
- maintaining centralised resources to provide best practice guidance,
- implementing a risk estimating strategy that counters common consequences of estimating heuristics,
- learn by monitoring outcomes of project activities relative to risk forecasts,
- using specialist consultancy expertise, and
- implementing an independent review of quantitative analysis forecasts.

The history of RMM assessments shows that the three most common problems that affect qualitative risk analysis are: failure to understand risks with the necessary clarity and depth, failure to cope with the administration overhead and faulty design of the prioritisation process (typically caused by a misapplication of the PIM technique). Of these three problems, poor understanding of risks is the most fundamental. Hence, if this weakness is identified, it should become the priority for improvement. There, is, for example, no point in designing an improved method for prioritising risks if the risks have not been properly understood in the first place. Actions for improving risk descriptions could include:

- Introduce a structured approach to risk descriptions that distinguishes between context (relevant facts), sources of uncertainty and consequences (effects),
- deliver training to practise writing descriptions using real project examples, and
- develop a simple dictionary of risk meta language to provide guidance.

Sometimes, the root cause of weakness in risk analysis is attempting to manage too many individual risks. This dilutes the attention that can be paid to each risk and hence affects the quality of risk assessment. In these circumstances, projects often fail to manage any of their risks effectively. Actions that address this problem may include:

- Using a sound risk description structure to aggregate associated risks up to a higher level, thus reducing the overall number of risks in a risk register, and
- making better use of the planning process to handle minor risks and issues.

Finally, many projects make elementary mistakes when designing a risk prioritisation system, particularly when using a PIM. Further guidance on this subject can be found in the APM's guide, *Prioritising Project Risks* (Hopkinson et al. 2008).

9 *Risk Responses*

In practice, the risk responses perspective has been found to be responsible for as many low Risk Maturity Model (RMM) scores as all the other five perspectives put together. Projects often seem to have real difficulty in making sure that planned responses are actually implemented. Whilst it might be relatively easy for a risk specialist to facilitate effective risk identification and analysis, the implementation of risk responses is usually outside their direct control. A corporate risk manager, speaking at a conference, once summarised the problem like this:

> *In the past, my company has been very good at risk identification, risk assessment and risk filing.*

If risk responses are not implemented, then effort expended on other parts of the process will be mostly wasted. At best, projects would have a more sophisticated forecast of their fate.

However, the implementation of responses is not in itself sufficient; selection of appropriate responses is also important. In practice, examination of a project's risk responses can often reveal them to be mundane. There is little to be gained by operating a formal process that generates actions that would have been undertaken anyway. Risk management will only add value if a project is able to respond to insights that might not have otherwise been understood through core processes such as planning and contract management. Mundane responses can be a consequence of weak risk analysis that produces a superficial understanding of risks. Mundane responses may also reflect a culture in which the ownership of risks is pushed down to lower levels in a team's management hierarchy.

It should be borne in mind that some of the most effective risk responses could be high-level decisions that address multiple sources of risk with a single overarching solution. These might include decisions about issues such as contracting strategy, choices between different products, tools or methodologies and mutually exclusive options for optimising project benefits. If the approach to risk analysis does not support the optimisation of key decisions then the project's risk response capability will be limited. A common example of where this may be the case is the practice of only regarding risk responses as being actions designed to reduce the probability and/or impact of risk on a risk-by-risk basis. Whilst this can add value, it neglects the wider opportunity to use the risk management process for making project strategy decisions; a key aspect of the concept of RMM Level 4.

The Project RMM is based on the premise that selection of the right responses and implementing them as planned are both critical to success. The questions weighting scheme reflects this by allocating equal weighting to each of these two aspects of the risk responses perspective. In practice, there are more questions that can be asked to find out if appropriate responses are selected. The one RMM question that is exclusively concerned with the implementation of responses (Question D6) is thus allocated a particularly high weighting.

Question D1: Utilisation of Fallback Decision Points

How does the project utilise fallback decision points?	
E	Not applicable (The project would not benefit from the identification and management of fallback decision points).
D	EITHER Fallback decision points are not identified; OR They are ignored.
C	Fallback decision points are sometimes passed without an appropriate review of the associated risk.
B	Risks are always reviewed at the fallback decision point, but sometimes this process fails to result in a clear decision.
A	There is a review at each fallback decision point. This results in a clear decision with respect to the fallback's implementation.
Perspectives affected: Risk Responses and Stakeholders	

One of the two types of fallback described under Question C10 (see Chapter 8) was 'a planned risk avoidance that could be implemented if deemed appropriate'. It is this type of fallback that should have a fallback decision point. The fallback decision point is the date or the point in the project's schedule at which a decision on implementing the fallback should be taken. It should be deemed appropriate to implement the fallback if the risk of continuing with the original plan is unacceptable.

The discipline of defining and using fallback decision points can prevent projects from continuing to chase their losses. As agents of change, project managers tend to be optimistic. Whilst there is much to be gained from this, not every opportunity proves to be fruitful. The use of planned fallback decision points offers project managers a mechanism with which to change plans if necessary. However, this mechanism needs to be used. There is no point in planning a fallback decision point if the decision is subsequently ducked.

Example 9.1 – A fallback decision point that was ignored

A defence equipment project involved the development of a computer suite with an architecture based on the next generation of a certain processor. Towards the end of the definition phase, prior to the main project approval, it became known that the processor development programme might be cancelled. Accordingly, a fallback decision point was identified which involved a review of the position three months after project approval. If the processor development programme was still in doubt, the fallback of adopting an alternative processor would be invoked. This would involve some additional costs, but would allow the project to keep on schedule.

In the event, the fallback decision point was ignored. This was despite the fact that the processor development risk had increased. By placing a fixed price contract after project approval, the government client believed that it had transferred the risk to its prime contractor. However, the prime contractor persisted in hoping that the new processor would become available. This position was influenced by the fact that its own parent company owned the processor and wanted to use the project to leverage further development. When development of the next generation processor was officially cancelled one year later, the project was set back the full year during which the fallback had been ignored. This affected the government client objectives as much as it did its prime contractor's.

The costs of reworking what had become an obsolete system design were also very high. Eventually, cost escalation on the project occurred on a scale whereby the government client had to provide significant additional funding. In effect its fixed price contracting strategy had not been wholly successful in transferring cost risk.

Not all projects will have fallbacks that require fallback decision points. It is often the case that the prevalence of this type of fallback declines as a project passes beyond its earlier phases. The RMM Assessor will therefore need to judge whether or not Question D1 is applicable, dependent on the project's circumstances. If fallback decision points should be in use but are not, then the D answer should be selected. If fallback decision points had been identified but had always been ignored then they would have been entirely ineffective. This would mean that they might as well not have been identified in the first place, so the D answer would still apply.

Selecting the C answer implies that, as a minimum, the fallback decision points are usually marked by an appropriate review of the associated risk. Use of the word 'appropriate' in this context means that affected stakeholders should be engaged in the review process if they have a legitimate interest in the decision. Selecting the B answer implies that this approach to reviewing fallback decision points is implemented in a consistent fashion. Selecting the A answer further implies that all fallback decision points are marked by a clear decision. This does not mean that the fallback is selected by default. A clear decision could involve a number of possibilities. What is important is that the risk position should be re-assessed and action taken accordingly.

Question D2: Different Risk Response Strategies

	To what extent are different strategies considered when selecting risk responses?
E	Not applicable.
D	Most risk responses are the first reasonable idea that occurs to the person concerned.
C	Risk responses tend to fall into one or two generic approaches, although some risks may show evidence of a more flexible or imaginative approach.
B	The nature of risk responses shows that a variety of different strategies are in use. However, there are some risks where viable response options have not been considered.
A	Consideration is given to all relevant risk response strategies, with the aim of identifying the actions and decisions that optimise the expected outcome of the overall project.
	Perspectives affected: Risk Responses and Stakeholders

A frequent weakness with project risk management processes in practice is that the action taken is the first reasonable idea that occurs to the person concerned. Such ideas are liable to comprise actions that would have been taken anyway. The risk management process then becomes little more than a procedure that documents the project planning process. This approach, as described in Answer D to Question D2, does not add value and is therefore symptomatic of a project with a Level 1 RMM capability.

Decisions as to how to respond to risk are almost always characterised by choice, even if one of the choices is to accept the risk and thereby do nothing. But to exercise choice, it is first necessary to identify the options that are available. The purpose of describing different risk response strategies is to prompt an exploration of all possibilities.

From an overall project perspective, risk response strategies can be viewed as being different types of decisions that can be made on the basis of risk analysis. These are the types of decisions that an early application of a top-down cyclical process could be designed to support. They might include:

- Selecting the parties involved,
- developing agreements between stakeholders that align risk with the ability to influence outcome,
- choosing and then using project authorisation decision points,
- choosing the most risk-efficient project solution from different options,
- adjusting project plans to make them more risk-robust, and
- developing appropriate targets for objectives and allowances for contingencies.

By influencing the overall project, response strategies such as these can contribute towards the management of many sources of risk with a single decision. By making such decisions early, they can also represent the best chance of optimising the project outcome. Selecting the A answer to Question D2 is therefore dependent upon the project using these types of response strategy to the extent that they are relevant.

Risk management strategies can also be described from the lower-level perspective of responding to individual risks on a case-by-case basis. Table 9.1 summarises risk management strategies of this type as they are described in three different guides.

Table 9.1   Risk management strategies identified by three guides

	UK Treasury Orange Book (2004)	PMBoK (2005)	PRAM (2004)
Threats	Terminate Treat – directive controls	Avoid	Avoid
	Treat – preventive controls Treat – detective controls	Mitigate	Reduce probability Reduce impact Plan fallback
	Transfer	Transfer	Share contractually Pool Insure
	Tolerate	Accept	Accept
Opportunities	Take	Exploit	Exploit
		Enhance	Enhance probability Enhance impact Plan option Invest
		Share	Share contractually Pool
			Reject
Contingent responses	Treat – corrective controls	Contingency planning	Reactive fallback
			Realise opportunity

The risk response strategies summarised in Table 9.1 can be criticised for treating all risks as being event-orientated threats or opportunities rather as being attributable, more generally, to a lack of certainty. However, the table can provide useful prompts for risk owners responsible for managing individual risks. Use of such prompts can be a good aid for identifying the various actions that could be taken to improve risk outcomes. In practice, for many risks, the best choice lies in a combination of actions. Whilst a risk management process based on responding to risks on a case-by-case basis may not be capable of optimising outcome from an overall project perspective, it can, nevertheless, add significant value. Projects only using such an approach may therefore still be able to able to select a B or C answer to this question.

Selecting the A answer to Question D2 is conditional on the project selecting responses that are likely to optimise the expected outcome of the overall project. This implies that risk analysis should be capable of providing a forecast of overall project risk and that this analysis allows selection of risk responses to be optimised. The application of Chapman and Ward's risk efficiency principle (for example, as described in Chapter 2 (pp. 22–4), and Chapter 3 (p. 49) is one way of achieving this level of capability. In effect, the appropriate risk response is to choose the most risk-efficient alternative from two or more mutually exclusive project solutions. Another approach might be to use models that simulate overall project risk to test the effectiveness of risk responses with a view to selecting the combination that provided the best value for money.

Since there are almost always choices to be made when selecting risk responses, and since the nature of these choices is usually diverse, it is difficult to envisage circumstances in which this question would be not applicable.

Question D3: Utilisation of Cost/Benefit Comparisons

	Is the selection of risk responses influenced by cost/benefit comparisons?
E	Not applicable.
D	Risk responses are taken with little consideration of cost versus benefits or secondary risks.
C	Risk response costs are informally taken into account when making decisions, but consideration of secondary risks and/or secondary effects is often weak.
B	Selected risk responses can be expected to stand scrutiny in respect of cost versus benefits although they may not always be formally recorded in this way.
A	Risk responses are formally supported by cost versus benefit comparisons that consider both the wider benefits of controlling secondary effects and the potential impact of secondary risks. Risks are accepted when it is economically rational to do so.
	Perspectives affected: Risk Responses

The overriding purpose of a project risk management process is to add value. If the process is worth carrying out, the costs of responding to risk must have a lower value than the consequences of doing nothing, that is, the benefits should exceed the costs. Conversely, some responses to risk might correctly be rejected on the grounds that their costs could not be justified on the grounds of added value. Developing the right risk responses is therefore not simply a question of reducing risk to the greatest extent possible. In practice, there is a limit beyond which further action would be counterproductive. The word mitigation is often used to describe risk reduction. It is a word that indicates that although risk can be reduced, elimination of risk is usually not the best choice.

As with Question D2 (Different risk response strategies) understanding how to answer Question D3 will depend upon the way in which the risk management process is being applied. One possibility is that of a project managing a number of risks by treating each one on its own merits. This would reflect the common practice of maintaining a risk register with each risk having its own response plan. In this situation, Question D3 can be addressed by examining whether:

- Risks have response plans (or response actions),
- the cost of response plans is understood and recorded,
- the benefits of responses have been understood and recorded, and
- risk owners can justify the cost of responses in terms of their benefits.

These questions often raise more complex issues than might at first be thought. One difficulty is that risk impacts typically have at least three dimensions: cost, time and product performance. Other impact dimensions (for example, reputation) might also be involved. The cost of responses is easy to compare to the cost impact dimension, but not the others. Even if the effect of schedule delays or product performance shortfalls can be translated into a cost equivalent, it is usually difficult to attribute their overall effect precisely to individual risks. A further problem arises as a consequence of secondary effects. Secondary effects are an important factor to consider, but they often cause complexity. For example, some secondary effects may be common to several risks.

Example 9.2 – The importance of secondary effects

A major communications programme was divided into several concurrent projects. The purpose of the smallest project was to develop a new modem. This was a technically demanding objective that involved a number of high risks. Moreover all the other projects were producing products designed to communicate via the modem. It was therefore critical to the whole programme. Despite this the modem project was allocated only a small contingency budget, commensurate with its planned cost rather than its risk exposure and its effect on other projects. As a consequence, cost-effective opportunities to invest in risk reduction were lost and the programme was delayed by modem availability.

When the project risk management process is reliant on responses to individual risks, it can therefore be very difficult to achieve the criteria required to select the A answer to Question D3. However, responsible risk ownership combined with regular project reviews of risk response effectiveness should make it possible to select the B answer.

Question D3 takes on a different perspective if project risk is being analysed and managed from an overall economic performance perspective. This involves supporting project strategy decisions with quantitative risk models in the manner illustrated in Chapter 3 (see pp. 37–56). If the risk model is built appropriately, the cost implications of the risk response decisions involved should be included within the analysis itself. This would fulfil the conditions for selecting the A answer.

Unfortunately, risk effects often can't be resolved into the single dimension of financial value for analysis purposes. This tends to be particularly true of projects owned by governments or not-for-profit organisations that are intended to serve a public rather than a business purpose. In practice, such projects may find themselves unable to select the A answer, whatever the quality of their risk management process. Whilst this might seem unfair, it should be remembered that achieving a Level 4 RMM capability does not require an A answer to be selected for every question.

Since any risk management process should add value, Question D3 should apply to all projects.

Question D4: Quality of Risk Response Plans

	What is the quality of risk response plans?
E	Not applicable. (The project is in an early cycle of a top-down risk management process during which risk responses are decisions rather than action plans.)
D	EITHER Significant risks often lack recorded responses; OR Risk responses tend to lack clarity, often describing what would have been done in any event.
C	Most significant risks have a response. However whilst some responses identify responsibilities clearly and tackle risks at source, many fail to do so.
B	All significant risks have a response. Most responses comprise tasks or actions with clear ownership that tackle risks at source where possible.
A	Risk responses are consistently identified in a way that sets out a clear plan for who is responsible for doing what by when. The majority of responses are designed to tackle risk at source.
	Perspectives affected: Risk Responses

This question is applicable whenever risk responses are based on actions or action plans. This will normally include any risk management process that uses an approach based on managing risks on a risk-by-risk basis. Typically, projects maintain a risk register for this purpose. One of the most important features of a risk register is its information on risk response actions and plans. In effect, the risk register becomes an action item database that can be reviewed and updated to ensure that all risk responses are implemented as planned. In some cases, the scope of certain risk responses may cause them to be transferred to the project's plans. Wherever the information is held, Question D4 is all about whether the plans for responding to risks are effective.

It should also be noted that all the answers to this question refer to *significant* risks. The RMM Assessor will have to make a judgement as to where to draw the line between significant risks and other risks that are of minor importance. This allows for the possibility that a project might enter a very large number of risks on its register, but reserve minor risks for monitoring purposes only.

The most effective risk responses tend to be those that tackle risk at source. Prevention is better than cure. Thus a key point to consider when answering Question D4 is whether or not the source of risks has been adequately understood. Much will depend upon the understanding of risks by their owners. Examining risk descriptions will provide a good indication of whether or not risks are well understood. As described under Question C1 (see Chapter 8, pp. 128–33), good risk descriptions capture information on the source of risk by articulating relevant facts and sources of uncertainty. Time that has been invested in developing this information will be repaid by the way in which it will help to identify pro-active responses.

Example 9.3 – An example of planning to act on risk at source

An engineering company was in the process of reducing its workshop capacity on the basis that subcontracted manufacture was becoming a cheaper option. However the quality of wiring work returned by some subcontractors had proved to be unacceptable, leading to serious delays. With this background, a project, with a strategically important production contract, identified wiring quality to be a significant schedule risk. This risk could be avoided if the company's management could be persuaded to keep the project's wiring work in-house. When this option was rejected, the project was forced to consider how best to reduce the risk.

Before sending out wiring work to subcontractors, the project identified the sources of the risk as being: 1. whether or not the subcontractor's best staff would be allocated to the work, 2. whether or not the subcontractor was familiar with the correct use of a particular tool, and 3. how quickly faulty work would be identified and corrected. The risk response tackled all three sources of risk. The project manager offered help to the subcontractor in the form of visits from a member of the project team who had wiring and inspection experience. They also discussed the possibility of follow on work should earlier work be done well. These two actions incentivised the subcontractor to use its best staff. Planned visits to the subcontractor were then used to check that tools were being used and to inspect work prior to finished units being delivered.

Although Example 9.3 is a simple one, it does illustrate how thinking through the sources of risk helps to identify effective responses. Of course, not all risks can be tackled at source. Sometimes, the only option is to be prepared to respond to a risk's occurrence. Allowance for this is made in the wording of the A and B answers to Question D4.

In addition to focusing on the sources of risks, response plans should record who is responsible for doing what, and by when. The ownership of plans and actions is particularly important. As with all management processes, actions without owners tend not to get done. Action or plan owners are not necessarily the risk owner, although they often might be. What matters is whether or not the right people are being tasked with taking effective action and whether or not everyone concerned is clear about what this involves.

Unfortunately, it is not uncommon to see unclear risk responses or responses that describe what the project would have done, even if the risk had not been identified. Examples, (taken from real risk registers) are:

- Closer co-operation with the supplier,
- improved monitoring, and
- rectify faults.

Vague statements such as these betray a lack of precision and detail in the risk owner's thought processes when considering their risks. They are typical of projects for which the D answer should be selected for this question.

Question D5: Monitoring of the Implementation of Risk Responses

How is the implementation of risk responses monitored?	
E	Not applicable. (Never – this question should always be applicable.)
D	The implementation of risk responses is rarely monitored.
C	The implementation of most risk responses is monitored, although this tends to be on an ad hoc basis.
B	The effectiveness and implementation of all risk responses is reviewed. However, EITHER planned reviews are sometimes missed; OR The project would benefit from increasing the frequency of such reviews.
A	The effectiveness of the implementation of each risk response is reviewed at agreed times (and where appropriate) at routine intervals.
Perspectives affected: Risk Responses	

Many projects monitor the implementation of risk responses as part of a programme of planned or routine risk reviews. Or, at least, that is their intention. In practice, best intentions are not always fulfilled. The causes of failure to monitor risk responses are usually either:

- Failure to keep to the programme of risk reviews, or
- distraction at risk reviews caused by other inadequacies in the risk management process.

As a consultant who has been involved with many projects, the author has found that the conduct and content of risk reviews quickly reveals many of the shortcomings of the process being operated. A typical shortcoming of weak processes is that the review is dominated by discussion about relatively unimportant matters such as the nuances of risk classification or scoring. The more important business of whether or not responses are being implemented and proving to be effective can be dropped, almost with no one noticing. The author's rule of thumb is that at least half of the time consumed by any risk review should be concerned with risk responses.

Question D5 should apply to all projects. Monitoring response effectiveness is an important means of improving the overall process. Although this is not one of the more heavily weighted Risk Maturity Model questions, the answer selected often proves to be a good predictor of how well the project scores on other questions including:

- D1 – Utilisation of fallback decision points,
- D4 – Quality of risk response plans, and
- D6 – Implementation of risk responses.

Question D5 will always be applicable. Even in cases where all risk responses are decisions rather than actions, it is still important that the decisions are actually implemented. Unless the implementation of responses is monitored it will not be possible to form a judgement as to whether or not they have been implemented as planned.

Question D6: Implementation of Risk Responses

Does the project implement risk responses as intended?	
E	Not applicable. (Never – this question should always be applicable.)
D	Little attention is paid to risk responses.
C	Attention is paid to risk responses, but progress against their planned implementation is only sometimes satisfactory.
B	Risk responses are usually implemented satisfactorily.
A	Risk responses are implemented in a consistently professional manner. Any actions not completed can be justified by changes in circumstances. This is confirmed by the process for reviewing risks.
Perspectives affected: Risk Responses, Stakeholders and Risk Management Culture	

This is the most heavily weighted question in the Project Risk Maturity Model. Implementing risk responses is critical to the capability of a risk management process. In the absence of response, the process can do no more than predict the range of potential consequences. Despite this, failure to implement responses is a frequent problem.

On the basis of more than 200 project assessments, it is this question that is the most frequent cause of low RMM scores. If a project tends not to implement its risk responses, it is important to find the underlying causes. These might include:

- Poor organisational skills/inappropriate prioritisation of activities,
- focus on short-term issues (firefighting),
- lack of senior management support,
- lack of belief in the results of risk analysis, and
- cutting corners (unwillingness to invest in risk responses).

Given this question's weighting, the RMM assessor should be particularly careful to select the appropriate answer. It can be easy for a project team to cite isolated examples of implementing risk responses and extrapolate from this a high overall success rate. Careful examination of a project's record often reveals a less satisfactory performance than might otherwise be thought. Of course, there may be occasions on which circumstances change in such a way that a planned risk response ceases to be the best option. The A answer to Question D6 accommodates this possibility. However, it should also be noted that selecting the A answer is conditional on monitoring responses. There is hence a clear link to Question D5. If responses are not monitored there would be insufficient evidence for the RMM assessor to select the A answer in any event. Selecting the B answer could also be difficult in these circumstances.

This question is applicable to all projects and during all project phases. The number of lines devoted to it in this book may be relatively few. But that is because it is an easy question to explain. Its importance should not be underestimated.

Question D7: 'Post Response' Risk Analysis

	To what extent is risk analysed using post response estimates?
E	Not applicable. (The project would not benefit from differentiating between pre- and post-response risk estimates.)
D	The benefits of risk responses are never estimated.
C	The benefits of individual risk responses are often assessed, possibly in the context of determining whether mitigation actions are good value for money. However, this principle is not extended to an analysis of the project as a whole.
B	The risk assessment process includes making pre- and post-response risk estimates. This is routinely used to assess the management of individual risks.
A	Risk analysis includes a pre- and post-risk response evaluation of the overall project risk in all relevant dimensions (for example, Timescale, cost or NPV).
	Perspectives affected: Risk Responses, Risk Analysis and Project Management

This question is applicable to all projects that would benefit from discriminating between two views of risk estimating and analysis:

1. Current risk exposure on the assumption that there will be no response to manage the risk (risk analysis based on pre-response estimates).
2. Current risk exposure on the assumption that planned risk responses will be implemented (risk analysis based on post-response estimates).

Discriminating between risk estimates in this way has become widespread practice. Accordingly, many risk register tools now accommodate two sets of estimates for the probability and impact of each risk. One argument in favour of this practice is that risk owners are able to account for the value that would be added by implementing responses to individual risks. Another is that the same estimates can be incorporated into an analysis of overall project risk so that the collective effect of risk responses can be assessed. For example, a project might produce two S-curve forecasts for its schedule, one based upon pre-response estimates and the other upon post-response estimates. The gap between the two curves indicates the time that can be saved by implementing risk responses.

However, despite there being good arguments in favour of making pre-and post-response risk estimates, there are also pitfalls. These tend to be less well understood. The most obvious problem is that making two sets of estimates increases the administrative burden. Discipline is required to make sure that all the estimates are kept up to date. In practice, this problem is often compounded by another issue: ambiguity about the basis for estimating. Whilst risk specialists may regard the concept behind pre- and post-response estimates as being intuitively obvious, other people frequently misunderstand it. For example, a risk owner might believe the basis for post-response estimates to be any of the following:

- Current risk exposure on the assumption that planned risk responses will be implemented,

- current risk exposure on the assumption that all identified risk responses will be implemented, including those for which there is no commitment,
- risk exposure that is likely to prevail at the time by which responses have been implemented (which is often zero), and
- a target risk exposure which the project should aim to achieve.

Ambiguity about the basis for risk estimates can undermine the risk analysis process, and hence provide misleading information. A common related problem is a tendency to overestimate the effect of risk responses and thereby forecast levels of overall project risk that are too optimistic. Organisations that base project approval decisions on post-response risk forecasts may be vulnerable to this effect.

Example 9.4 – Optimistic post-response risk estimates

A risk manager being audited during the implementation phase of a major project admitted that every one of the risks that had occurred had had an impact greater than the post-response estimates recorded in the risk register. When risk owners were interviewed, it became apparent that they usually made reasonable pre-response estimates for risks, but when doing so often already had ideas for a suitable risk response strategy. In effect they were already taking into account the risk response when making the pre-response estimates. When making the post-response estimates, they then felt under pressure to reduce estimates further. Risk owners also often reduced both the probabilities and impact estimates of adverse risks when close inspection of each response strategy showed that it would only affect either probability or impact.

A further problem with the common-practice use of pre- and post-response risk estimates occurs if it is assumed that data maintained in the risk register can be transferred automatically into quantitative risk models. The pitfalls of this assumption should be evident from the discussion of quantitative modelling issues in Chapter 8 (see pp. 150–61). A consequence is that the forecasts of overall project risk distinguishing pre- and post-response scenarios may be misleading. This would undermine one of the arguments in favour of the approach.

Finally, it should be noted that for projects using high-level quantitative models to make risk-efficient decisions, the concept of pre- and post-response estimates may be irrelevant. Use of this approach to risk analysis (as illustrated in Chapter 2, Example 2.1, pp. 22–4) is an effective means of achieving Level 4 RMM capability. Proponents of this approach may argue that the common-practice application of pre and post response estimates is actually a barrier to best practice.

In practice, operating a risk management process using pre- and post-response risk estimates may therefore have a number of unintended adverse consequences. The RMM assessor should therefore only apply this question to projects for which there is good reason to expect that maintaining pre- and post-response estimates will be of net benefit.

Typical Actions for Improvement

This section provides guidance for the identification of process improvement actions related to the risk responses perspective. The identification of actions for improvement will be affected by whether or not the root cause of weakness lies in response selection or response implementation. The latter is often the more obvious problem. It is not uncommon to find risk registers full of actions representative of good intentions that are unfulfilled. However, the cause of this problem may be that the people responsible for implementing these actions know that there are more important or more urgent things to do. Hence, on closer inspection, the root source of the problem may lie in the selection of ineffective or mundane risk responses. Responses might be ineffective because they fail to address the source of risk, are identified at too low a level, or are allocated to the wrong people.

In the event that responses fail to address the source of risk, the remedy may lie in improving risk analysis. If risks are not well understood or if the project's quantitative analysis lacks credibility, risk responses are liable to be ineffective. The solution would be to implement risk analysis improvements and capitalise on them through the risk review process.

Some of the most effective risk responses are decisions or actions taken at high level. These may include matters concerned with developing the project solution, maintaining its alignment with the interests of the organisation and the project's commercial strategy. If the risk management process fails to address risk associated with project strategy, its effectiveness will be limited. Potential actions for improvement include:

- Making use of a top-down multi-pass approach to risk management, and
- retaining the ownership of some risks at a senior level.

The problems of allocating risk responses to the right people tend to increase with project size and complexity. On a complex project with a geographically dispersed project team, it may be difficult to identify or communicate with the person who is best placed to implement the most effective response. Equally, the risk owner might not know that certain possibilities even existed. This is a problem that an effective risk manager can help to overcome by working across team boundaries and by recognising that other teams could be affected by the impact of risks. Carefully managed use of a multi-user concurrent access risk database tool can also help.

If, despite identifying effective responses, risk responses still tend not to be implemented, the most practical solution is usually to follow a disciplined programme of project team risk reviews. These do not have to be time-consuming; but they do have to be focused on the effectiveness and implementation of responses. They also need overt support from the project manager and, if possible, from the project sponsor.

Despite such measures, some projects fail to implement risk responses because of the sheer volume of short-term issues. This is symptomatic of a project in difficulties that is continuing to attempt to achieve objectives that have become unrealistic. Ultimately the solution to this is to adjust the objectives. Doing so will require the project sponsor to be engaged with the risk management process.

10 *Project Management*

This perspective concerns the extent to which risk management is integrated with the overall project management process. It embraces two activities that are part of the core risk management process shown in Chapter 2, Figure 2.4 and on the right hand side of Figure 2.5 (see pp. 25 and 27):

1. Initiating the process, and
2. Managing the process

Together these activities should ensure that the process is tailored to the purposes of the project, implemented as intended and evolved as and when appropriate. Failure to do these things would prevent the process from being effective.

The *Project Risk Analysis and Management (PRAM) Guide* describes process initiation as defining the project and focusing the risk management process. Effectively this involves aligning the process with the project's purpose and understanding how it will co-exist with other project management processes. Without taking care over these matters, risk management can become an isolated process that has little impact on other project activities. The Risk Maturity Model (RMM) questions primarily concerned with process initiation are:

- E1 – Alignment of the risk management process with the project's purpose,
- E2 – Project Team Risk Management Responsibilities,
- E3 – Cyclical Development of the Project Solution, and
- E4 – Relationship between Risk and Project Plans.

The *PRAM Guide* describes the purpose of the Manage Process activity as being to ensure that the risk management process remains effective. The RMM questions primarily concerned with this are:

- E5 – Maintenance of Project Risk Records,
- E6 – Quality of Risk Reporting,
- E7 – Arrangements for Risk Reviews,
- E8 – Use of Risk Information for Project Cost Forecasting, and
- E9 – Assessment of the Project's Risk Management Capability

The arrangements for risk reviews can be particularly important. Projects can evolve rapidly. Thus, unless risk is reviewed on a continuous basis, the information on which risk management is based can become stale. People working on the project know this; they are unlikely to have confidence in any process based on stale information.

Question E1: Alignment of the Risk Management Process with the Project's Purpose

	Is the risk management process aligned with the project's purpose?
E	Not applicable. (Never – this question should always be applicable.)
D	The project's purpose is inadequately defined or is subject to some fundamental disagreements.
C	The project's purpose is adequately defined and has been agreed upon within its owning organisation. However, the risk management process is inadequately aligned with the project purpose.
B	The project purpose has been crystallised into recorded objectives to the extent appropriate to the project phase and with the formal agreement of the project sponsor (or project board). The risk management process is aligned with the achievement of these objectives.
A	Sources of uncertainty that could affect the purposes of the project are managed as strategy risks via the project sponsor or by the project board.
	Perspectives affected: Project Management, Risk Analysis and Risk Identification

The capability of a project risk management process cannot be assessed without understanding whether or not it is aligned with the project's purpose. Thus one of the first things that the RMM assessor should do is to understand and verify the purpose of the project.

The purpose of a project can be described as being its reason to exist. Many projects have the same fundamental purpose: to add economic value to the owning organisation's business. Sometimes this can be easy to overlook. For example, it would be easy to describe a project purpose as being to 'build a new office block' or to 'develop a new vaccine'. But, the ultimate purpose of most projects like these is for the project owners to make money. If their risk management process is not aligned with this purpose, it will fail to deliver best value.

Internal projects often have a similar purpose; they support some form of change to add economic value. Thus the business cases for projects such as IT infrastructure, rebranding, and relocation are founded on the principle that their economic benefits outweigh the costs involved. If the project risk management process fails to consider risk to benefits, it will therefore be flawed. Project success can be more than a matter of delivering product on time and to costs.

However, some projects have non-economic purposes. For example, government bodies fund projects related to defence, law and order and social services, for the national good rather than an economic return. Similarly, many charity-owned projects have no direct economic return. For projects like these, attempts to translate all risk effects into cost equivalents are liable to be irrational. Risk modelling in this environment can become more complex because of the number of different dimensions in which success is measured.

Some projects may also have more than one purpose. Examples include commercial projects in which the secondary purpose is to develop the organisation's capability to undertake similar projects in the future. Government bodies and charities are particularly likely to sponsor projects that have multiple purposes.

Example 10.1 – A project with more than one purpose

The London Millennium Dome project involved two major purposes. The first was to hold an exhibition that would capture the public imagination and attract 12 million visitors in one year. The second purpose was to provide a legacy that would help long-term regeneration of the local area.

Viewed in some ways the project was a success. For example, the Dome itself was an impressive piece of engineering and was completed on time and to budget. However, viewed in the light its two major purposes, the Dome was less successful. Actual visitor numbers were only half of those expected, for reasons that, in retrospect, might have been anticipated. The Dome's legacy was also affected by a lack of planning about how it would be used subsequently.

Finally, it should be noted that projects that involve contract procurement will have different purposes to the different organisations involved. Commercial contractors can be expected to treat the project purpose as being to make a profit. In contrast their customer may treat the project as having a wider purpose. Both points of view would be valid and reasonable. Objectives tend to become narrower as one goes down a project's contract hierarchy. Accordingly, the RMM assessor needs to be clear as to which organisation's management of risk is being assessed at any one time. RMM results for one party are often different to that of the other parties involved.

Question E1 is concerned with whether or not the risk management process is aligned with the project purpose. If it is not, this will be for one of two reasons:

1. The project purpose is ill-defined or subject to fundamental disagreements, or
2. The risk management process is not tailored appropriately to the project.

The first of these two conditions is described by the D answer to Question E1. Projects that lack clarity of purpose tend either to waste time and resources in their early phases or to produce outcomes that, in retrospect, are unsatisfactory. Whatever the cause, lack of clarity of purpose will undermine both the project and its risk management process.

Understanding purpose is a fundamental aspect of any project and an essential component of project strategy. However, it would be naïve for an organisation to let project managers develop purposes for their own projects without governance controls. Hence, defining (or at least, authorising) a project's purpose and ensuring that it is crystallised into approved and measurable objectives (including benefits) is a responsibility borne by the project sponsor. In the case of multi-owned projects, the sponsorship role might be carried out by a project board. Lack of clarity about project purpose might arise in a number of ways, including both a lack of direction and conflicting direction. Projects that lack effective sponsorship or projects with multiple sponsors are particularly vulnerable.

Example 10.2 – A project with multiple sponsors and conflicting objectives

A project owned by a public transport infrastructure organisation had several sponsors including managers representing financial, technical and customer service functions. The project was set a number of objectives, including targets for financial efficiency, completion dates and the minimisation of customer disruption. However, as alternative project solutions were studied, it became evident that none of them would meet all objectives. Whilst each objective appeared to be reasonable in itself, the combination of objectives produced conflicting requirements.

Since the project team could not identify an ideal solution, it failed to gain approval to pass on to the next phase. Instead, time and effort was spent on recycling the business case, only to have it rejected for different reasons. This was unproductive work for the project team and caused delays and lost opportunities. This was not a problem that the project could solve. The solution lay in resolving a disagreement amongst the project sponsors as to the primary purpose of the project.

Assuming that a project does have clear and agreed purposes, the RMM assessor will need to consider whether or not the risk management process is designed appropriately. Typical causes of alignment shortfalls include:

- Weak linkage between the project business case and the methods employed for risk analysis,
- focusing on risks to the completion of the current phase (for example, project definition) rather than the wider project purpose,
- failure to take into account risk over the extended the project lifecycle (for example, cost of ownership risks and risks to project benefits), and
- exaggeration of the importance of certain types of impact as compared to others (neglecting what should regarded as being reasonable trade-off between effects).

Shortfalls such as these should limit the RMM assessor to selecting the C answer to Question E1. However, if there is good alignment between the project's purpose and its risk management process, the RMM assessor will be able to choose between the B and the A answers. Differentiation between these answers then depends upon whether the risk management process influences project strategy decisions or whether it is restrained to the tactical management of risks to objectives.

The B answer represents a project with a risk management process operated in the context of fixed project objectives. This is typical of much project risk management in practice; the purpose of the process is to maximise the chances that the project objectives will be achieved. Whilst this is a laudable purpose, it is essentially a tactical one since key strategy decisions such as the specification of objectives are assumed to be outside the remit of the process itself.

In contrast, selecting the A answer requires the risk management process to include project strategy decisions. Since these could involve decisions about the purpose of the project, this will involve the active engagement of the project sponsor, and, possibly, other parties within the organisation. Project strategy decisions will be linked to an organisation's governance of projects.

Whilst clarity of purpose is a project necessity, this does not mean that the purpose of a project cannot change. Rather it means that the project's purpose should be clear at any point in time. In practice, there may be significant sources of uncertainty that could either change or even invalidate a project's purpose. These might be related to conflicts between objectives. They could also be related to internal changes to the project-owning organisation or to other external sources of uncertainty. Whatever the source of uncertainty, potential changes to purpose would represent project strategy risks. As the custodian of project strategy, the project sponsor (or project board) should be responsible for making sure that the implications of such risks are managed effectively. In many instances, the project sponsor may be the most appropriate risk owner. This is the principle that is written into the A answer.

Since all projects have (or should have!) a purpose, Question E1 is applicable in all cases.

Question E2: Project Team Risk Management Responsibilities

	How are risk management responsibilities carried out within the project team?
E	Not applicable. (The project is managed by a one person acting alone.)
D	There is no nominated risk manager for the project.
C	There is a nominated risk manager. However, the risk manager is not sufficiently engaged with the project team to acquire good quality risk information.
B	The risk manager has specified appropriate responsibilities for all other project team members and provides sufficient facilitation to ensure that these responsibilities can be carried out.
A	Risk owners are fully accountable for the management of individual risks, but make use of the risk manager's specialist skills when it is appropriate to do so.
	Perspectives affected: Project Management

Question E2 concerns the engagement of project team members in the risk management process. Project team members will normally be engaged in a number of different processes, such as planning and the management of technical tasks. If they are not also involved in the risk management process then the process will either lack relevance to significant aspects of the work or lack input from people who have important contributions to make.

The project risk manager is responsible for planning how the risk management process should be conducted and then ensuring that the planned process is implemented. Depending upon the project's size and complexity, this might be a full-time or part-time role. On small projects, the project manager might choose to assume the role themselves. On other projects, they should delegate responsibility to a member of their team. In either case, there should be clarity about who the risk manager is. In the absence of such clarity, the D answer should be selected.

Assuming that there is a nominated risk manager, one of two issues might prevent the process being implemented effectively across the project team:

1. The risk manager working in isolation from the team, or
2. The risk manager lacking sufficient resources.

An effective risk manager will recognise that other members of the team usually have a better understanding of risks than they do themselves. Equally, these people are liable to be busy; some might regard the risk management process as being a distraction. It therefore requires tactfulness, skill and commitment on behalf of the risk manager to acquire high quality risk information.

It helps considerably if project team members believe that the risk management process is contributing to the effectiveness of their own work. An effective risk manager will enable risk owners to develop new insights into their own work and its interactions with other activities and decisions. They can also help to promulgate and monitor the effectiveness of risk responses. In effect, the risk manager can make significant contributions to communication and, in the process, build up a particularly wide understanding of the project.

In contrast, an ineffective risk manager may be wedded to their own computer, generating information with little sense of ownership from other members of the project team. Whilst this could be the result of inexperience or a lack of confidence, even very capable risk management professionals can find themselves in this position. In the absence of support from the project manager and project sponsor, risk managers can find it very difficult to be effective. Whatever the source of the problem, a project in this position should not select an answer to Question E2 better than C.

Another common cause of poor project risk information is a reliance on risk owners to generate it without advice from someone with risk expertise. This would also normally prevent the selection of an answer better than C. Risk owners have expertise in different fields; it is not reasonable to expect that they all also have a high level of risk expertise. They may also be unfamiliar with how their information is used, particularly if quantitative analysis is involved. Left to their own devices, risk owners tend to produce disconnected information of variable quality. This problem may be particularly evident if the project has deployed a multi-user concurrent access risk database tool on the assumption that risk owners will populate it appropriately. It may also be caused by a lack of risk manager resource.

Assuming that there is sufficient engagement between the risk manager and other members of the project team, it would be appropriate to select either the A or B answer to Question E2. Differentiation between these two answers is dependent upon the behaviour of risk owners. Ideally, risk owners should, of their own volition, seek advice from the risk manager as and when appropriate. If they do, this would lend itself to selecting the A answer.

This question will be applicable to all projects that have a project team. Some small projects may be managed by one person acting alone. In that case, that person will undertake all the roles required to manage the project. In these special circumstances, Question E2 is not applicable.

Question E3: Cyclical Development of the Project Solution

How effectively are risk management cycles applied prior to project implementation?	
E	Not Applicable. (The project is in its implementation phase – Question E4 applies)
D	Risk management is only applied when plans for the project implementation phase are mature.
C	Risk management is applied as plans for the project implementation phase approach maturity. As a consequence significant opportunities for optimising the project solution from a risk perspective are lost.
B	Risk management cycles are used in conjunction with the development of the project solution throughout all appropriate project phases.
A	Each risk management cycle uses risk identification and analysis to introduce a greater level of understanding of the project's exposure to risk. This influences the project solution by improving its risk efficiency and/or risk robustness in line with stakeholders' objectives.
Perspectives affected: Project Management	

Question E3 is applicable to projects in stages prior to the main implementation phase. If using the project life cycle shown in Figure 2.1 (see Chapter 2, p. 20), this would include all projects in the concept or definition phases. The purposes of these earlier phases include:

- Developing measurable objectives aligned to the project purpose,
- choosing between project solution options,
- making contracting strategy decisions,
- reducing risk to an acceptable level prior to full project implementation,
- setting targets and contingencies for project objectives, and
- developing project implementation plans.

These purposes include the development of project strategy. It is not until major project strategy decisions have been taken that stable plans can be developed for the implementation phase. This should affect the design of the risk management process during different stages. Techniques that are appropriate to making risk-efficient choices between project strategy options are not necessarily the same as those that help a project remain on track with its plan during the implementation phase. Chapter 3 provides an illustration of how the risk management process may evolve through different phases.

A simple and common approach to project risk management is to identify, assess and manage potential deviations from project plans. Whilst this approach of managing risks on a case-by-case basis has the merits of being simple to operate, it is only rational if the project plans themselves are well-defined. This simple approach is also very limited in its ability to verify whether or not the plans themselves are optimised. For reasons discussed in Chapters 2 and 3 (see pp. 20–26 and pp. 48–53), optimisation of the project solution can only be supported by a risk process based on the analysis of overall project risk; and this is dependent upon having a sound top-down iterative approach to the risk management process. An effective risk management process will therefore employ an iterative process, such as the *PRAM Guide* process shown in Figure 2.4 (see Chapter 2, p. 25), prior to the main project implementation phase.

In contrast, if risk management only commences when the project implementation plans have become mature, opportunities for optimising the project solution from a risk perspective will be lost. This would undermine a major purpose of the earlier phases, that is, to reduce risk. Accordingly, the D answer to Question E3 should be selected for projects in which this is the case.

An improved, but still limited, approach would be to introduce the risk management process as implementation plans were taking shape. This could have the effect of influencing the plans so as to make them more risk-robust. However, it would be unlikely to affect project strategy decisions such as contracting strategy or choosing between project solutions. Since project strategy has an important influence over risk, this would result in lost opportunities for project optimisation. As a result, this would limit the project to selecting the C answer at best.

Selecting the B answer should be conditional on the project using the risk management process to help develop the project solution throughout all early phases. Risk management would thus have to be relevant to the decisions being taken as a consequence of the concept and definition phase activities. To verify whether or not this is being done, it will be necessary for the RMM Assessor to understand the purposes of these phases in the context of the project's overall purposes. This should be distinguished from the idea of managing risks to the delivery of the concept and definition phases themselves.

Further to this, selecting the A answer is conditional on the risk management process being delivered in an iterative manner, with each cycle building upon the insights and responses identified in previous cycles. In practice, some risk management cycles may be conducted in phase with similar top-down processes used to develop the project solution. For example, if an engineering project uses a formal system design approach, the early iterative development of user requirements and system and specifications might be phased in with the risk management process. This would make risk management directly relevant to engineering activities. Best practices for a variety of project processes such as planning and contractual design have a strong top-down element. Risk management should be no different. It should also be relevant to these other processes.

Question E3 is applicable to any project that is still developing its project solution. If the project has a stable solution and the risk management process cannot therefore be expected to contribute further to project strategy decisions, the question may be not applicable. In these circumstances, the next Question, E4 will always be applicable. There are no circumstances in which both questions are not applicable, and in some circumstances (for example, a programme with projects in different phases) both questions will be relevant.

Question E4: Relationship between Risk and Project Plans

\multicolumn{2}{l}{What is the relationship between project planning and the risk management process?}	
E	Not applicable. (The project is in a very early phase and thus, justifiably, has no baseline plans for the phases that are the primary focus for risk management.)
D	Project planning and risk management are conducted as separate activities.
C	Some use is made of the project plans for the identification and assessment of risk. However, risk responses tend not to be worked back into the plans to the extent that the planning process normally requires.
B	Project plans are used to aid risk identification and assessment on a regular basis. The implications of planned risk responses are usually present in plans although they may not be explicitly identified as such.
A	Project plans are used to aid risk identification and assessment via a process of routine planning reviews. Fallback decision points and risk responses with significant work content are included in plans.
\multicolumn{2}{l}{Perspectives affected: Project Management}	

A project should always have a plan, even if only at a very high level. Even at the outset of a project, it should have an identified purpose. The plan would thus be to achieve this purpose. Of course, as a project progresses through its earliest phases, planning detail tends to increase. At a high level, plans also become more stable. Accordingly, it becomes increasingly rational for the risk management process to progress to lower levels of detail. The status of plans should thus influence choices about how to operate the risk management process.

A project's plans provide important context for the identification and assessment of risk. For example, individual risks might be assessed in terms of their effect on plans. Planning assumptions are also often required to structure risk models. Moreover, the aim of most risk analysis is to identify how project plans can be improved. Understanding the relationship between risk and plans is therefore always of importance. In practice, most people realise this. What is required is clarity of thought when making connections. The RMM Assessor should be able to find out whether or not this happens.

A project's plans should reflect what it intends to do. Hence, project plans should incorporate planned risk responses. Whilst this is also widely understood, the implications often cause difficulties. For example, many projects lack the discipline to ensure that the costs of risk responses are included in plans or fail to adjust plans to accommodate significant additional activities. At the other extreme, some projects impose discipline with counterproductive bureaucratic procedure. For example, a project that required a new cost number to be raised for any risk mitigation action found that team members simply avoided raising new risks and actions. What is needed is consistent exercise of professional judgement; significant new work arising from risk responses should be added to plans in the same way as any new work.

Since all projects should have plans, it is difficult to envisage circumstances in which this question would be not applicable.

Question E5: Maintenance of Project Risk Records

	How efficiently and effectively is risk information maintained?
E	Not applicable.
D	EITHER Risk records are not maintained; OR Risk records cannot be retrieved reliably.
C	Risk records are maintained using means that are capable of maintaining master copies of relevant information. However, much of the information is not updated on a sufficiently regular basis.
B	Risk records are maintained using tools that are regularly used to update master records of all relevant information. However the retrieval of information and production of reports could be made more efficient.
A	Risk management information is maintained and updated routinely. There is sufficient historical information to provide a good audit trail. All people with an interest in risk data have convenient access to the relevant information.
	Perspectives affected: Project Management and Risk Analysis

For many projects, this question will concern the recording of information in risk registers or risk database tools. If they also use quantitative analysis techniques, risk records will also include information in risk models, including estimates and the rationale that lies behind them. However, some projects may not maintain a risk register, particularly if they are working with relatively simple high-level risk information. Such projects could choose to maintain risk data in the tools used for quantitative modelling. What is important is that there are good records of the information that is used for the risk management process that are readily available to all people who have an interest in it. Ideally, there should also be an audit trail. This can help people to understand when and why information was changed and may also contribute to lessons learned to be used by other projects.

In recent years, there has been a growth in the use of computerised risk database tools. These structure risk records in a consistent manner and allow data to be extracted using filters, sort orders and reports. Many also include an audit trail function. Some enable multi-user concurrent access to a database via a network connection. Use of computerised risk database tools may thus help to improve a project's capability in respect of this question. However, the use of such tools can also have drawbacks. For example, the administrative load imposed by a complex database may prove to be counterproductive. Using a specialist tool might also limit the readiness with which data is available to the project team. Hence, investment in a specialist tool may solve some problems but create others. If projects are to get the best out of risk database tools they need to understand how and why they use the information that is stored and to be able extract and report the information efficiently.

Projects that do not use a risk database tool might, nevertheless, be able to select the A answer to this question. For example, an audit trail can be provided by a series of date-stamped documents or electronic files. However, there may be configuration control problems that break the principle that there should be a single master record for each item of data. This can be particularly problematic if there is a lot of data or if a number of different people are able to change it.

Question E6: Quality of Risk Reporting

	How effective are risk reports produced by the project?
E	Not applicable.
D	EITHER There is no planned basis for producing risk reports; OR Most risk reports leave recipients little the wiser.
C	Risk reports are produced on a planned basis. However, at least one key audience for risk information is poorly served by risk reports either because of omission or lack of clarity.
B	All relevant audiences for risk information receive risk reports that they consider to be both helpful and timely.
A	Risk reports contain relevant, realistic and concise data that allows all target audiences to assimilate data on risk both efficiently and in a manner that is focused on decision making processes.
	Perspectives affected: Project Management and Risk Management Culture

Risk information needs to be reported to the right people at the right time. Reports might take a number of different forms including snapshots of data extracted from risk tools, presentations and formally authorised documents. They can also be promulgated by different means, including hard copy, e-mail and placement at network locations accessible by the intended audience. It helps if the audience for each risk report knows what to expect in terms of its purpose, content and timing.

Thought also needs to be put into understanding the purposes of risk reports. What decisions will recipients make as a consequence of the information that they glean? Different audiences for risk reports will use them for different types of decisions and at different levels of management. Hence reports should be tailored with a clear understanding of purpose. Table 10.1 summarises typical types of risk report, together with the nature of the decisions that they support.

Table 10.1 Typical purposes of risk reports

Risk Reports	Examples of decisions supported
Prioritised list of risks	Selection of risks for management attention.
Risk details (for example, one page per risk)	Support of decisions made at risk reviews, for example, identification of new responses.
Risk decision analysis	Support of specific decisions, for example, choosing between different project solutions.
Cost risk analysis	Decisions to allocate, increase or reduce the level of financial contingencies.
Schedule risk analysis	Strategic placement of milestone objectives. Prioritisation of schedule.
Business case risk assessment	Support of project authorisation decisions.
Customer risk status report	Joint approach to management of key risks.

Of course not all the report types shown in Table 10.1 will be used by all projects. What is important is that each project understands how risk information should influence decisions and to have planned the content, scheduling and target audience for its risk reports accordingly.

In practice, responsibility for producing good quality risk reports will usually fall on the risk manager. Reports are key risk management products and should hence be an important issue when planning the process. A lack of any planned basis for reports would betray a fundamental planning shortfall.

Assuming that risk reports have been considered when planning the process, differentiating between answers better than D is dependent upon whether or not all key audiences for reports have been identified and reports are tailored to their needs. If they have not, the A and B answers would be invalid.

Selecting the A answer to Question E6 is dependent on risk reports containing relevant, realistic and concise data. Data is unlikely to be relevant and concise unless the purposes of each report have been thought through. It should also be noted that risk data will not be realistic unless other parts of the process have been carried out to a high level of capability. In considering the answer to this question, the RMM assessor should therefore also take into account answers provided to RMM questions related to risk identification and analysis. Examples include those concerned with risk estimating (Question C7, see Chapter 8, pp. 144–9) and quantitative analysis (Questions C8 and C9, Chapter 8, pp. 150–55 and pp. 156–61). Taking this into account, differentiation between the A and B answers to this question is stronger than might at first appear to be the case.

If a networked tool is being used to maintain the project's risk information, it might be argued that access to the tool and its database makes the production of risk reports redundant. Such tools usually have report functions, so the way in which this question is addressed should include the risk tool capability. However, providing multi-user access to such a tool often fails to optimise the quality of risk reporting in practice. Although it is helpful for users to produce reports when they need them, they often lack the necessary skills. For example, if quantitative risk analysis reports are produced, unskilled use of a risk database tool is unlikely to produce rational results. Moreover, such reports usually need to include contextual information such as a list of key simplifying assumptions.

It is therefore difficult to envisage circumstances in which this question would be not applicable. Within any project risk management process there will be some degree of separation of responsibilities between analysis and decision making. Even on very small projects on which circulation of reports within the project team was not required, the project sponsor would still have an interest in risk information.

Question E7: Arrangements for Risk Reviews

What are the arrangements for risk reviews?	
E	Not applicable.
D	EITHER Risks are not reviewed; OR Risk reviews are so infrequent that the review process has little effect.
C	EITHER Risks are reviewed but with insufficient regularity or frequency; OR Risks are reviewed regularly, but the reviews are often too cursory or superficial to be effective.
B	The project uses a risk review strategy designed to make the management of risks effective. Most risk reviews are held as required by this strategy, although some may be either missed or not achieve sufficient depth.
A	The risk review strategy ensures that there is a regular review of a) all individual risks, and b) overall project risk. The frequency and depth of such reviews and the management levels at which they take place are consistent with optimising value added by the risk management process.
Perspectives affected: Project Management	

If risk is not reviewed on a regular basis, changing circumstances on the project will cause risk information to become stale. Eventually, its quality will become so poor that it ceases to provide a good basis for decisions. Regular risk reviews are therefore both an enabler and an indicator of good practice. In contrast, failure to review risks can cause the risk management process to enter into a vicious circle in which the project team makes increasingly less use of the process because of a lack of confidence in its own information.

Risk reviews may take on a number of forms, including:

- Reviews of individual risks by risk owners,
- risk interviews or workshops facilitated by the risk manager,
- reviews of selected (for example, high priority) risks by the project team, or sub-team at risk review meetings,
- review of overall project risk at strategic points,
- reviews of key risk decisions at appropriate decision points,
- risk included as an agenda item in other meetings, for example, technical reviews, and
- joint reviews with the project stakeholders.

A common complaint is that risk review meetings take too long or that people find that their time is not well spent. If true, this would reflect poor practice. A potential source of the problem is poor quality input data. Another is that people attending the meeting only have an interest in part of the agenda. The solution to such problems often lies in preparatory work. For example, if a team meeting is to work its way through a list of risks, it is important that risk owners have already reviewed each risk and that all the information is relevant and up to date. An effective risk manager will have provided sufficient facilitation to ensure that such information is of a consistently good quality. The team meeting can then focus on matters such as whether or not there are additional overarching or cross-cutting risk responses that would add value but that would not have been identified by risk owners thinking or acting as individuals.

Example 10.3 – A simple risk management effectiveness metric

During the definition phase of a major project, the prime contractor's project director, initiated a monthly traffic light report to monitor the effectiveness of each project process. The risk manager suggested focusing on the percentage of risks that had been reviewed. The risk management process would be allocated a green light if at least 95 per cent of risks had been reviewed appropriately by their risk owner during the month and a red light if the percentage dropped below 80 Per cent.

The project director was surprised at this approach. They had expected the metric to be based on a risk count, for example, a red light if the number of risks had increased. However, the risk process manager pointed out that regular in-depth risk reviews were both a success factor and a success indicator. The project customer was fully supportive of this view and gained confidence in the process's effectiveness as a result. Increased quality of risk data also enabled joint risk reviews to operate more effectively.

It is helpful for risk review meetings to progress at a reasonable pace. Whilst the purposes of risk review meetings should include gaining assurance that risk information is realistic, it is easy to get slowed down by estimating issues. Realistic risk estimates require time and an appropriately structured process. This is work that may be better done outside meetings. Instead, meetings should primarily be an opportunity to identify new insights, make decisions and verify that risk responses are effective and being implemented. As with all meetings, the chair makes a significant difference to productivity. Injecting fun into the process can also help.

Example 10.4 – Introducing fun to a risk review

A risk manager introduced a fun idea to raise spirits in a project team risk review. New insights or suggestions for new risk responses were rewarded by the chair with jelly babies. The stock of red jelly babies (for high risks) and black jelly babies (for escalated risks) dwindled rapidly. It would be easy to criticise this idea as being infantile. However, the participants were an exceptionally able group and didn't regard it so. The meeting proceeded with good humour and subsequent reviews were well attended.

The project should plan risk reviews with the cost effective use of people in mind. Having done so, it should then adhere to this plan save for exceptional circumstances. Frequently missed risk reviews are a sure sign of weak risk management capability.

Finally, it should also be recognised that risk reviews may occur at different levels and support different decision making forums. Thus whilst individual risks tend to be reviewed routinely, the review of specific risk decisions will be planned at particular points in time. Likewise, reviewing the implications of overall project risk will be dependent upon when the project chooses to undertake the associated risk modelling. Whilst this might be done regularly, it is unlikely to be done as frequently as a more tactically orientated review of individual risks.

Question E8: Use of Risk Information for Project Cost Forecasting

	Does the risk management process support realistic project cost forecasts?
E	Not applicable. (The project cost is not important – an unusual choice!)
D	EITHER There is no relationship between risk information and cost forecasts; OR Budgetary constraints preclude risk responses that would otherwise be implemented on the basis of being good value for money.
C	There is a recorded relationship between the risk management data and the project budget. However this relationship is insufficiently robust to provide assurance that the project's exposure to cost risk is within the appropriate bounds of tolerance.
B	There is adequate assurance that the project budget includes appropriate cover for the project's overall exposure to cost risk. Funding for effective risk responses is not constrained by contingency budgets.
A	A robust and rational risk-based analysis contributes towards setting the project budget. Planned costs include implementing the risk management process and the implications of planned risk responses. The budget also includes a separate component for unidentified risk that could emerge in the future.
	Perspectives affected: Project Management

Figure 10.1 shows different categories of money used for the purposes of financial planning by a typical project. Whilst different organisations use different labels for the terms shown in Figure 10.1, most organisations follow the same underlying principles. When setting a budget, there should be a differentiation between planned cost, calculated deterministically using a cost breakdown structure, and project contingencies, based on the implications of uncertainty. For projects delivered under contract, profit is then added to the budget. For such projects, profit realisation is usually a key measure of project management effectiveness.

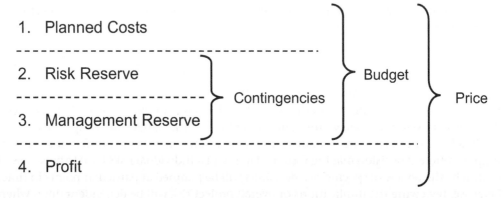

Figure 10.1 Typical labelling and purpose of project financial contingencies

By providing a source of uncommitted funds, contingencies allow a project to invest in new risk responses. Hence if contingencies are too low, a project will lack the flexibility to respond to risk effectively. Contingencies can also be used to absorb the effects of risk as they materialise. Hence there should be a sound relationship between contingencies and risk analysis. This question is about whether or not the risk management process is used to identify realistic cost contingency estimates.

As illustrated in Figure 10.1, contingency is often broken down into two elements: risk and management reserves. This differentiation is often reflected in management responsibilities. Typically, responsibility for estimating and controlling the risk reserve is delegated to the project manager, whilst spending money from the management reserve would be authorised by the project sponsor. In practice, the management reserve might be part of a risk pool for a programme or project portfolio maintained by the organisation or project sponsor.

A risk reserve should be based on the effects of known unknowns. In contrast, the management reserve would be primarily designed to cover the implications of unknown unknowns. Whilst the risk reserve can therefore be estimated on the basis of a cost risk analysis, the management reserve cannot. It would, for example, be irrational to estimate management reserve from the S-curve forecast for overall project risk.

The wording of answers to Question E9 reflects the fact that unknown unknowns fall outside the scope of project risk management. However, their effects should not be ignored. Whilst risk analysis cannot be used to estimate unknown unknowns, failure to allow for their effects could still leave a project with inadequate contingency, and thus constrain risk responses. Assessing whether or not there is good evidence that contingencies are appropriate (as required for the B answer) inevitably involves a degree of subjectivity.

In assessing whether cost risk analysis contributes appropriately towards contingency estimate, the answer is likely to be closely coupled with the answer to Question C9, 'Quantitative Risk Analysis for Overall Project Economic (or Financial) Performance' (see Chapter 8). For example, the C answer to Question C9 is: risk modelling for the project's economic outcome has significant weaknesses that may introduce bias to the forecasts produced. If there are significant risk analysis weaknesses that could introduce optimistic bias, a risk-based estimation of project contingency is likely to be insufficiently robust. Hence a C answer to Question C9 often indicates that the answer to this question should also be no better than C. If contingency funding is so low that the project rejects risk responses that would be likely to save money, then the D answer should be selected.

Compliance with the A answer to this question requires a rational cost risk analysis that includes the implications of all sources of risk, but avoids duplicating effects. This is easier said than done. Before selecting the A answer, the RMM assessor should therefore review the evidence gathered in connection with previous questions related to quantitative analysis. In addition to Question C9 (Chapter 8, pp. 156–61), these include:

- C3 – Assessment of Risk Impacts (Effects),
- C4 – Analysis of secondary effects, and
- C7 – Risk estimating.

On this basis, many, if not most, projects may be found to lack a realistic and rational cost risk analysis. When this occurs, the RMM assessor will have to investigate other evidence to judge whether or not the project budget includes appropriate cover for the project's overall exposure to cost risk, thus potentially meeting the conditions for the B answer to this question. This may be a difficult judgement to make. However, there are two points that should be borne in mind.

The first point is that rules of thumb for estimating of project contingency can be grossly misleading. When asked what a realistic level contingency should be for a project many people will offer an estimate of 10 per cent of the overall project cost. This 10 per cent figure is, in effect, rule of thumb. Example 10.5 shows how misleading this can be.

Example 10.5 – Cost of the Scottish Parliament building

The initial estimate for the Scottish Parliament building in Edinburgh was £40million. At this point, use of the 10 per cent rule of thumb for project contingencies would have suggested that the project could be approved with a £4million allowance for risk. However, after project approval by the Scottish Parliament the project's costs escalated rapidly. The final cost was £431million. There is therefore a reasonable case to assert that a realistic level of contingency associated with the original estimate would have been almost £400million; a factor of 100 greater than the £4million contingency calculated by rule of thumb! Of course, any risk analyst suggesting this at the time would have probably been deemed both incompetent and insubordinate.

Judging whether or not a project's budget includes appropriate cover for its overall exposure to cost risk should take into account the project environment and the degree to which self-interest may have introduced bias into cost forecasts. It should also take into account inherent level of risk and the extent to which risk has been transferred using commercial arrangements. Some low risk projects do not need contingency levels as high as 10 per cent of the overall budget. Example 10.6 describes a project approved with contingency funds of approximately 5 per cent of costs, and which, in practice, returned all this to the business as profit.

Example 10.6 – A low risk project

A company received an order to deliver a one-off version of a computer system that had been manufactured on four previous occasions. The majority of work was subcontracted at fixed prices using detailed drawings to define the product required. Under these arrangements, the retained risk was associated with drawing changes (for example, caused by component obsolescence) and failure to co-ordinate the timing of work being undertaken by different subcontractors. In practice these risks were fully mitigated.

Any project should make provision for risk as part of its cost forecasts. Inadequate provision for risk is liable to cause budget overruns and/or lost profit. Projects that lack adequate contingencies also find it difficult to invest in effective risk responses. This question should therefore apply to any project on which cost is used as a measure of success. In practice, there will be very few exceptions.

Question E9: Assessment of the Project's Risk Management Capability

In what ways is the project's risk management capability assessed?	
E	Not applicable. (The project life cycle is less than one year.)
D	The project's risk management process effectiveness is never reviewed.
C	The project manager or project sponsor is sufficiently engaged with the risk management process to form an assessment of its effectiveness. Areas for process improvement are acted upon as a consequence.
B	The project's risk management capability is formally reviewed on a regular basis. Actions for improvement are identified and implemented.
A	The capability of the risk management process is formally audited, as a minimum, on an annual basis. Priorities for process improvement are identified and implemented as appropriate.
Perspectives affected: Project Management and Stakeholders	

As with any process, the effectiveness of the risk management process should be monitored and action taken to improve it as appropriate. Moreover, the requirement to do so should be led from the top of an organisation. In some cases, this is underpinned by regulatory requirements. For example, in the case of companies listed on the London Stock Exchange, compliance with the Turnbull Guidance requires the board of directors to seek regular assurance that its risk-based system for internal control is functioning effectively. They are required to confirm that this has been done in the company's annual report to shareholders.

There are a number of ways in which a project may assess its risk management capability. The simplest way is for the project manager or project sponsor to challenge ineffective practice where they see it and ensure that improvements are made. However, this approach does have limitations. For example, the managers involved may lack the expertise to drive improvements beyond a certain point. Best practice risk management is more than a matter of formalised common sense. Some sources of process weakness might also be identified more readily by someone with greater independence.

Using a formal review of risk management capability may help managers to structure their assessment of the process more systematically. For example, the risk management process could be reviewed against the organisation's risk management policy or descriptions of best practice. Alternatively, of course, this book advocates the Project RMM as being the best available structured approach to the assessment of risk management capability! A regular formal self-assessment that identifies and monitors actions for improvement qualifies a project to select the B answer to this question.

Further to this, selecting the A answer is conditional on the process being audited. Such audits should be conducted by people with appropriate expertise and independence. A process for conducting audits using the Project RMM is described in Chapter 5 (see pp. 89–91). Two advantages of using the RMM for this purpose are that it identifies priorities for improvement and enables the monitoring of improvements. Being able to do these are also conditions for fulfilling the A answer criteria.

Typical Actions for Improvement

This section provides guidance for the identification of process improvement actions related to the project management perspective. The starting point for action identification should be to identify which questions received the poorest answers. This can show that the root cause of the problem might be concerned with instigation (and design) of the process or with its ongoing management.

If the cause of weakness is concerned with process design, it should be noted that the project management perspective includes two of the most heavily weighted questions in the model:

1. E1 – Alignment of the risk management process with the project's purpose, and
2. E3 – Cyclical Development of the Project Solution.

Whilst Question E3 is usually only applicable to earlier project phases, Question E1 is always applicable. Thus, although issues of process design are always important at the outset, they may continue to be important at any time. Actions to address issues of process instigation and design typically include:

- Appointment of an experienced and capable risk manager,
- tailoring the risk management plan to the project's circumstances,
- clarification of the project's purposes with the project sponsor, and
- clarification of roles and responsibilities for risk management.

Assuming that process design is not the priority for improvement, attention can be shifted to issues of process implementation. The causes of failures to implement a process as planned can be both cultural and practical. If cultural barriers are the source of difficulty, it would be usual to find that the RMM measurement for risk management culture would be low compared to the measurement for other perspectives. If this is the case, the best remedies might be found amongst 'Typical Actions for Improvement' listed at the end of Chapter 11.

In some countries and organisations, the prevailing culture drives adherence to the planned process. However in other countries (the UK and the Netherlands being examples) the culture is often one in which people are disinclined to follow a process that does not make sense personally. Hence the solution to what may appear to be a cultural problem may have practical solutions. If project team members find risk management to be too time-consuming, complicated or not sufficiently helpful to their own objectives, the process can fall into disuse. The root cause of this can be addressed by actions such as:

- Improving the usability, accessibility and simplicity of the risk database tool, and
- improving communication on risks that cut across team boundaries.

Finally, it should be noted that having an effective programme of risk reviews is usually a critical success factor in managing the process. Question E7 (Arrangements for Risk Reviews) often provides a good indication of the overall RMM capability level. The history of RMM assessments shows that improved use of risk reviews is one of the most frequently recommended actions for improvement.

11 *Risk Management Culture*

Risk management culture is often discussed, but is frequently not well defined. Two meanings of the word 'culture' are relevant. The meaning of the word referring to the characteristics of a society is relevant in the sense that a project team is a social group that exhibits behaviours that may be constructive or otherwise. Another meaning of the word referring to the concept of being refined or educated is relevant in that people using the risk management process need to understand it. Using these two ideas, risk management culture can be defined as being the collective willingness and ability of the people involved with a project to use the risk management process for purposes intended to optimise the overall project outcome.

An indicator of weak risk management culture is compliance with the mechanics of the process being achieved in a box-ticking manner. This can produce information that appears to satisfy the process's requirements, but fails to provide new insights or to challenge preconceptions about the project appropriately. Another indicator of a weak risk management culture is the alteration of risk information (albeit sometimes unconsciously) in order to comply with the expectations of managers or peers. A weak risk management culture can undermine any aspect of the risk management process. Thus improvements to other aspects of the process may, in practice, require attention to enablers of risk management culture.

The influence of risk management culture is reflected in the Risk Maturity Model (RMM) weightings structure. More questions in the model contribute to the risk management culture perspective than any of the others. As a consequence, the assessment score obtained for this perspective on each project tends towards the average scores for the other five perspectives. The score obtained for this perspective can therefore be regarded as good general indicator of the health of the overall process. Despite this, there have been a number of project assessments for which risk management culture has been either the weakest or the strongest score obtained.

Projects with a relatively good risk management culture score are more likely to make rapid progress with actions to improve other aspects of the process. In contrast, a project with a relatively poor risk management culture may find process improvement actions are difficult to implement. In this situation the best approaches to improvement are likely to be found by first identifying the key enablers of risk management culture that need to be addressed. Typically these include tackling issues such as the engagement of senior management in the process and the effectiveness of risk management training.

Finally, it should be noted that risk culture should not just be regarded as being a soft issue. A disinclination of people to use the process can also be produced by the fact that they find the process to be time-consuming relative to the value that it adds to their own work. Bureaucratic procedure producing detailed information that often goes unused can therefore be an obstacle. Another key enabler of good risk management culture is therefore designing a process that is as simple and user-friendly as it can be, given its scope and purposes.

Question F1: Scope of Freedom to Act

	Do people involved with the project understand and use their freedom to act?
E	Not applicable.
D	People working on the project have little understanding of their responsibilities with regard to risk management.
C	There may be insufficient clarity about scope of freedom to act. As a result, managers tend EITHER To own too many risks to manage effectively; OR Fail to learn of significant new risk information within a satisfactory timescale.
B	People working on the project have clear boundaries of responsibility. However, in practice, these may not be sufficiently well related to the operation of the risk management process.
A	Significant risks are escalated to the appropriate level of management. Below this level of risk, project team members make full use of their scope of freedom to act, identify, assess and respond to risks.
	Perspectives affected: Risk Management Culture

The Project RMM identifies management roles at three levels within an organisation:

1. Project sponsor.
2. Project manager.
3. Project team members.

On large projects a management structure within the project team might create additional levels. At each level in this hierarchy, managers will have delegated responsibilities and a scope of freedom to act, as implied by delegated resources and decision making powers. Ambiguity about these matters or mismatches between responsibilities and scope of freedom to act can become significant sources of difficulty for any project management process. The risk management process is no different.

Lack of clarity about responsibilities and scope of freedom to act can cause confusion about risk ownership. Ideally, risk owners will be motivated to manage their risks effectively, even if some of the secondary effects would impact on aspects of the project being managed by other team members. In a dysfunctional team, lack of clarity can cause team members to avoid responsibility for risks.

Example 11.1 – Lack of clarity about management responsibilities

On an IT infrastructure programme, a business continuity risk was identified. This concerned whether or not the new infrastructure would be compatible with the organisation's business continuity plan. However, no one working on the programme felt that they were either responsible for owning the risk or qualified to manage it. This problem extended all the way up to the programme sponsor. The programme thus simply proceeded on the assumption that its design would be adequate.

However, clarity of responsibility is not in itself sufficient. Misalignment of responsibilities and scope of freedom to act can similarly cause risk to be managed poorly. The most common problem is delegation of responsibility without the necessary resources or decision making powers. This leads to the disempowerment of managers at lower levels in the management hierarchy.

Example 11.2 – Bureaucratic obstacles to empowerment

On a complex programme, the programme director instigated a procedure intended to manage contingency funds more tightly. Under this procedure, any new risk response had to be supported by a full business case subject to formal approval by the programme director or his deputy. In order to fund this process, contingency funding that had previously been delegated to project managers was centralised.

In practice, the new procedure was counterproductive; its bureaucratic implications had the effect of reducing the number of new risk responses. Moreover, any responses that were raised tended to be reactive measures to absorb the costs of risks as they materialised. Effective preventative approaches to risk mitigation were thus ignored, particularly if the risks were liable to impact on other projects. Project managers were also inclined to bid for as much money in each business case as they could get away with. Thus, the risk management process evolved into one in which risks were only escalated to the programme director when project managers knew that the need for additional funding had become inevitable. Ironically, what had started off as an initiative to put more control into the programme director's hands led to their losing information on risks until opportunities for proactive responses had passed.

Of course, responsibility can also be delegated to too great an extent. Project sponsors and project managers should not expect to delegate the ownership of all risks. Project strategy risks and risks that have overarching responses should be owned at senior levels. Team members also have to understand the basis on which risks should be escalated. Risks may be escalated on the grounds of significance. However, they may also be escalated on the basis that the required response is beyond the owner's scope of freedom to act. Thus, what is required is a professional approach to delegating and escalating responsibilities for risks that aligns the ownership of such responsibilities with the project roles that people undertake.

When selecting the answer to this question, the RMM assessor will find that evidence related to Question C2 (Risk Ownership) (see Chapter 8, pp. 134–5) may be helpful. For example, it will be difficult to find evidence to select the A answer if risks lack nominated risk owners. Another previous question to consider is E7 (Arrangements for Risk Reviews) (see Chapter 10, pp. 192–3). One of the purposes of risk reviews should be to escalate and delegate risks and risk responses to appropriate levels. Hence, in the absence of regular risk reviews the management of risks is unlikely to be well-aligned with scope of freedom to act.

This question should be applicable to all projects. Even projects without a project team should still have a sponsor and project manager to whom this question can be applied.

Question F2: Climate of Trust Within Project Team

Is risk management fostered by a good climate of trust within the project team?	
E	Not applicable.
D	Project team members have little understanding of their responsibilities with regard to risk management.
C	Some project team members are reluctant to disclose risks until their effects are almost inevitable. This may be due to a project culture that fails to distinguish between targets and commitments.
B	Project team members are willing to be open on the reporting of most risks, but there have been occasions in which the reaction of the project's senior management has been unsupportive.
A	There is a climate of trust such that a realistic disclosure of all significant risk information is encouraged and valued by all levels of management.
Perspectives affected: Risk Management Culture	

Communication of new information when it matters is the foundation for a climate of trust. Since the management of risk recognises that things might not go to plan, one of the benefits of a risk management process should be that it fosters communication of new information on subjects that matter. Fostering a climate of trust should therefore be one of the benefits of effective risk management. However, having a climate of trust is also an important pre-condition for effective risk management. People are unlikely to identify risks if they think that the information will be received badly.

In the author's experience, working with many projects and in different industries, the quality of internal communication is a key factor differentiating between effective and ineffective project teams. In an effective project team, there is a culture in which people communicate new information to others of their own volition. This is also an essential ingredient of a good risk management culture. In contrast, in dysfunctional project teams, there can be an inclination to avoid communicating new information on the grounds that it may not be in your self-interest. The prevailing culture is often set by the ethos and practices of the owning organisation.

Example 11.3 – Professional culture based on open communication

The author's career in project and risk management started at Ferranti Computer Systems Ltd. Ferranti had a well-founded reputation as being a company in which there was a constructive professional culture based on open communication. The fundamental question asked of members of staff conducting job interviews was 'Would you like to work with the interviewee?' Working at Ferranti, it was noticeable that customers would comment favourably on its openness and performance relative to competitors. This is not to say that everything went to plan. However, when Ferranti worked alongside other companies on the same projects, it was often able to take advantage of their lack internal communication.

In the author's experience, the overwhelming majority of people who work on projects, at all levels in an organisation, are willing to work hard to make them a success. However, this goodwill can be eroded if people lose confidence that others are willing to make the same effort as they are. Sometimes the causes of this can be as simple as the existence of unrealistic expectations. Perhaps the most common point of breakdown occurs between different levels of management.

Inevitably, managers involved with projects face a dilemma when setting objectives. Since, by definition, every project is unique, projects know that some, if not all, activity estimates are subjective; there is uncertainty about their realistic duration values. Managers are also aware that if project teams are given easy targets, they will tend to do no better than meet those targets. This is predicted by Parkinson's Law which states that 'work expands so as to fill the time available for its completion'. Another of Parkinson's maxims, 'expenditure rises to meet income', describes why the same effect also applies to costs. However, setting unrealistically optimistic objectives can also be a mistake. Attempts by a project to achieve unrealistic objectives can be counterproductive as the adverse consequences of short cuts start to unfold and team morale suffers from the routine occurrence of failure. Unrealistic objectives also foster a culture of short-termism and the denial of inconvenient risks and issues. In turn this leads to a loss of trust between the people involved. Setting objectives that are either too easy or too difficult to achieve are thus both errors of management strategy.

Given that the cost and/or duration for a piece of project work may be uncertain, it makes sense for a manager to set a target at the optimistic end of the plausible range of outcomes. To do otherwise would spurn the opportunity of efficient performance. However, when doing this, the manager should recognise that the target is not unlikely to be missed. Failure to recognise this will put the team under unfair and, potentially, counterproductive pressure. In return for recognising this, the team should do two things. First, they should be willing to work towards the target and achieve it or get as close to it as possible. Second, they should commit to complete work within a specified longer period of time and/or higher cost, with a very low probability of failure to deliver on this commitment. The gap between the manager's target and the team's commitment can be managed as risk.

Chapman and Ward (2002), identify distinguishing between targets, commitments and expected outcomes as being an important benefit of risk management. Effective risk management can thus become part of the solution for fostering trust within projects. Of course, as the presence of Question F2 (see above) in the RMM indicates, trust is also a key enabler of effective risk management. One of the arts of good management is to ensure that trust is not lost in the first place. This question will be applicable to any project with a project team of two or more people.

Question F3: Climate of Trust with Stakeholders

Is risk management fostered by a good climate of trust between stakeholders?	
E	Not applicable.
D	Some stakeholders are reluctant to divulge new information on risks. Previous experience may have shown that it is counterproductive to their interests.
C	All stakeholders are open in the disclosure of new information on many risks, but fail to divulge relevant information in other cases. The motivation in such cases may be related to commercial advantage or covering up shortcomings.
B	All stakeholders are open in their disclosure of new information on most relevant risks, but careful not to disclose significant information in specific cases on matters affected by legitimate issues of commercial confidentiality.
A	There is a climate of trust such that all risk information relevant to the project and its stakeholders can be disclosed as a matter of mutual interest.
Perspectives affected: Risk Management Culture and Stakeholders	

Issues affecting trust between stakeholders are important to the effectiveness of risk management for much the same reasons as they are within a project team. However, the consequences of mistrust between stakeholders can be even more pronounced and intractable. As with relations within project teams, conflation of targets and commitments is a frequent underlying cause of mistrust. This is particularly so when the project includes contracted sub-projects placed after a competitive tendering process.

Contracting strategy may cause difficulties establishing trust. For example, it could be against the interests of competing contractors to disclose risks. Open disclosure of risks during a tendering process may cause a client to choose another (less scrupulous) contractor. After contract award, disclosure of risks can still be against a contractor's commercial interest. Even if they default on their own obligations, circumstances may arise in which the client or another party is obliged to fund project delays. The case in Example 11.4 is one that the author heard of 20 years ago. Whilst some details in the story might be apocryphal, it does illustrate how contracting practice can influence openness of risk disclosure.

Example 11.4 – Missile flight trials

The development of a missile system involved a number of projects to develop related subsystems. When the missile was undergoing early flight trials, contractors were required to monitor their systems during the launch countdown. Each contractor was supplied with a button to be pressed in the event that the countdown should be stopped. However, pressing the button carried a financial penalty, burdening the offending contractor with the full cost consequences of trials delay.

At the first flight trial, most contractors knew that their system was not sufficiently reliable to proceed with the flight. Nevertheless, they all continued with the countdown in the hope that another contractor would stop the launch first. As the countdown proceeded, tension mounted. All parties knew that when the countdown reached ten seconds to go, the launch reached a point of no return. It rapidly dawned on everyone that timing the button press was going to prove to be a critical skill. Between the counts of eleven and ten several buttons were pushed surreptitiously. The launch was stopped and the unlucky contractor who had made electrical contact first was announced. The others were able to make a claim for contract change.

Project clients need to know about contractor-sourced risks that could impact upon their own control of the project. Knowledge of risks and their implications is important to making correct contracting choices. It also helps the project to respond to risks that emerge during project delivery. Despite this, in many cases, it is fair to observe that project clients get the degree of openness of risk disclosure that their contracting strategy deserves. Simply asking for a risk register is often insufficient.

Following contract award, it is not uncommon for the client to become aware that risks effects have emerged that were foreseeable at the time of contract award, but not disclosed. The reaction of the client is then important to the future effectiveness of the risk management process. Example 11.5 illustrates an occasion on which the client's reaction to bad news was counterproductive.

Example 11.5 – A client that mandated irrationally detailed planning

On a project to develop and manufacture a complex and technically advanced defence electronics system, the client became increasingly frustrated by schedule delays. These delays were attributable to the contractor's failure to manage a number of technical design risks effectively. However, the contractor had failed to disclose these risks and their effects. As a consequence, the client concluded that the poor schedule performance was due to the contractor's inability to plan. In response the client threatened to cancel the contract if the contractor did not produce a detailed 'inch stone' schedule with all work broken down to tasks lasting a maximum of a few days.

The contractor produced the detailed schedule as demanded. However, the effort of doing so distracted the project team thus producing further delays. Furthermore, the ongoing effects of unmanaged risks meant that the schedule was unworkable. In effect, the level of planning detail implied unrealistic degrees of certainty about what was possible. Internally, everyone working for the contractor knew this and coped by ignoring the schedule. The primary purpose of the project planning process then became one of maintaining a work of fiction that satisfied the client's appetite for detail. Project performance declined further, as did trust between the two parties. In the meantime, risks causing these problems remained unmanaged.

In contrast to the above example, other projects have transformed their working relationships with clients by being more open about the implications of risk. The same can be said for relationships with other stakeholders. The discussion above that accompanies this question focuses on the client–contractor relationship because that is often the one that is most fraught. However, the RMM assessor should take into account other stakeholders relationships as well. The selected answer should reflect conditions as they affect the weakest relationship.

Since all projects have at least one stakeholder (for example, the sponsor for an internal project) this question should always be applicable.

Question F4: Risk Management Plans

	Is there an appropriate risk management plan that is used in practice?
E	Not applicable. (The project is small and conforms to a generic type, allowing it to adopt a standard risk management plan specified by its owning organisation.)
D	There is no project-specific risk management plan.
C	There is a project risk management plan. However, EITHER This is inadequately tailored to the project; OR Practice on the project is significantly at variance with the plan.
B	The project's practice is mostly consistent with its risk management plan. However some people involved may either be insufficiently aware of its contents or fail to provide sufficient support to the process.
A	The risk management plan has been tailored appropriately to the purpose and context of the project. Risk management practice is consistent with the plan.
	Perspectives affected: Risk Management Culture

Many projects maintain a document called a risk management plan. This plan is a project-specific explanation of the risk management process for anyone who needs to know. As with all plans its scope is neatly summarised by the following lines from Rudyard Kipling's *Just-So Stories*.

I keep six honest serving men
(They taught me all I knew);
Their names are What and Why and When
And How and Where and Who.

As with all aspects of project management, it is difficult to defend not having a plan. If something is worth doing, it is worth thinking through the associated purposes, means and logistics. Equally, however, it is all too easy to spend too much time on planning and too little on doing. Many projects plan to an irrationally low level of detail. In risk management, one should expect the purpose and details of the process to evolve through the project life cycle, so the plan should have sufficient flexibility for this to be allowed to happen. A frequent problem with risk management plans is that they focus on the minutiae of procedure rather than explain how and when the process's products will add value by supporting decisions.

Example 11.6 – A culture of planning rather than doing

A new recruit to a consultancy company had previously worked in an organisation that was one of the consultancy company's major customers. When asked about their experience of risk management in this organisation, the new recruit found it difficult to comment. In effect, they said, so much effort was spent in developing and authorising risk management plans that projects took a long time to start implementing the process. Moreover, other priorities then often took over, with the result that risk management was never implemented as planned.

Another problem with risk management plans is that the actual process is not conducted as planned. There is little point in making a plan and then ignoring it. Whether or not the risk management process is conducted as planned may depend upon wider organisational and national cultural influences. In the USA, for example, there is often stricter adherence to process than in the UK. Nevertheless, it is also important for a project to review the value of its process and make changes where it makes sense to do so. What is required is a plan that fosters the right behaviours and underpins a process that is light on procedures but rich on intelligence. The best plans are short, concise and accessible to all the people that they affect.

Most project-based organisations will have centralised risk management guidance. In the absence of this, reference can always be made to standard guides. There should therefore be no need to pad out a risk management plan with theory. Instead, thought needs to be given to how the risk management process is tailored to the purposes and circumstances of the project. Key aspects of a risk management plan may include:

- Purpose of the process – particular benefits to the project,
- linkage between project decision points and the management of risk,
- risk management roles and responsibilities,
- risk management products, their purposes and their audience,
- reference to selected tools and techniques, with project-specific explanations of adaptation where appropriate, and
- interaction with other project stakeholders and other project management functions, including implications for planning and contract management.

In order to select any answer better than D to Question F4, there must be a risk management plan tailored to the purposes and circumstances of the project. Reliance on a homogeneous centralised process or procedure takes the brain away from the project-specific problems at hand. The risk management plan does not have to be long. At the outset of a project it might comprise a simple statement about the scope of a first cycle of the process. Even later, and on large projects, it should be possible to read in 10–15 minutes. As with all plans, a key test is whether or not people working on the project actually use it; and this is a good indication of the team's risk management culture.

Selecting the B answer is conditional on most project team members acting in accordance with the risk management plan. Barriers to all team members doing so may include lack of time or understanding of the process. Selecting the A answer is conditional on overcoming such barriers and thus securing the engagement of project team members with a role to play in the process. It is also conditional on the risk management plan being tailored appropriately to the project's purpose and context. In practice, this should mean that the risk management plan evolves as the project progresses through different phases.

Some projects may be sufficiently small and low risk for it to be sufficient for them to refer out to their organisation's risk management guidance in lieu of producing a project-specific risk management plan. However, since all projects are unique, even small projects may benefit from tailoring such guidance for their own purposes. Project risk management plans do not have to be long-winded: just project-specific. This question should therefore be applicable in most cases.

Question F5: Early Use of Risk Management

From what point did the project risk management process commence?	
E	Not applicable. (The point at which risk management commenced no longer influences project culture.)
D	The use of risk management was only considered when the project was in difficulty or when it was imposed by senior management.
C	Risk management is used during the main project implementation phase(s).
B	Risk management was used from the point of project team formation.
A	Risk management commenced from the point at which the need for the project was identified.
Perspectives affected: Risk Management Culture, Stakeholders and Risk Identification	

The greatest benefits of risk management usually occur during the earliest phases of a project. This is when the significance of known unknowns it at its greatest. As described in Chapters 2 and 3 (see pp. 20–26 and pp. 37–56), risk management can be used to resolve questions of project strategy and to establish realistic targets for objectives. Once these matters have been settled and the project is in its implementation phase, the risk management process tends to tackle risks at a lower level.

However, effective risk management during the earlier phases of a project is often more conceptually demanding. Most people find it easier to identify and assess risks in the context of a project with stable objectives and defined stakeholder obligations. But these are luxuries that usually do not exist at the point of a project's conception. Hence the willingness of an organisation to engage in the risk management process from the outset is a good test of its risk management culture. The fact that this is the point at which the process may add the greatest value makes Question F5 doubly important. Selecting the A answer is dependent upon risk management commencing at the earliest opportunity, thus allowing it to influence plans for the concept phase.

Commencing risk management at the earliest opportunity is likely to be dependent on the project sponsor being actively engaged in the process; another indicator of good risk management culture. An alternative, as represented by the B answer, is to wait until the project team starts to become formed. Deferring the process until this point would be common practice, but indicative of a project sponsor's expectation that the management of project risk is a responsibility that can be fully delegated. Moreover, the project team may not take shape until later in the concept or definition phases.

The C and D answers to Question F5 are both indicative of an organisation that uses risk management primarily as a tactical approach to keeping projects on plan. Delaying the process to the implementation phase neglects the value that risk management can add to project strategy decisions. It also engages stakeholders in the process at a point when it is too late for them to make a fundamental difference. However, there may be cases of very long projects, where selecting either of these answers would have been true at one time but which is now an unfair reflection of the project culture. Hence for projects in the implementation phase that have used a risk management process for long enough for it to become well-embedded, this question might be deemed not applicable.

Question F6: Recognition for Good Risk Management Practice

What is the project's approach to individuals responsible for the management of risks?	
E	Not applicable.
D	There is no active recognition or support for good risk management practice.
C	Good risk management practice is sometimes recognised by the management, or within the project team, but this tends to be only on occasions on which it has achieved marked success.
B	There is a healthy regard for risk management within the project team. This can, at least in part, be attributed to support from the project leadership.
A	Good risk management practice promotes project team morale and is actively rewarded by management, even when the outcome is less than ideal.
Perspectives affected: Risk Management Culture	

Outstandingly effective project risk management processes seem to be invariably led by project sponsors and project managers who provide active and overt support. Active engagement by these people bolsters their own confidence in the process and demonstrates their belief in its importance to other members of the project team.

Example 11.7 – Engaging a project director in the process

When a new risk process manager was appointed to a £multi-billion project, the project director asked how they could help improve the process. The new risk process manager asked for them to do two things. The first was to take personal ownership of at least one risk (of their choice) from the risk register. The second was to approach senior members of the project team from time to time to discuss the management of any particular risk that they owned.

The project director became more familiar with both the process and the risk register. They also discovered that ad hoc risk discussions with senior team members often revealed interesting information. From the risk process manager's perspective, the payoff was that a culture of interest in risk information was passed downwards through the management team.

Since risk management concerns uncertainty, there is no guarantee that any decision will prove to have been the best when looked at with the benefit of hindsight. Selecting the A answer to Question F6 is conditional on management supporting people implementing the process even if some of its outcomes are less than ideal.

In contrast, the benefits of decisions made in respect of known knowns are predictable and easy to account for. Reliance on the certainties that these decisions bring can impair commitment to the risk management process. Selecting the B answer would indicate that the project team understands this dilemma, and supports risk management accordingly. In practice they need management support to do so. Since a project manager needs the support of the project sponsor, this includes even the smallest projects. Question F6 is therefore always applicable.

Question F7: Recognition of the Value of Risk Taking

What is the project's record in respect of the acceptance of risk?	
E	Not applicable.
D	EITHER The management style is dominated by a defensive ethos aimed at the minimisation of mistakes; OR The project takes excessive risks and fails to manage them adequately.
C	Opportunities intended to improve the project outcome may have been taken. However, the decisions involved are often taken independently of the risk management process, even if they could have significant risk implications.
B	There is evidence of opportunities being taken to enhance the project outcome. Decisions to accept such opportunities usually take into account a risk assessment of the implications. This may (but does not have to) be achieved by the maintenance of opportunities data within the risk register.
A	Opportunities for the improvement of expected project outcome are actively sought. Such opportunities may increase the project's exposure to variance in outcome but are adopted when risk analysis shows that, on average, outcome can be improved.
Perspectives affected: Risk Management Culture	

It is easy to perceive project risk as being undesirable. It is then but a short mental step to believe that it would be desirable to authorise and deliver projects with zero risk. The evidence that an organisation had achieved this would be that it was able to deliver all projects precisely as planned. Each project's products would be delivered to the intended quality, and cost and schedule overruns would be eliminated. Would this state of affairs be desirable?

For most organisations, eliminating risk from projects is not an option. Commercial organisations are usually subject to pressures of competition. They would not wish to authorise projects with the contingencies required to gain absolute assurance that cost overruns were impossible. Government and other not-for-profit organisations are also usually reluctant to do this, due to limited financial resources combined with aspirations to deliver more projects than they can afford. Most organisations are similarly under time pressure and therefore set tight project timescale objectives with minimal schedule contingencies. Finally, organisations are inclined to specify ambitious targets for project products. The least risky projects are often not the ones with the best potential to drive organisational productivity or growth. Hence, project risk is often not only inevitable, but is also, to an extent, desirable.

However, organisations that manage to deliver almost all projects to time and cost can be found. Usually, they are shielded in some way from the effects of competition. Alternatively, they might have a management that is so aggressively intolerant of any project overrun that project managers would not dare to accept risk. Thus, the question as to whether or not a zero risk approach is an effective way to run projects is still relevant. Example 11.8 illustrates the consequences of using this approach.

Example 11.8 – An organisation that delivered all projects to time and cost

A large national organisation divided its operations into a number of regions each with its own management. In order to maintain operations, a number of different types of project had to be implemented in order keep the organisation's infrastructure updated and reliable. Each year, regional managers were required to plan these projects in detail in order to secure central authorisation for the funding involved. Their performance was then judged on whether or not the projects were delivered within budget. Regional managers also knew that the budgets authorised each year set a precedent that anchored central management's expectations in the subsequent year and were therefore motivated to submit expensive project plans. Central management was well aware of this; its requirement for detailed plans was driven by a desire to verify whether or not all costs were justified.

Unfortunately, regional managers lacked sufficient internal resources to cope with the planning burden. They coped by persuading contractors to contribute to the planning effort free of charge. Over the years, these contractors became skilled at presenting plans that were acceptable to management yet contained unnecessarily high contingencies. The same contractors were subsequently employed to deliver the projects on cost-plus terms. Unsurprisingly, all projects were delivered on budget. Equally unsurprisingly, the overall project portfolio was very expensive given the work involved.

In a capitalist economy, commercial organisations take risk to make money for their shareholders. Profits and growth are, to some extent, a reward for taking risk. The value of risk is also recognised in the pricing of financial products. In the long term, the financial return on more volatile financial products such as shares is expected to be higher than the return on more predictable products such as government bonds. Thus, the commercial world treats risk as having desirable properties. In principle, project risk should be no different; riskier projects might be justified on the basis of delivering, on average, better returns. For the same reasons, projects with zero risk are liable to be economically inefficient.

However, experience shows that taking too much or unnecessary risk can be a serious mistake. At a macro-economic level, the 2007 credit crunch and its consequent recession are a reminder of this fact. This seems to be a lesson that societies have to relearn periodically. In project management, it sometimes seems to be a lesson that is being learned continuously. Thus, taking either too little risk or excessive risk is a sign of an immature risk management culture. Should a project be taking either of these approaches, the D answer should be selected for Question F7.

Assuming that the project does not fit either of the D answer criteria, the answer selected for this question will depend upon the way in which the risk implications of opportunities are handled. The use of opportunities to manage improvements to the project outcome is evidence of a good project management culture. However, incorporating opportunities into a project plan often alters the project's risk exposure. Opportunities should therefore be accepted if the risk implications are acceptable, but rejected if they are not.

As used by this question, the word 'opportunity' should be interpreted broadly. The intention of the Project RMM is not to mandate the formal inclusion of opportunities in the risk register, although this might be helpful in certain circumstances. Rather, the word opportunity refers to any action, decision or outcome that would, or would have the potential, to improve project performance. If, in practice, there is inadequate linkage between the management of such opportunities and the risk management process, then the answer selected for this question should be no better than C.

From an opportunity management perspective, the most fruitful periods of a project are usually the phases prior to the main project authorisation point. These tend to be the periods during which alternative project solutions are considered and project strategy decisions made. Project plans are honed to capitalise on the increasingly detailed understanding of the project built up by the project team. By both inclination and their sponsor's insistence, most project managers will plan for success rather than plan to accommodate failure. Opportunities for project enhancement are thus naturally built into a project's plans during the earliest phases of its life cycle. A formal opportunities register may help with this process, but is not essential. What matters is that project risk is analysed and managed effectively as plans for the project are developed.

After the main project authorisation point, opportunities for project enhancement may still exist. There may be a number of ways in which this can be handled, any of which could be reasonably interpreted as contributing towards the selection of the A answer to this question. A common approach is to maintain a risk register that includes both threats and opportunities. This provides a risk-by-risk approach to mitigating threats and capitalising on opportunities. Clearly, this approach includes the explicit management of opportunities. However, the potential to mitigate threats can be also interpreted as being a form of opportunity in the wider sense of the word. In order to select the A answer to Question F7, the RMM Assessor would have to be satisfied that due account was taken of secondary effects of responses to both threats and opportunities.

In practice, many projects running a threats and opportunities risk register find that their opportunities are heavily outnumbered by threats. There may be a number of reasons for this, particularly after the main project approval point. First, the imposition of tight timescales and budgets may leave only limited opportunities for improvement. In effect, work done during the concept and definition stages would have already resulted in opportunities having been built into plans. Second, subsequent to project approval, stakeholders may become resistant to the idea of exploiting opportunities. For example, a contractor identifying opportunities may discover their customer reluctant to find additional funding.

When collecting RMM data an assessor therefore needs to judge what may be a reasonable ratio of threats to opportunities. This judgement should take into account where the project is in its life cycle, the overall difficulty of meeting its targets and the nature of any commercial arrangements that are in place.

Example 11.9 – An opportunity register that the customer preferred to ignore

As part of the scope of a large project delivered under contract to a customer, the contractor had been contractually required to maintain a formal risk register. As the end of the implementation phase approached, the contractor suggested augmenting what had been a threat-orientated risk register with opportunities. The customer encouraged this initiative as they were aware that the formal management of opportunities in risk registers was increasingly being recognised to be good practice.

However, when the customer saw the opportunities identified by the contractor, they immediately realised that there was an underlying commercial agenda. Accepting any of the opportunities was dependent upon customer funding. In most cases, the opportunities were product enhancements for which the contractor had solutions ready to hand, but was demanding a high price. In other cases, the opportunities were simply commercial arguments supporting contract changes for product performance already delivered. Thus none of the opportunities appealed to the customer; a weakness that was fatal to the prospects of any being accepted.

An alternative approach to managing opportunities in the context of risk management is to recognise that, in many cases, the range of potential outcomes implied by a risk can include both positive and negative effects. The bridge project first pass risk analysis described in Chapter 3 (see pp. 41–4) can be used as an example to illustrate this. One of the risks in this example was the time that would be required between 'time now' and the commencement of bridge operations: the point at which the revenue stream would commence. The most optimistic estimate for this time was three years and the most pessimistic, seven years. A uniform probability distribution was assumed on the prudent basis that any period of time between these dates might be equally possible. Figure 11.1 illustrates the probability distribution.

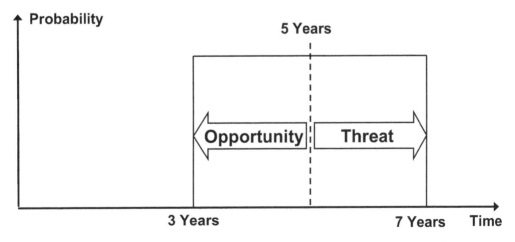

Figure 11.1 Example of a risk that includes both threat and opportunity

Figure 11.1 also illustrates how the probability distribution includes the implications of both threat and opportunity. It should be borne in mind that, since this is part of a first pass analysis, the risk is a composite of many risks that would be identified later. Drawing a threat/opportunity boundary through the distribution at its mean value of five years can therefore be criticised as being arbitrary. However this should not distract from the main point, which is to recall that when combined in an analysis with other risks, the implications of all schedule risks are taken into account regardless of whether future target setting results in them being defined as threats or opportunities.

A project using a top-down quantitative approach to risk analysis should thus be able to understand the risk implications of opportunities and accept them where it is rational to do so. This meets the criteria required to select the A answer to Question F7. In particular, it should be noted that application of Chapman and Ward's risk efficiency principle (see Chapter 2, p. 24) lends itself to this approach.

Whatever approach is used for risk management this question should apply to all projects, save perhaps for an exceptional case in which the sponsor cannot tolerate any failure to achieve all objectives.

Question F8: Lead time to Implement Risk Responses

How consistently does the project implement timely responses to risk?	
E	Not applicable.
D	EITHER Risk responses tend to be based on rapid decisions based on a weak understanding of the alternatives; OR Delays between risk identification and the implementation of responses renders many potential responses ineffective.
C	The lead time to implement risk responses is sometimes, but often not appropriate to optimising their effectiveness.
B	Most risk responses are implemented without unnecessary delays.
A	Risk responses are consistently implemented within a time that reflects a sound balance between the benefits to project schedule control and the benefits arising from insights created by risk identification and analysis and associated decision making processes.
Perspectives affected: Risk Management Culture and Risk Responses	

A simple thought experiment can be used as an analogy to explain the rationale behind this question. Imagine driving a car which had an inbuilt two-second delay that affected all controls. For example, the front wheels would not turn until two seconds after the steering wheel had been rotated. Similarly, the brake pedal would have to be depressed two seconds before the brakes started taking effect. Whilst it would be possible to drive such a car, the experience would be deeply unsettling. Although the timescales involved on projects are much longer, delays between deciding to do something and actually doing it often reduce the action's effectiveness. This is frequently an issue that reduces the effectiveness of risk responses.

Following the above argument, it might be easy to believe that any identified action should be implemented with the minimum of delay. However, ill-considered actions are often counterproductive. The car analogy can also be used to illustrate this point. The safest driving strategies involve creating sufficient thinking time to identify and analyse circumstances as they evolve. In some situations this involves understanding alternative courses of action in advance. In contrast, driving at high speed close behind another car distracts attention from more peripheral sources of risk. The need for emergency responses becomes more likely and some may prove to be not well-judged. Of course one can also take the defensive driving idea too far and make poor decisions or become too slow (and hence a danger to other traffic) as a consequence of over-analysis.

A similar principle applies to risk management; it is important to identify the right risks and analyse their implications before taking action. It is also important to conduct risk identification and analysis efficiently and to avoid over-analysis. Hence, although Question F8 might at first appear to concern risk responses only, it should be understood in the context of the overall risk management process. Given the circumstances of the project, is the time taken to transfer from a situation of risks being identifiable to implementing responses appropriate?

Selecting the appropriate answer to this question will depend upon the RMM assessor being able to make a reasonable subjective judgement. The circumstances of different projects are so varied that it would be unwise to suggest any rule of thumb for what constitutes a reasonable period of time to allow for analysis and decision making. Moreover, the context of risk analysis changes from one phase to another. For example, during the definition phase, the risk management process might undertake cycles that are phased in with the iterative development of implementation phase plans. Many risk responses would then comprise amendments to these plans or associated commercial agreements. Appropriate timeliness of response implementation could hence be judged by whether or not the planning, commercial and risk management processes were synchronised. In contrast, during the implementation phase the emphasis on risk management might be more heavily weighted towards the tactical control of individual risks. The response timeliness to emerging risks would then be driven by issues such as the frequency and effectiveness of risk reviews and the performance of risk owners. Example 11.10 is taken from the implementation phase of a project. In most respects this project had an exceptionally mature risk management process. However, misjudgements made by the risk owner in the case of this example affected the response timeliness.

Example 11.10 – Response to an emerging risk during ship construction

During the construction of a ship, a new risk was identified by fitters with the new design being used for pipe couplings. They had realised that if the problems that they were experiencing could not be corrected, and that if more pipes continued to be manufactured, then there would be major delays and rework. Supervising engineers alerted the risk process manager promptly and a risk was immediately entered into the risk register. However, the risk owner underestimated the level of risk. Thus although the senior project management team became aware of the risk, they failed to appreciate its severity. The risk owner also failed to take sufficient early action to mitigate the risk's effects to the extent that they could have been. The risk had a significant impact on the ship's date of introduction into service.

Question F8 encompasses a range of issues about the capability of the risk management process and how these issues could be different from one project to another. However the common underlying issue concerns whether or not relevant members of the project team manage risks collectively. Delays in identifying risks, understanding their implications to the overall project, identifying effective responses at the right level of management and then implementing these responses in a timely manner can all impair the process's effectiveness. These actions are often carried out by different people, thus making a wide appreciation of risk management and communication on risks important to success. This question is therefore a key test of risk management culture. It is also a test that large projects with complex management structures may find it particularly difficult to score well on.

This question should be applicable to any project on which timeliness and efficiency are issues. It is hard to conceive of any project for which this would not be the case.

Typical Actions for Improvement

This section provides guidance for the identification of process improvement actions related to the risk management culture perspective. The tone for project culture is led from the top management level in the project and sometimes from a level above. Thus actions for improvement usually have to address management issues at a senior level. Whilst actions such as the training of project team members are helpful, their effects will be limited unless the process receives overt and constructive management support.

A common source of difficulty for risk management lies in the unrealistic expectations of project sponsors and other senior management personnel involved in project approvals processes. In practice, the risk associated with projects is often greater than is acknowledged in their business cases. Typically, an organisation's system for governing projects adjusts for this by setting risk-averse project approval criteria. In such an environment, if a project does include a realistic risk analysis in its business case, senior management may react counterproductively. Projects that have made realistic risk-based forecasts are liable to be closed or made to rework their plans. The result is a vicious circle in which effective risk identification and analysis is squeezed out by internal politics. Breaking this circle requires actions such as:

- Project risk management training for senior managers,
- development of models for project risk based on previous projects,
- introducing measures making sponsors accountable for benefits realisation, and
- formal management of project strategy risks owned at the appropriate level of management.

Immediately below management levels with governance direction responsibilities, the project manager is the key figure for establishing a sound risk management culture. Actions that the project manager can take to help in this respect include:

- Helping to shape the design of the risk management process,
- sponsoring reviews of risk management process capability,
- owning risks in their own right,
- chairing project risk reviews,
- rewarding good risk management practice, and
- enquiring informally about the status of risks and responses to them.

The risk manager also has an important influence on risk management culture. In order to exert this influence, they need credibility as being both a specialist in the field of risk management and having experience of the type of project work involved. Risk management requires insight, experience and flair, but is a somewhat specialist career choice. Organisations with weak project risk management resources may need to consider the career development implications for people making this choice in order to attract people with the qualities that are required.

Finally, it should be remembered that commercial strategy has an important effect on risk management culture. Failures of contracting parties to disclose risk or manage risk constructively are often the consequence of inappropriate risk transfer or a lack of mutual interest in the risk outcome. Correcting this requires a contracts solution.

Appendix A
Attributes of Risk Maturity Model Levels

Taken from Hillson, D. 1997. Towards a risk maturity model. *International Journal of Project and Business Risk Management*, Volume 1, Issue 1, March.

	Level 1 – Naïve	Level 2 – Novice	Level 3 – Normalised	Level 4 – Natural
Definition	Unaware of the need for management of risk. No structured approach to dealing with uncertainty. Repetitive and reactive management processes. Little or no attempt to learn from past or to prepare for future.	Experimenting with risk management, through a small number of individuals. No generic structured approach in place. Aware of potential benefits of managing risk, but ineffective implementation, not gaining full benefits.	Management of risk built into routine business processes. Risk management implemented on most or all projects. Formalised generic risk processes. Benefits understood at all levels of the organisation, although not always consistently achieved.	Risk-aware culture, with proactive approach to risk management in all aspects of the business. Active use of risk information to improve business processes and gain competitive advantage. Emphasis on opportunity management ('positive risk').
Culture	No risk awareness. Resistant/Reluctant to change. Tendency to continue with existing processes.	Risk process may be viewed as additional overhead with variable benefits. Risk management only used on selected projects.	Accepted policy for risk management. Benefits recognised and expected. Prepared to commit resources in order to reap gains.	Top-down commitment to risk management, with leadership by example. Proactive risk management encouraged and rewarded.
Process	No formal processes.	No generic formal processes, although some specific formal methods may be in use. Process effectiveness depends heavily on the skills of the in-house risk team and availability of external support.	Generic processes applied to most projects. Formal processes, incorporated into quality system. Active allocation and management of risk budgets at all levels. Limited need for external support.	Risk-based business processes. 'Total Risk Management' permeating entire business. Regular refreshing and updating of processes. Routine risk metrics with consistent feedback for improvement.
Experience	No understanding of risk principles or language.	Limited to individuals who may have had little or no formal training.	In-house core of expertise, formally trained in basic skills. Development of specific processes and tools.	All staff risk-aware and using basic skills. Learning from experience as part of the process. Regular external training to enhance skills.
Application	No structured application. No dedicated resources. No risk tools.	Inconsistent application. Variable availability of staff. Ad hoc collection of tools and methods.	Routine and consistent application to all projects. Committed resources. Integrated set of tools and methods.	Second-nature, applied to all activities. Risk-based reporting and decision making. State-of-the-art tools and methods.

Appendix B
Project Risk Management Principles

The following list of 12 principles is offered to readers as a checklist to identify significant gaps in their risk management process. Whilst not all Project Risk Maturity Model (RMM) questions apply to all projects, these principles should do so. Thus, this list may serve as a useful supplement to the Project RMM. It also provides readers with short summary of what, in the author's opinion matters most about a project risk management process.

1. Risk management is concerned with the implications of uncertainty

Uncertainty in this context means lack of certainty. This principle helps to define the concept of what is meant by the terms 'a risk' and 'overall project risk'.

A project is risky if its outcomes are uncertain and if the extent of this lack of certainty matters. A risk can be described as being any aspect of the project or its environment that contributes towards its overall level of risk.

2. Risk management matters most during the earliest phases of a project

This principle follows on from the first. Uncertainty tends to reduce as a project progresses through its life cycle, so it follows that risk management's greatest potential to add value should occur in the earliest phases. One implication is that the risk management process should be capable of influencing the project objectives as they become firmed up into specific targets and commitments.

3. The risk management process should ensure that the most important sources of uncertainty are investigated first so that they become a focus for discovering more detailed risk insights

This principle indicates that a multi-pass process is required, at least in the initial stages. Failure to do so frequently results in a detailed but fragmented list of risks that lacks the breadth to cover some of the most important sources of risk and lacks a structure that allows the project to gain those insights that can make the most telling contribution to decision making.

4. The purpose of risk analysis is to support decisions

Risk analysis that does not support decision making is a waste of time. The decisions involved may range from strategic choices (for example, project go/no go decisions) through to the selection of treatments for individual risks. Decisions are also likely to include prioritisation and escalation of risks and risk responses.

5. The most effective risk treatments tend to be those that tackle risks at source

In project risk management prevention is usually better than cure. The primary purpose of risk assessment is to create an understanding that leads to effective risk treatment. It follows that risk assessment should have a strong source-orientated basis.

6. To quantify overall project risk one has to understand both source and impact

The relationship between sources of risks and their impacts may be complex; one cannot construct rational models for analysis unless the most important features of such complexity are understood. This usually involves including a top-down element to the development of any analysis and is another reason why a multi-pass process is usually best practice.

7. All the components of the core risk management process are essential to its overall effectiveness

The various guides and standards available have tended to coalesce around a similar core standard that involves 1) establishing context, 2) risk identification, 3) risk analysis, 4) planning of risk responses, 5) implementation of risk responses and 6) management of the process including the use of reviews. If any of these components are omitted, the overall process may be totally ineffective. For example, if you don't implement the decisions made as a consequence of the process, any amount of risk identification, analysis and reviews will be a waste of time.

8. There should be clarity about the ownership of responsibility

This really applies to any process; if individuals are not clear about their responsibilities, things tend not to get done. Risk owners and the people responsible for taking action to treat risks need to be identified and must know what is expected of them. Commercial or organisation ownership of risk is also an important issue.

9. Leadership by the project sponsor and project manager is essential to the health of the process

Overt support for the process from the most senior managers is critical. Risk management is about acting on the things that could make the most difference to the project outcome. The senior project personnel need to be active in their management of risk rather than simply being the recipients of reports on risks from other people.

10. The elicitation processes for risk estimates should counter prevailing sources of bias

Risk estimates are affected by the project environment and by the effects of heuristics. Structured techniques can be used to counter some of these effects. However, in circumstances where bias is not unlikely, the use of independent advice should be considered prior to major project decisions.

11. A culture of open communication on risk is essential

Open communication is about people taking the trouble to communicate information to others when they need to know. It is also about being willing to discuss difficult issues realistically. Risks often concern inconvenient truths, which, if hidden or suppressed, cause more damage than they need to have done.

12. Risk management must add value to the project and complement its other core processes

Data used to define or organise a project lies in the domain of processes such as requirements management and planning; these are core processes that risk management should be seeking to assist with decisions but not be seeking to replace.

Appendix C
Governance of Project Management

In 2004, the Association for Project Management (APM) published the guide *Directing Change: A Guide to Governance of Project Management*, (GoPM Specific Interest Group). The guide describes the governance of project management as concerning those areas of corporate governance that are specifically related to project activities. Some aspects of corporate governance guidance and legislation are explicitly related to risk. For example, the Sarbanes–Oxley Act (SOX), which applies to companies with shares listed publicly in the USA, regulates risk associated with the accuracy of financial reports to shareholders. For companies listed on the London Stock Exchange, the Turnbull Guidance is recommended by the Combined Code as a risk-based approach to internal control.

However, prior to the publication of *Directing Change*, there had been a gap between the disciplines of corporate governance and project management. For example, the Sarbanes–Oxley Act, its associated accounting standard and the Turnbull Guidance all fail to distinguish between project and non-project activities. Similarly, project management standards such as the bodies of knowledge published by the APM and the Project Management Institute had failed to make adequate connections with corporate governance principles. Since projects should only exist if they align with the purposes of the organisations that own them, this was a significant gap. Figure C.1 illustrates the space filled by governance of project management.

Figure C.1   Governance of Project Management (APM 2004)

Project-related risk can have significant corporate implications. In the case of contractors, the majority of the organisation's business is often project-based. Even organisations whose main purpose or business is dominated by non-project operations are usually reliant on significant projects to deliver change. In both cases, the implications of project risk may have to be managed at the board level. In some cases, the existence of an organisation may hinge on project performance. Given this, the Project Risk Maturity Model (RMM) has been designed to take the significance of corporate governance into account. Whilst corporate governance requirements such as the Turnbull Guidance have provided important input, the APM's governance of project management guidance has been used to fill in some of the project-specific detail.

Directing Change contains 11 principles applicable to the governance of any organisation's portfolio of projects. A number of these can be related to the strategic use of project approval points. As described in Chapter 4 (see pp. 70–71), the Project RMM can be used as a means to provide assurance as to whether or not risk-based information provided to project approval authorities is reliable. Further to this, *Directing Change* identifies the governance of project management as having four components:

1. Project Portfolio direction,
2. Project Sponsorship,
3. Project Management – effectiveness and efficiency, and
4. Disclosure and reporting.

The typical hierarchical relationship between these components within an organisation is illustrated in Figure C.2. The Project RMM does not address project portfolio direction directly since it has been designed to assess individual projects. However, as illustrated in Chapter 4 (see pp. 71–2), if the RMM is used to assess multiple projects it may contribute towards the governance of a project portfolio. The RMM also addresses each of the other three governance of project management components directly.

Disclosure and reporting is addressed by a number of RMM questions. For example the effectiveness of risk reports is addressed by Question E6 (Chapter 10, pp. 190–91), 'Quality of Risk Reporting'. This is backed up by the need to maintain risk data as addressed by Question E5 (p. 189), 'Maintenance of Project Risk Records'. However, the existence of reports and data is not sufficient in itself. In order for the risk management process to function effectively, there has to be a culture of open and honest disclosure. The RMM addresses this in a combination of ways. Cultural aspects of disclosure are most obviously addressed by various questions in the risk management culture perspective. However, they are also important to many of the questions related to risk identification and analysis. Finally, it should be noted that a number of questions in the Stakeholders perspective address the question as to whether or the organisation's management is informed about significant risks.

The project management component of *Directing Change* is concerned with whether or not the board is assured that its organisation's project management capability is adequate. The Project RMM is, of course, itself an assurance tool. However, it also embraces a number of key questions built into the *Directing Change* guidance. For example, *Directing Change* asks whether all projects have clear critical success criteria and whether or not they are used to inform decision making. Likewise the Project RMM Question E1 (Chapter 10, pp. 180–81) concerns whether or not the risk management process is aligned with the project's purpose.

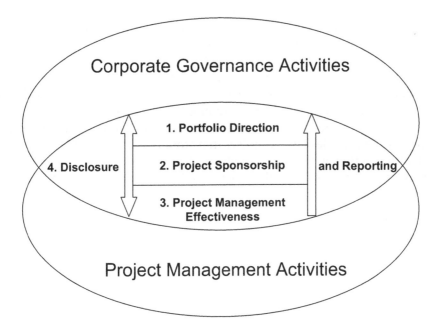

Figure C.2   Governance of Project Management: four components

Critical success criteria are a useful means of summarising a project's purpose. Aligning the risk management process with critical success criteria ensures that they are implicitly used to develop risk-based decisions. All other questions in the *Directing Change* project management component that are relevant to risk management can be associated with RMM questions in similar ways.

The project sponsorship component is a key feature of *Directing Change*. The guide describes the project sponsor as being the route through which project managers directly report and from which project managers obtain their formal authority, remit and decisions. There are certain matters on which the project manager should be able to contribute advice but not make the final decision. These include setting project objectives, approving project contingencies and making project go/no go decisions. *Directing Change* implies that these decisions are governed by project sponsors. Since an effective project risk management process can be expected to contribute to all of these decisions, the Project RMM recognises the project sponsor's role. The way in which it does this is explained in the text accompanying Questions A1 and A2 (see Chapter 6, pp. 96–7 and 98–9). For internal projects, the project sponsor is also treated as being the project's customer, in which case, Question A4 (see pp. 102–3) also applies.

Directing Change covers the governance of project management within a single organisation. However, the ownership of some projects is shared between two or more organisations. Since most organisations would not accept an individual from another organisation being the sole sponsor for a project that they co-own, this creates a special case for project sponsorship. Guidance on how to manage the implications of project co-ownership is provided by another APM guide: *Co-directing Change: A Guide to Governance of Multi-owned Projects* (GoPM Specific Interest Group 2007). From a project sponsorship perspective, arrangements will usually be made for the project to be directed by an owning board with owner-sponsors representing each of the owning organisations. For the purposes of Project RMM assessments the owning board then represents the senior management referred to in Questions A1 and A2 (see Chapter 6, see above).

Although co-ownership of projects can cause commercial difficulties, there are a number of potential benefits. One is that the organisations can share risk. Moreover, if the different strengths available from amongst each organisation are aligned with project responsibilities the overall project team capability can be greater than any one organisation could provide. Thus a project that would be unacceptably risky for any of the organisations acting on their own, might be viable if risk can be shared constructively with other parties. Some of the world's biggest and most complex projects are co-owned for this reason.

Appendix D
QinetiQ

QinetiQ is a leading international provider of technology-based services and solutions to the defence, security and related markets. QinetiQ is the UK's largest research and technology organisation with over 14,000 employees and revenue of over £1.6 billion in 2009. Approximately half of the company's employees are shareholders. QinetiQ develops and delivers services and solutions for government organisations, predominantly in the UK and US, including defence departments, intelligence services and security agencies. In addition, it provides technology insertion and consultancy services to commercial and industrial customers around the world.

QinetiQ is one of the UK's leading recruiters of graduates and continues to strengthen its presence at key universities. The quality of people recruited is regarded as being a critical factor to the success of a business that is reliant on innovation and expertise. Equally, the company invests heavily in the ongoing professional development of its people. Personal membership of professional bodies is both encouraged and funded. One consequence is that the company produces a wealth of papers published in academic and professional journals.

In 2004, QinetiQ bought HVR Consulting Services Ltd, a privately owned company founded in 1993 (the HVR name was derived from the name of the company's founder; Harry Victor Rogers). The Project Risk Maturity Model was one many tools and techniques that HVR had developed. Other HVR tools include FACET (a knowledge-based cost forecasting tool) and the Top Down Risk Model (trade named TDRM). By purchasing HVR, QinetiQ also acquired the proprietary rights to these tools.

By 2004, HVR had grown organically to a size of approximately 100 staff by developing an excellent customer reputation in areas including risk management, cost modelling, operational research and safety management. HVR had previously rejected numerous approaches to purchase the company. A critical factor that led to the acceptance of QinetiQ's offer was that, like HVR, QinetiQ kept itself at the leading edge of professional and technical development by fostering innovation amongst its staff. It also allowed HVR to maintain an independent approach to the delivery of its services. However, in 2009, increasing synergy between HVR and QinetiQ's wider consultancy business led to HVR being fully merged into its parent company.

QinetiQ's approach to its consulting business is based on the achievement of client impact through a combination of insight, innovation and integrity. It draws upon QinetiQ's unique combination of technical and process insight to provide advice including decision and project support for both civil and defence customers.

References

Association for Project Management 2004. *Project Risk Analysis and Management (PRAM) Guide* (2nd Edition). Princes Risborough, UK: Association for Project Management.

Association for Project Management 2006. *APM Body of Knowledge* (5th Edition). Princes Risborough, UK: Association for Project Management.

Berstein, P.L. 1996.. *Against the Gods: The Remarkable Story of Risk.* New York, USA: John Wiley & Sons Inc.

Carnegie Mellon Institute 2006. *The Capability Maturity Model: CMMI for Development, The SEI Series in Software Engineering.* Reading, Massachusetts: Addison-Wesley.

Chandra Sekar, Y. (ed.) 2005. *Project Risk Management: Principles and Practices.* Hyderabad, India: ICFIA Books, ICFIA University Press.

Chapman, C. 2006. Key points of contention in framing assumptions for risk and uncertainty management, *International Journal of Project Management*, Volume 24, Issue 4.

Chapman, C. and Ward, S. 1997. *Project Risk Management: Processes, Techniques and Insights* (1st Edition). Chichester UK: John Wiley and Sons Ltd.

—— 2002. *Managing Project Risk and Uncertainty: A Constructively Simple Approach to Decision Making.* Chichester, UK: John Wiley and Sons Ltd.

—— 2003. *Project Risk Management: Processes, Techniques and Insights* (2nd Edition). Baffins Lane, Chichester, UK: John Wiley and Sons Ltd.

Chapman, R.J. 2006. *Simple Tools and Techniques for Enterprise Risk Management.* Chichester, UK: John Wiley and Sons Ltd.

Cooper, D. et al. 2005. *Managing Risk in Large Projects and Complex Procurements.* Chichester, UK: John Wiley and Sons Ltd.

Comptroller and Auditor General 2008. *Ministry of Defence Major Projects Report 2008.* Buckingham Palace Road, London: UK National Audit Office.

Earned Value Specific Interest Group. *Earned Value Management: APM Guidelines.* Princes Risborough, UK: Association for Project Management.

Flyvbjerg, B, Bruzelius, N. and Rothengatter, W. 2003. *Megaprojects and Risk: An Anatomy of Ambition.* Cambridge: Cambridge University Press.

Rt Hon. Lord Fraser of Carmyllie 2004. *The Holyrood Inquiry Final Report.* (available at www. holyroodinquiry.org).

GoPM Specific Interest Group 2004. *Directing Change: A Guide to Governance of Project Management.* Association for Project Management. (available at www.apm.org)

GoPM Specific Interest Group 2007. *Co-directing Change: A Guide to Governance of Multi-owned Projects.* Princes Risborough, UK: Association for Project Management.

GoPM Specific Interest Group 2009. *Sponsoring Change: A Guide to the Governance Aspects of Project Sponsorship.* Princes Risborough, UK: Association for Project Management.

HM Treasury 2004. *The Orange Book: Management of Risk – Principles and Concepts.* London, UK: (available at www.hm-treasury.co.uk).

HM Treasury 2009. *Risk Management Assessment Framework: A Tool for Departments.* London, UK: (available at www.hm-treasury.co.uk).

Hillson, D. 1997. Towards a risk maturity model. *International Journal of Project and Business Risk Management*, Volume 1, Issue 1, March.

—— 2002. *Use a Risk Breakdown Structure (RBS) to Understand Your Risks*. San Antonio, Texas, USA: PMI Annual Seminars & Symposium.

—— 2004. *Effective Opportunity Management for Projects: Exploiting Positive Risk*. New York, USA: Marcel Dekker Inc.

—— and Murray-Webster, R. 2005. *Understanding and Managing Risk Attitude*. Farnham, UK: Gower Publishing.

Hopkinson, M. 2000a. Using Risk Maturity Models. *Kluwer's Risk Management Briefing*, Issue 40, (May), 4–8.

—— 2000b. The Risk Maturity Model. *Risk Management Bulletin*, Volume 5, Issue 4, (November), 25–29.

—— (2001). *Schedule Risk Analysis: Critical Issues for Planners and Managers*. London, UK: PMI Europe Conference.

——and Brown, R. 2002. *Measuring Risk Maturity in UK MoD Projects*. Project Manager Today, Risk Management Conference, London, UK.

—— and Lovelock, G. 2004. *The Project Risk Maturity Model – Assessment of the UK MoD's Top 30 Acquisition Projects*. Prague, Annual PMI Congress Europe.

Hopkinson, M. et al. 2008. *Prioritising Project Risks*. Princes Risborough, UK: Association for Project Management.

Hulett, D. 2009. *Practical Schedule Risk Analysis*. Farnham, UK: Gower Publishing.

Kerzner, H. 2001. *Strategic Planning for Project Management using a Project Management Maturity Model*. New York, USA: John Wiley & Sons Inc.

Leitch, M. 2008. *Intelligent Internal Control and Risk Management: Designing High-Performance Risk Control Systems*. Farnham, UK: Gower Publishing.

Lichtenberg, S. 1989. *The Successive Principle: A New Decision Tool for the Conception Phase*. Atlanta, US:, Joint Project Management Institute/IPMA Symposium.

Lichtenberg, S. 2000. *Proactive Management of Uncertainty using the Successive Principle*. Copenhagen, Denmark: Polyteknisk Press.

Mackay, C. 1852. *Extraordinary Popular Delusions and the Madness of Crowds*. Wordsworth Edition Ltd, Ware, Hertfordshire (1995).

Murray-Webster, R. and Hillson, D. 2008. *Understanding and Managing Group Risk Attitude*. Farnham, UK: Gower Publishing.

Parliamentary Office of Science and Technology. *POST Report 200* (2003). 7 Millbank, London.

Project Management Institute 2004. *A Guide to the Project Management Body of Knowledge (PMBOK)* (3rd Edition). Philadelphia, USA: Project Management Institute.

—— 2009. *Practice Standard for Project Risk Management.*, Pennsylvania, USA: Project Management Institute Inc.

Reuvid, J. (ed.) 2007. *Managing Business Risk: A Practical Guide to Protecting Your Business* (4th Edition). London, UK: IRM (Institute of Risk Management).

Simon, P., Hillson, D. and Newland, K. 1997. *Project Risk Analysis and Management (PRAM) Guide* (1st Edition). High Wycombe, UK: Association for Project Management.

Turnbull, N. et al. 1999. *Internal Control: Guidance for Directors on the Combined Code*. London, UK: Institute of Chartered Accountants.

Turner, R.J. 1999. *The Handbook of Project-based Management*. Maidenhead, UK: McGraw Hill Publishing Company.

Vaughan, D. 1996. *The Challenger Launch Decision: Risky Technology, Culture and Deviance at NASA.* Chicago: Chicago University Press.

Vose, D. 2008. *Risk Analysis: A Quantitative Guide* (3rd Edition). Chichester, UK: John Wiley and Sons Ltd.

Williams, T. 2002. *Modelling Complex Projects.* Chichester, UK: John Wiley and Sons Ltd.

Software User Instructions

Now you've tried it your way, read this to try it our way!
Instructions sheet enclosed with a self-assembly kit.

The disk that comes with this book will enable you to run your own Project Risk Maturity Model (RMM) assessments. The software is written in Microsoft Access but is packaged with an Access run time licence, making it unnecessary to have a copy of Microsoft Access itself. The software should be compatible with common Microsoft Windows operating systems, including XP, Vista, Windows 7 and other contemporary windows operating systems that are found in the workplace. Although compatibility is not guaranteed, it can be noted that almost all most software issues fixed after testing were identified by users of Vista. The licence is unlimited in terms of both time and the number of assessments that can be made.

As with most software applications, the licence conditions have to be accepted by the user during the installation process. However, two conditions should be noted at this point. First, there is no user help line; the software is relatively simple and these instructions should be sufficient. Second, the licence is for one computer only. If you want to transfer it to another computer, the software should be uninstalled first. This second condition is intended to prevent the software from being used by people other than the owner of the book. If other people want a copy of the software they should buy the book! After all, the book provides a lot of additional information that should be regarded as being important to achieving accurate assessments. Using the software without this information should be discouraged.

Software Installation

After being loaded in the computer's CD drive, the Project RMM installation application may start automatically. If it doesn't, installation can be initiated by opening the QQPRMMSetup application file that can be found on the disk, for example, by using Windows Explorer.

The software will install after the licence conditions have been accepted (click on the acceptance box at the bottom left to enable installation). By default, the application will be installed on the Programmes directory in a folder created using the path Program Files/QinetiQ/Risk Maturity Model Book Software. However, this default can be changed to an alternative path name at the user's discretion. As the installation process continues, it displays a Windows box stating that Access Runtime 2003 is being reconfigured. This only affects the RMM software and should not alter the configuration of your computer in any other way. The installation process should also create a desktop shortcut in the form of the RMM icon.

Software Launch

The software can be launched in any of the following three ways:

1. Double-click on the QinetiQ Project Risk Maturity Model icon (a white box with RMM in light blue letters).
2. Use the Windows Start button to select Programs/QinetiQ Risk Tools/Project Risk Maturity Model.
3. Use Windows Explorer to locate and open the qqprmm application file following the path selected during the installation process.

As the software is launched, a blue QinetiQ/Project Risk Maturity Model flash screen will be displayed for a short period. This will then be replaced by the RMM control panel shown in Figure 1.

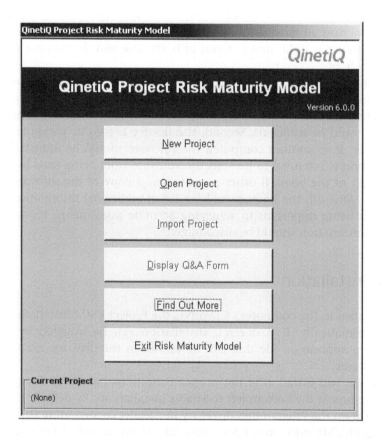

Figure 1   Control panel

The control panel enables you to create assessments for a new project or to open a file previously created for a project. On the first occasion that the software is launched, there will be no previously created files, so a new project has to be created.

To create a new project, click on the New Project button and then enter a file name for the new project in the Windows dialogue box that appears. The browser at the top of the dialogue box can be used to select an appropriate folder for the file to be saved in. After entering this information, click on the Save button. This will create an RMM type file in the chosen folder. The Save button also returns you to the Control Panel. This time, however, the Display Q&A button will no longer be greyed out. Click on the Display Q&A button to enter the RMM itself.

Assessment Data Entry

Clicking the Display Q&A button takes the user to the data entry screen shown in Figure 2. By default, having entered the model, you are shown the details of Question A1: the first of the RMM's 50 questions. The other questions can be viewed in turn by selecting Records at the bottom left of the screen. However, assuming that a new project has just been created, it should be noted that the radio buttons (circular buttons to the left of each of the five answers) do not yet respond to mouse clicks. In order to start the data entry process, you have to create a new review (that is, RMM assessment).

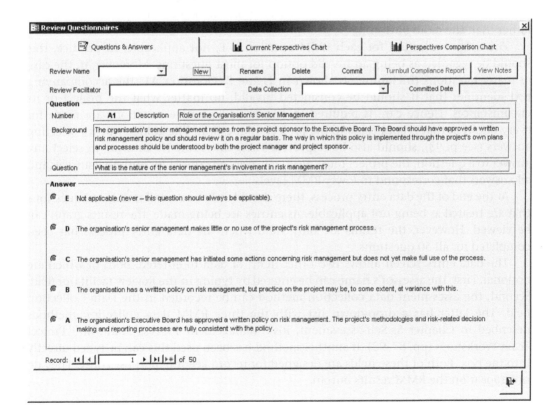

Figure 2   Data entry screen

To create a new review, click on the New button, found towards the top left of the screen. This causes a small dialogue box to appear instructing the user to 'Enter the name of the review you want to create'. The name that is entered here will later appear on the results graph. It is therefore good practice to differentiate each review from the others recorded in each project file by including both the project name and a date. Typically projects have short names, often in the form of mildly amusing acronyms. Hence, for example, one might enter the name 'SCRUM May 2011'. Having entered this name in the dialogue box, accept it by clicking on the OK button. If a typing mistake is found after this procedure, it can be corrected by clicking on the Rename button and editing the review name.

Once accepted, each new review name is added to the Review name drop-down list to the left of the New button. The review name selected from this drop-down list corresponds to the data that is entered for each of the RMM questions and the results graph produced in response. Having created a new review name, it should be noticed that the five radio buttons to the left hand side of the screen will have become active and can be selected by mouse clicks.

Having selected a review name, answers to each of the RMM questions can thus be entered in turn by clicking on the appropriate radio button and then moving to the next question by clicking on the right-pointing Record selection arrow. For convenience, answers can subsequently be selected by clicking on the text of the appropriate answer rather than the radio button.

The default selection for each RMM question is E; not applicable. In practice, this should be regarded as being an invalid option for most questions. Moreover, in the case of many questions (including, as shown in Figure 2, Question A1) the accompanying text identifies that it should be considered invalid, no matter what the project or its circumstances. Hence care is required to ensure that positive selections are made for every question that is applicable to the project in question. The golden rule for selecting answers (see p. 93), should also be respected. The golden rule is: 'In order to select any answer to a question, the project must meet or exceed all criteria for both that answer and all answers that correspond to lower RMM levels'.

At the end of the data entry process, there should only be a small number of questions that are treated as being not applicable. As entries are being made, the results graph can be viewed. However, the results are only valid when the data entry process has been completed for all 50 questions.

The data entry screen allows two other items of data to entered, both of which are optional. First, the assessor's name can be entered by typing in the Review facilitator field. Second, the assessment data collection method can be recorded in the Data Collection field. The latter has a drop-down list with the three RMM data collection methods described in Chapter 5: Self-assessment, Risk Management Process audit, and Project Team Workshops (pp. 87–92). If another method has been used this can be typed directly into the box. Both of these fields are designed for record keeping purposes only. They do not appear on the RMM results output.

Viewing and Using the Results Graph

To view the result graph, click on the Current Perspectives Chart tab at the top of the screen. This replaces the questions data entry screen with a results chart equivalent to that shown in Figure 3.

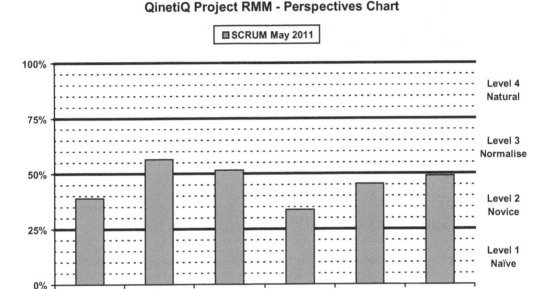

QinetiQ Project RMM - Perspectives Chart

Figure 3   Example of a Project RMM results chart

As explained in Chapter 1 (see pp. 7–8), the overall RMM assessment is read from this chart as being the level corresponding to the lowest bar. Hence, for example, Figure 3 shows a project with a Level 2 RMM capability.

The results chart can be exported into other applications such as Microsoft Word or PowerPoint by clicking on the Copy to Clipboard button and then pasting into the other application. The best results are obtained by using Paste Special to paste the chart as a metafile or a Microsoft Graph Chart Object.

To return to the data entry screen, click on the Questions and Answers tab at the top of the screen to the left of the Current Perspectives Chart tab.

Protecting Data Entered for a Review

When the data entry has been completed for a review, it can be protected from further change. To do this, click on the Commit button. After this action, it should not be possible to amend any of the answers selected for the RMM questions and, hence, alter the results shown by the results graph.

Viewing Case Studies

The software comes with seven one-page PDF files. Please note that Adobe Acrobat Reader is required to open and read them. Six of these files are case studies related to each of the RMM perspectives as labelled on the Results chart. To view a case study, go to the Current Perspectives Chart screen and click on a RMM label (for example, Risk Identification). A hyperlink on the label opens the relevant case study. All case studies are based on project risk management work on real projects. The other PDF file provides background information on QinetiQ and the Project RMM and can be opened by clicking on the Find Out More button on the Control Panel.

Exiting the Risk Maturity Model

To exit the Risk Maturity Model, click on the Close Screen button at the bottom left of the data entry screen. Alternatively, you can close the screen by clicking on the box with the cross at the top right hand side of the application window. Finally, click on the Exit Risk Maturity Model button on the Control Panel.

Opening and Using an Existing Project RMM file

After opening the application to view the Control Panel, click on the Open Project button. This will open a Windows dialogue box with which you can find the project to be opened. RMM files created by the Project RMM are created and saved with a .prm extension. By default, this dialogue box will browse the last folder that was used by Risk Maturity Model. If the file you are looking for is not in that folder and you cannot remember where it is stored, one approach is to search your computer disk for all files with a .prm extension. Having found and selected the right file, click on the Open button. Finally, from the Control Panel, click on the Display Q&A Form button to start using the project file.

When the data entry screen is first displayed, none of the reviews previously created in the project file will be selected, all the radio buttons on the left hand side of the screen will be inactive. To start using the tool, select a previous review using the Review Name drop-down list. Alternatively, click on the New button and enter and OK the name of the new review you would like to create.

Functions not Enabled in the Software Provided with the Book

For the purposes of the book release, some software functions are disabled that are available to QinetiQ consultants and client organisations that have bought rights to use their own bespoke versions of the tool. These functions are:

- The Perspectives Comparison Chart (which enables the results of different reviews to be displayed side by side, but which will show a blank graph if selected using this software).
- The Notes function (which opens up notes fields for maintaining associated audit records).

- The Turnbull Compliance Report (which identifies aspects of the project risk management process that fail to comply with standards of internal control required for companies listed on the London Stock Exchange).
- A reports function that prints hard copies of the Project RMM content and the results entered for selected project assessments.

A full copy of the Project Risk Maturity Model (and other similar models such as the Business Risk Maturity Model) can be negotiated with QinetiQ. Organisations interested in this option also often choose to make minor alterations to the words in the model so as to tailor it to their in-house terminology.

Index